Faulkner in America

FAULKNER AND YOKNAPATAWPHA

1998

Faulkner in America

FAULKNER AND YOKNAPATAWPHA, 1998

EDITED BY
JOSEPH R. URGO
AND
ANN J. ABADIE

UNIVERSITY PRESS OF MISSISSIPPI
JACKSON

www.upress.state.ms.us

Manufactured in the United States of America
09 08 07 06 05 04 03 02 01 4 3 2 1
∞

Library of Congress Cataloging-in-Publication Data

Faulkner and Yoknapatawpha Conference (25th : 1998 : University of Mississippi)
Faulkner in America / Faulkner and Yoknapatawpha, 1998 ; edited by Joseph R. Urgo and Ann J. Abadie.
p. cm.
Proceedings of the 25th Annual Faulkner and Yoknapatawpha Conference, held at the University of Mississippi, July 26–31, 1998.
Includes bibliographical references and index.
ISBN 1-57806-375-2 (alk. paper)—ISBN 1-57806-376-0 (pbk. : alk. paper)
1. Faulkner, William, 1897–1962—Knowledge—United States—Congresses. 2. Literature and history—United States—History—20th century—Congresses. 3. National characteristics, American, in literature—Congresses. 4. United States—In literature—Congresses. I. Urgo, Joseph R. II. Abadie, Ann J. III. Title.

PS3511.A86 Z78321186 1998
813′.52—dc21 2001026169

British Library Cataloging-in-Publication Data available

In memory of William Shaver

Contents

Introduction

The beauty—spiritual and physical—of the South lies in the fact that God has done so much for it and man so little. I have this for which to thank whatever gods may be: that having fixed my roots in this soil all contact, saving by the printed word, with contemporary poets is impossible.

—WILLIAM FAULKNER, 1925[1]

This was the American Dream: a sanctuary on the earth for individual man: a condition in which he could be free not only of the old established closed-corporation hierarchies of arbitrary power which had oppressed him as a mass, but free of that mass into which the hierarchies of church and state had compressed and held him individually thralled and individually impotent.

—WILLIAM FAULKNER, 1955[2]

1

Two things are new to the Faulkner and Yoknapatawpha series this year. One is me, as coeditor of the volume. Don Kartiganer has coedited each volume of essays from the annual Faulkner and Yoknapatawpha Conference with Ann Abadie since 1991. Before that, Ann coedited with Doreen Fowler and before that, with Evans Harrington. Don asked me to coedit this year as the first of what is planned as a series of guest editors. The second new thing is in the volume title. For years the conference (and book) has been called Faulkner and something else—such as "Faulkner and Ideology," "Faulkner and Gender," "Faulkner and Film." The 1998 conference began, in its planning stages, with the form dictated by tradition, "Faulkner and America," but the conjunctive, as it turned out, slipped its yoke and gave way to a preposition, with the result that the conference and this volume would become "Faulkner in America." The preposition raises appropriate questions regarding William Faulkner's place in American literature, his location in literary studies, and his relation to United States culture—and to address such issues, one must take time to define what we mean by the phrase *Faulkner in America*. My hand as guest editor for this volume, in the long run, signifies very little because I can take neither credit nor blame for the slippage but, as author of this introduction, I am compelled to comment on it because, I would say, it signifies a great deal.

A conjunctive relation indicates irrefutable fact of union; a prepositional relation, on the other hand, is another matter. The title "Faulkner and America" was designed to attract attention to the relationship between Faulkner and his national affiliation. The impulse is peculiarly American, as one can hardly imagine a conference on "Proust and France" or "Shakespeare and England." Americanness, in the United States, is a matter of political and ideological scrutiny, and one can envision a host of conferences that examine the American qualities of various national authors. However, at some point in the interplay of language and reality the conjunctive must have struck the conference organizers as presumptuous.[3] How can one discuss Faulkner *and* America until some agreement has been reached on where Faulkner (and his native soil, Mississippi) is to be located *in* America? Here arise the ghosts of Faulkner's own hand: Quentin introducing Shreve to Henry Sutpen and Charles Bon, their Harvard roommate-shades; Hightower visited by ancestral warriors; Isaac McCaslin greeting animistic forefathers. Surely, Faulkner mused: How is Mississippi in America? William Faulkner embodied the question; he was rooted in it biographically. When he thought *America* Faulkner thought about being left alone, as if being "in America" either meant privacy or it meant nothing meaningful. He felt the same way about being "in literature," achieving notoriety for his distance from literary circles in his own time. But, without a doubt, Faulkner was a literary man and he was in America. Or, rather, he was sustained by literature and by America. To borrow his logic from the essay on the American Dream, "We did not live *in* the dream: we lived the Dream itself, just as we do not merely live *in* air and climate, but we live Air and Climate."[4] Faulkner, from our vantage point in the twenty-first century, did not merely live *in* America, either.

I have begged the question, however, of how Mississippi is in America. It has been begged for some time. The literary status of Faulkner hinges on the response. Attending the Modern Language Association Convention each year, one would not suspect that William Faulkner is second only to Shakespeare in the volume of critical study produced by scholars in the United States. When decorative literary quotation is needed, Faulkner's words are not the first choice of pundits and journalists. Maybe it's because of the question we are begging. If Faulkner is not merely *in* America but is America itself, then surely Mississippi is America as well, and not merely a state, or merely a Southern state. Conceptual challenges arise, however, when Mississippi (and Faulkner) are situated centrally, definitively. Our national rhetoric of revolution-won freedoms and independence rings less loudly in a region where subsequent impulses were quashed by force. That question, ever on the shore of Faulkner's consciousness, about why God let the South lose the War, translates, even in the iron New England dark, into how it was that a nation of united states came to force unity upon states where federation was no longer desired. How it was, furthermore, that a state and a region that did not want to be "in" was forced to be so. And for our purposes, how is it that the strongest and most articulate literary voice in this nation emerged from such defeat? Faulkner was always, literally, "in" America, but centrally? marginally? Would one have argued in 1925 or 1955 that Lafayette County is the center of the United States? Or, given Faulkner, how does one dare argue otherwise?

Faulkner avoided the nation's literary institutions and establishments. He attended the University of Mississippi for a while, but probably because it was right next door. One cannot imagine William Faulkner applying for a grant, or even a job for that matter. He is famous for running from all associations with poets and writers and critics unless compelled to participate, and there is plenty of Faulkner lore disparaging those like me (and maybe you) whose lives are consumed by writing and talking about literature. And yet it is this aloofness, this separation, which, in its way, is responsible for the American quality that undeniably marks and is marked by Faulkner. The refusal to join, the distancing of the self from centrality, the detachment from the humming and buzzing of American culture—and then, the plunge into its very soul (if that is the right term), in Hollywood—these moves are inextricably Faulknerian. It is as if the Mississippi landscape itself is embodied by and in turn embodies Faulkner. The state, Mississippi, perhaps the deepest of the deep South, is bracketed and asterisked in many studies of America (economic, social, historical) so that we don't mistake Mississippi for what is typical America. But then we know that can't be right, that must be a mistake, because of the origin of American blues, because of the incubating realities of a multiracial United States culture, because of the testing of American laws that claim freedom and individualism and associations freely entered. It may be, we suspect, that Mississippi (and Faulkner) bear a relation to America more heady than conjunctive; and so we move from "and" to "in," to an inextricably prepositional relation. "Mississippi begins in the lobby of a Memphis, Tennessee hotel and extends south to the Gulf of Mexico." Faulkner wrote this in 1954, in an autobiographical essay written for popular consumption.[5] We now know that Faulkner spent his adult life and his literary career explaining how far north Mississippi extended: encompassing and overpassing the North, even to Alberta, Canada, I believe.

The 1998 conference asks, what is the relationship between Faulkner and America and where in America is Faulkner? Faulkner has been called the twentieth century's great American writer, the Shakespeare of modernism, the writer whose work will one day come to be synonymous with the American century, perhaps with American civilization itself. But that would mean that the literary, cognitive, and aesthetic capital of the nation is in Mississippi, and that to know America one must know Faulkner and one must also know Mississippi: Not New York, not California, not even Kansas or Michigan, but Mississippi. Nonetheless, when the nation imagines itself, and when the world imagines the United States, it is unlikely that Mississippi plays a synecdochical function. If a filmmaker wants to project the image of a typical American town, the screen is unlikely to fill with courthouse and town square. If it should, most Americans, even those in the South, will note that this is to be a *Southern* town, not a typically American scene, and the narrative that follows will be Southern, not American—or rather, it will be Southern and American—no, that's not right, either; it will be Southern *in* America. One suspects that for many readers in the United States, Faulkner occupies the same problematic relation to the national culture. There is no question that Faulkner is *in* America, the question is, where. When one opens a book by Faulkner one expects a novel about—America?—the South?—so much so that Faulkner's attempt to leave his Southern materials, in *A Fable*, resulted, for decades, in almost no response by critics, save complaints. It seems no coincidence that at this conference, where Faulkner in America was the question on everyone's mind, *A Fable* was discussed interminably.

William Faulkner knows this: In the South, you are in America but you are in the South. These are not two different places; but, neither are they interchangeable or identical. You are never in one or the other exclusively; and when you are in Mississippi, you are, as such, even more so. And, most importantly, if you are in America and you are also in Mississippi, you are where you are not entirely by the freely made historical choice of the people, but at least in part by defeat, by military order. If you are in Wyoming you are also in America, in the West, and the state will tell you when it was that Wyoming chose to join the Union. In Mississippi, and in the South generally, warfare compelled union; there was no choosing. So it just can't be "Faulkner and America" because it's not that simple. Melville and America, James and America, Cather and America—these relationships, while arguably complex, fit comfortably within conjunctive bounds. However, Faulkner's *and* is not simply an academic complexity but the very source of his authorial stature. The figure of William Faulkner as an American writer depends on and extends from that problematic placement and context. To paraphrase (and add preposition to) Gertrude Stein, there is so much more *in there* than simply "there" in there, leaving Faulkner both in and out of America. He is in by fact of geography, and he is out by the memory of historical contingency. Quintessentially marginal, Faulkner's identification as an American writer cannot be explored without unearthing every ghost and demon that we associate with the nation—racial chaos (to use his phrase), power relations that define the limits of democracy, class division, hereditary privilege, the problematic right to be left alone—it all comes crashing through the gates with Faulkner in America.

Nationality may be chosen freely, the product of successful revolt or the declaration of newly arrived allegiance. Conversely, one's national identity may be the product of defeat, of the failure to extricate from powerful economic and political concerns, producing a sense of conjunctive purpose and national existence bordering, if not overpassing, to the compulsory. It would be interesting to know which condition most Americans identify with today. Clearly, Faulkner located himself with the defeated in America, those for whom the federal government was (to borrow Marthe's warning about the Old General in *A Fable*) "something which all the earth had better beware and dread and be afraid of."[6] Among Faulkner's more controversial public statements about power relations, during the Civil Rights era, was one made to Russell Howe in 1956, when he said (and later denied) that "if it came to fighting I'd fight for Mississippi against the United States even if it meant going out into the street and shooting Negroes."[7] Maybe he said it, maybe he didn't. He probably did. My sense of the statement being Faulkner's is based on the essential consistency between Faulkner's predicament and the principle it embodies and also, not insignificantly, on the raw, crude way in which the principle is phrased. Perhaps it would have been less offensive had Faulkner substituted "federal officers" or "the FBI" for "Negroes." Anti-authoritarianism is far less repulsive when not confused with racism. Intertwined throughout Faulkner's comments to Howe on race—and running throughout Faulkner's thinking in the Civil Rights era—are concerns about the relation between federal power and Mississippi or, for our purposes, the place of Mississippi in America. When Faulkner thought *America* he thought as often about compulsion and loss as he did of freedom and liberties gained.

If the statement about shooting Negroes is a fact, then it is one which we should probably consider in a Faulknerian way. The relationship between the facts on which we focus and the truth of our utterances was never far from Faulkner's mind when he was thinking about politics, and in the Howe interview, the phenomena of fact and truth emerged once again. Faulkner explained, "Truth says this and the fact says that. A wise person says, 'Let's use this fact. Let's obliterate this fact first.' " I'd suggest we use the "fact" of the controversial statement about defending Mississippi and shooting federally empowered Negroes to indicate nothing more or less controversial than a troubled relationship to the nation held by a man from a state whose presence in the Union exists by historical, military coercion. We know from his writing that the fact of the War interfered profoundly with his vision of the nation. In speculating about his place in America, the War stood between him and his national identity like one of those ideas or images that Quentin, in *Absalom, Absalom!*, cannot pass. I do not think such blockage stemmed from the bare fact of military loss but rather was tied inextricably to Faulkner's capacity for articulation *in* America, to his identity as an American. One finds no romantic images of Italian immigrants arriving in New York or New Orleans, pursuing the American Dream, in Faulkner's work. Arriving by choice seems not to have been among the tools on his famous workbench. To be American, in Faulkner, is to be compelled, driven, and ultimately, to relive certain paradigmatic moments of coercion and confrontation with violent wills in the guise and under the banners of freedom.

In his subsequent denial of the original remark to Howe, Faulkner went to the heart of the matter: "The statement that I or anyone else would choose any one state against the whole remaining Union of States, down to the ultimate price of shooting other human beings in the streets, is not only foolish but dangerous. Foolish because no sane man is going to choose one state against the Union today. A hundred years ago, yes. But not in 1956. And dangerous because the idea can further inflame those few people in the South who might still believe such a situation possible." Faulkner's consciousness provides access to something not given full play in nationally mediated conceptions of America, the contingency represented by the "Union of States" and the option, however foolish, to choose one state against that Union. In Faulkner's mind, and throughout the historical South, the memory of defeat and forced union make highly problematic the *place* of the South in the national culture. Fourth of July rhetoric about independence and freely chosen courses of events emerge as ironies under the shadow of the confederate soldier's statue on the town square in Oxford and throughout the state. The conceptually invigorating signification of the phrase "Faulkner in America" is one of provisionality. Foremost in Faulkner's mind, in interviews as well as in the aesthetics of the apocryphal Yoknapatawpha County, is the fact that whoever and whatever is "in" America got there by a wide variety of factual means in United States history, by battles won and lost, by emigration and enslavement, by choice and by compulsion. We ought not forget, as Americans in any part of the nation, that the War between the States freed slaves but also enforced allegiance to the federal government, forever defining the Union of States as indivisible by any means save force, and aligning freedom with inclusion. The answer to Rousseau is that in America, indeed, citizens have been forced to be free.

2

> A national literature cannot spring from folk lore—though heaven knows, such a forcing has been tried often enough—for America is too big and there are too many folk lores: Southern negroes, Spanish and French strains, the old west, for these always will remain colloquial; nor will it come through our slang, which also is likewise indigenous to restricted portions of the country. It can, however, come from the strength of imaginative idiom which is understandable by all who read English. Nowhere today, saving in parts of Ireland, is the English language spoken with the same earthy strength as it is in the United States; though we are, as a nation, still inarticulate.
>
> —WILLIAM FAULKNER, 1922[8]

Regarding Faulkner's place in American literature, we can safely say he wrote his way in, and that Faulkner in America is characterized above all by "the strength of imaginative idiom" which he brought to bear on the national culture. The quotation above is typical of early Faulkner, particularly of the series he wrote for *The Mississippian* in the early 1920s under the column "Books and Things." Faulkner began his career with an ambitious sense of becoming, in words used twenty years later, "articulate in the national voice";[9] of expressing, in the language of the nation, truths of the American civilization. His sense in 1922 was that few writers had found the language to write themselves into America, though many had gotten from its regions various and useful American materials. However, region to Faulkner meant not folklore but words, imaginative idiom, and creation. Of all the "dramatic material in this country," Faulkner asserted in 1925, "the greatest resource [is] our language."[10] Faulkner's understanding of the potential of the literary in America was tied not to its peculiar or exceptional history, and neither was it connected to the depth of knowledge a writer might bring to what he called its local and regional folk lores. The organ of creativity in Faulkner was, and remained throughout his writing life, his ear—the spoken as well as the unspoken, the conscious and unconscious elements of the English language in America. When readers find his prose mesmerizing, enthralling, or simply dazzling, this is what they are hearing.

Region and raw material, subject matter and theme, such content variety was not as vital as the use of language toward achieving an American aesthetic signature. "Sound art . . . does not depend on the quality or quantity of available material," Faulkner explained. On the contrary, "wealth of material" is incidental to literary creation as Faulkner, in his apprenticeship, estimated it. "One rainbow we have on our dramatic horizon: language as it is spoken in America."[11] Language, however, cannot be understood as a static tool of expression. Language is both the product and the source of social relations; and as such, it is (as Faulkner would say) always in motion. "Our wealth of language and our inarticulateness (inability to derive any benefit from the language) are due to the same cause: our racial chaos and our instinctive quickness to realize our simpler needs, and to supply them from any source."[12] Such "instinctive quickness" he associated with writing for the mass media, and with books such as the popular social-commentary novels of Sinclair Lewis. What Faulkner may have meant by "racial chaos" is made clear by the writing he left behind, by his own ability to derive linguistic benefit from the racial encounters that have contributed to what it is one finds in America.

No doubt, his understanding of language as the core of the literary—a truism that may tend to get lost in our work to establish accuracy of social context—contributes to Faulkner's stature in the academy and, to return to my initial point, reserves that place *in* America for the narrative energies that surround his name today. However, Faulkner's interest in language was never simply a matter of refinement, of esoteric or aesthetic Being, apart from the everyday world where fingernails get dirty and boots collect the dust of work and travel. It was not a pure interest in linguistic form that drove Faulkner to literary creation, but the fusion of language and location, the recognition that language springs from the relationship between human beings, their time, and their environment. For this reason, perhaps, Faulkner felt it necessary to assert his connection to traditions outside the literary, and to shun overdetermination by aesthetic influences. This sentiment, strong in his apprenticeship ("that having fixed my roots in this soil all contact, saving by the printed word, with contemporary poets is impossible"), would also become a part of his profile as an elder man of letters. Faulkner's claim throughout his career as a writer was that he was not a literary man but a simple farmer, a man of the soil who also wrote books. His essay entitled "Verse Old and Nascent: A Pilgrimage" outlines an aesthetic program for the young author in 1925, including a call to creation which Faulkner accomplished in time: "Is not there among us someone who can write something beautiful and passionate and sad instead of saddening?"[13] Faulkner's language is taken from the idiom of the South—whites, blacks, Spanish and French strains, the frontier. Faulkner's language lays claim not only to being "in" America but to informing the nation itself, reflecting its narrative predicaments and possibilities, producing through language a body of work that is beautiful and passionate and sad and *American* without becoming jingoistic, patriotic, celebratory—or anything like it which is, in literature, truly saddening.

Two essays from the 1998 conference deal specifically with Faulkner's use of language. Richard Godden studies Faulkner's syntax and diction with a level of precision not often found among contemporary critics. In "A Phenomenological Reading of *The Hamlet* as a Rebuke to an American Century," he configures the equation of land and language through the trope of penetration and insemination. Godden reads the episode about Ike Snopes and the cow within a nexus of "comparative idiocy" that links Ike to Benjy Compson, Isaac McCaslin, Rider, Henry Armstid, and Jim Bond. What connects these characters into a recognizable and socially significant pattern is the autochthonous qualities they share: each seems drawn—sometimes fatally, always consequentially—back to the earth of his indigenous place. Ike Snopes provides the paradigmatic example of a character who reenters the earth, in his case through what Godden argues is a seminal relation with the cow. His sexual penetration of the bovine creature returns Ike to the soil, and his attraction for the cow is an articulation of his longing for such restoration. Isaac McCaslin, on the other hand, rejoins the natural world through less physical but equally, if not more consequential means, by locating his ancestry there when he identifies the snake as his grandfather. Rider is drawn to the earth as an articulation of his love for Mannie, his dead wife. In each case, Faulkner's particularized, signature language, deftly scrutinized by Godden, conjoins land and articulation into seamless continuity.

Godden's intricate reading of these characters leads to an interpretation of Faulkner in America that is far less dependent on recently dominant modes of social and cultural analysis—Marxist, sociological, and psychological—and so is less likely to identify in Faulkner's prose the kinds of ideological posturing we've grown used to in literary criticism. Rather, Godden leans toward anti-Lockean and ecocritical implications, seeing in the earth a gravitational ecology whereby agricultural tenancy alienates human beings from spiritual fulfillment, and traps them into situations where, like Henry Armstid at the end of *The Hamlet*, they quite literally are seen to dig from the earth their own social identities through their labor. As a result, Godden is able to acknowledge but transcend standard readings of *The Hamlet* which see in the onset of market capitalism an intrusion on a benevolent agricultural economy. The ground revealed throughout Yoknapatawpha contains "practices of exchange which should not be simply assimilated into market terms" but rather situated within the contexts of the physical, ecological, and emotional relationships which both precede and will outlast capital. Faulkner's language, his artistry, emerges at Godden's hand from an aesthetic in which the very soil of Yoknapatawpha produces an autochthonous condition of linguistic fatality, making Faulkner's art an organic product both of the pull of the soil and the response of human articulation.

The difference that the employment of language makes to one's predicament is taken up by Hortense Spillers in "Faulkner Adds Up: Reading *Absalom, Absalom!* and *The Sound and the Fury*." Faulkner critics have noted the difference of opinion between Mr. Compson and his son, Quentin, over which is the saddest word in the English language. Mr. Compson nominates "was": the loss of event, emotion, or thought into the irretrievable nothingness of the past. Compson's life embodies the nomination, as he mourns the loss of even his ability to mourn losses. Quentin counters his father's "was" with "again," which he posits is the sadder word because it repeats into meaninglessness the very signifier, we might say, which ought to have secured meaning. Quentin's suicide can be seen as his final argument, which Faulkner himself undermines, as Quentin has indeed committed suicide over and over again, since 1929, in the reading. Spillers's insight is that it is in the combination of these anxieties that we find the novel's ultimate statement of loss. Faulkner's words continuously double back on themselves when they ought to have long disappeared, or they return after having been banished from the family lexicon (like the trope of caddie/Caddy); and words that do return do not necessarily produce repetition. Sometimes, words double back as synonyms, traces, complex regressions which seem like "again" but are also very much "was," in the past, yet. The fluidity between repetition and loss marks a particularly Faulknerian mode of existence, a psychology, intricately tied to history and duration. "We can only mean the repetition compulsion and the complex of regression, then, in a shadow dance to the psychoanalytic sphere," Spillers argues.

Spillers's intersection accounts for the overwhelming sense of loss we know in a book like *The Sound and the Fury*, a loss magnified because it is not experienced as *was* but seems ever on the brink of recurring, *again*. In America, Spillers says, Faulkner makes grief "a gift to the national culture," a way to comprehend modernism and regionalism, for one, and to recognize the implications of loss that the novel provides. Spillers begins by inquiring into Faulkner's avant-garde status, speculating profitably on Faulkner's dual identity as experimental modernist and as Southerner, native to the nation's backward region, who by ordinary would be thought immune to national aesthetic currents. Spillers wonders, what might have been the impression made by a novel like *The Sound and the Fury*, not on Mississippians but on minds who thought something in particular when they thought Mississippi in 1929. As Mr. Compson says in *Absalom, Absalom!* (and Spillers echoes), it just does not explain. However, the burden of explanation lies not with those who lived and performed the deeds in question, but on those who've taken it upon themselves to make sense of it. One of the underlying arguments in this collection is that the failure to see Faulkner in America, the recognition of the statement as problematic, only identifies the distance we've yet to go, as critics, toward fully accounting for the centrality of Faulkner's mind to American intellectual traditions. Or rather, those traditions must be inadequately articulated if they, in turn, cannot account in full for Faulkner's presence on the intellectual landscape.

A second pair of essays address such concerns directly. Noel Polk in " 'The Force that through the Green Fuse Drives': Faulkner and the Greening of American History," revisits Faulkner's meditation on the past through two characters particularly troubled (or, tragically untroubled) by historical forces, Isaac McCaslin and Thomas Sutpen. Polk begins with Gavin Stevens's deceptively simplistic "The past is never dead. It's not even past," and teases out the tangled implications of the statement. Does Stevens mean that we are, universally, victims of time, circumstance, heredity, and environment? "If so," Polk asks, "what is the point of human striving?" The animating spirit of the American culture we know more readily is not found in Stevens's formulation, but is more likely phrased as "The past is never here. It's not even in the past." Remaking the world, making it new, starting again: these are American imperatives. The Puritans did not come to the New World to perpetuate the Old, but to remake their faith, to start Christianity over again. Nonetheless, by the time of Faulkner, history could not be set aside so conveniently, or geographically. For the Mississippian, slavery, in particular, left the slate in an uncleansable condition.

By juxtaposing Isaac McCaslin with Thomas Sutpen (and the novels, *Go Down, Moses* with *Absalom, Absalom!*), Polk yields a significant crop. Sutpen wagered everything, and lost it all, attempting to create an Isaac McCaslin of himself. The driving force behind his attempt was an American belief that history—time, circumstance, heredity, and environment—could be set aside to make room for Thomas Sutpen. And the force prevailed, initially, as it has on occasion in America. Sutpen became a successful planter. But when he applied this formulaic America to himself and to the circumstances he created, when he thought that he could set aside *his own son* and the biographical history he had left behind him, the formula blew up in his face, and Sutpen fell into history. Isaac, in contrast, is painfully aware of his time, circumstance, heredity, and environment—to the point of intellectual paralysis. Fashioning himself and his condition as chosen by God for some particular judgment in time, Isaac seeks an apotheosis (much like Quentin, in *The Sound and the Fury*) worthy of divine expurgation. But alas, Isaac acts historically, not divinely, and thusly not very well. The irony is that Isaac is in a position to accomplish the ends of equity he says God has in mind, but can do so only by accepting and not repudiating history. Together, the novels articulate Faulkner's sense of historical responsibility. Polk's articulation of that perspective escapes oversimplification, but does not err in presenting Faulkner's challenge, the refusal to believe in victimization by events or anonymous forces. McCaslin and Sutpen make definitive choices and know just what they are doing, even as they contemplate disaster and ask God (or General Compson) how they could have failed.

The second contemplation of Faulkner's place in American intellectual traditions is Peter Nicolaison's, "William Faulkner's Dialogue with Thomas Jefferson," an extensive consideration of the significance of "Jefferson" to Faulkner. Briefly considering the fictional account of the town's naming in *Requiem for a Nun*, Nicolaison is more interested in the intellectual dialogue engaged in by Faulkner with Thomas Jefferson starting in 1926, when he first used the name for the Yoknapatawpha County seat, through the publication of *A Fable*, read by Nicolaison as written in part "to refute Jefferson." Over the course of three decades, Faulkner engaged Jeffersonian ideas on a wide variety of issues, ranging from independent farming, rural democracy, and governmental interference, to race, slavery, and miscegenation, and to questions about individual liberty and autonomy. Ultimately, however, Faulkner engaged Jefferson on the questions of power, authority, and rebellion. *A Fable* is thus "a direct attempt to come to terms with Jefferson's position on the liberty of the people, and the power of an entrenched establishment bent on defending its privileges." After locating Jeffersonian traces in a range of novels, including *The Hamlet, Go Down, Moses*, *If I Forget Thee, Jerusalem,* and *The Unvanquished,* Nicolaison concludes that there is a crucial "affinity between the two men" which has to do with a shared awareness "that the great democratic experiment in America might have a dark underside."

Reading Faulkner's texts against Jefferson's, particularly *Notes on the State of Virginia*, Nicolaison yields a fresh and important set of insights into Faulkner as a major intellectual presence in America in the twentieth century. In the dialogue Nicolaison constructs between Faulkner and Jefferson, we see each thinker concerned with a set of questions running parallel and remaining central to their respective time and place in the eighteenth, nineteenth, and twentieth centuries. Questions Faulkner raised through the creation of Jefferson, Yoknapatawpha, for example, are rooted in the life, writing, and legacy of Thomas Jefferson. Faulkner consistently revisited issues that have remained salient for three centuries in America, no less vital and explosive in Faulkner's era than they were in Jefferson's. Faulkner's concerns are consistently Jeffersonian, according to Nicolaison, "questions about power, for instance, about race, and, especially in his late fiction, about structures of authority and the freedom of the individual." Nicolaison thus contributes to an important but infrequent project of mapping Faulkner's intellect. Through an engagement of Faulkner's lifelong dialogue with Thomas Jefferson, Nicolaison raises Faulknerian exegesis from literary criticism to intellectual history. No less troubling a figure, Faulkner the intellectual raises problematic issues reminiscent of the controversies surrounding the notion of Jefferson's own independence of thought on matters of race, authority, and individual freedom.

Nicolaisen's study of *A Fable* is one of three essays that focused on that novel in the 1998 conference. The second, Catherine Gunther Kodat's "Writing *A Fable* for America," redefines the terms on which we read this novel, away from the biographical ("late Faulkner") or the evaluative ("bad Faulkner") toward the literary, economic, and cultural implications of the text, both in terms of its production and its contribution to its time. Specifically, Kodat places *A Fable* in context of the collapse of high modernism, the rise of the consumer economy in the Cold War, and the reemergence, at the same time, of the sentimental—particularly in the form of American sentimental Christianity. As a result, Kodat's *A Fable* represents a complex postwar intersection of particularly American cultural integers: sentimental Christianity, consumerist mass culture, and the decline of modernism. She provocatively labels *A Fable* Faulkner's *Uncle Tom's Cabin* because of the sentimentality with which it casts political issues as family dramas (e.g., the General and the corporal, the General and Marthe). Kodat implicitly raises questions that redefine the novel: If sentimental fiction recognizes sympathetic feeling as the glue holding together the social, then in the novel that glue is simultaneously weakened and replaced by the wedge of military authority, so that corporate-military hierarchies replace sympathetic connections as the phenomena of social cohesion. Kodat ingeniously connects the desire for such ties to the persistence of Freemasonry in the text, a matter which has confounded critics of the novel. The Masonic "brotherhood" is the masculine counterpart to what is often considered feminine sentimentality; Freemasonry is thus sentimentalism masculinized and reified as a social organization. In Kodat's understanding, the presence of the Masonic, its signals and mysteries, contributes to the sentimental project of *A Fable*.

Much has been obscured about Faulkner and America because of critical lapses in reading Faulkner's great novel of the Cold War era. Kodat suggests that "the frustrating and ungainly aspects of *A Fable* are best accounted for when we read the novel as a book about America" that includes "Faulkner's most sustained meditation on American philosophies and American aesthetics at the moment of the Unites States' ascension to global power via the twin forces of military victory and mass cultural expansion." The novel has intimate and originary ties to Hollywood, it boldly appropriates the Christ story for its specific narrative purposes, and it connects self-interest inextricably to communal purposes. At the same time, Kodat shows how *A Fable* nearly collapses into itself by the weight of what it attempts to accomplish. It may well be that the novel itself is our best evidence for the collapse of the high modernist project. On the other hand, as a literary response to the Cold War, the artist so closely associated with raising loss to the level of an aesthetic project is seen, in his "magnum o," as lamenting the loss of loss itself—much like the Mr. Compson of Hortense Spillers's essay. When American culture achieved hegemonic status among the victorious nations of World War II, it could no longer cast itself as "the runner" among nations; it had become, despite its national rhetoric of revolution and youth, the Generalissimo of nation-states. Faulkner's struggle in the novel is personal, aesthetic, and epochal.

In "Where Was that Bird? Thinking *America* through Faulkner," I offer the third essay on *A Fable*, continuing the inquiry into Faulkner's aesthetic program in that novel by casting it in performative, rather than representational terms. Evidence for the critical methodology employed is taken from the text. In its preface, Faulkner credits James Street's book, *Look Away*, as the source of a specific passage in *A Fable* about a hanged man and a bird. However, upon investigation, we learn that Street's novel does not contain what Faulkner credits it with; on the contrary, the best that can be said is that Street's book includes a story about a hanging (but no bird)—and hanging tales are in no short supply in American literature. So why would Faulkner credit the story to Street? The argument proffered is that the relationship between the story of the hanged man and the bird in and its "source" in *Look Away* is emblematic of Faulkner's aesthetic practice in *A Fable* and elsewhere. "It is not so much a representation of America that we find in Faulkner," I argue, but something of far greater importance, "a way to *think* America, a cognitive practice rooted in an American cultural ecology." That ecology is a tendency toward the performative, beginning with the Declaration of Independence (performing United States) and running through Sutpen's articulation-foundation, "Be Sutpen's Hundred." Included in the essay is a minor compendium of those occasions when Faulkner would deny the centrality of mimetic, thematic, or symbolic aspects of his fiction. Instead, he would refer to the tools of his trade, the lumber of his fictional constructions—always drawing his questioner's attention away from representation toward language, toward craft and articulation.

The way of thinking *America* accessed through Faulkner's art draws our attention to the "strength of imaginative idiom" on this continent, to the link between utterance and act. Language is powerful in America, from the naming of the continent itself for an Italian explorer to the naming of *Indians*, an act which linguistically displaced native peoples. Faulkner's artistry seems rooted in an awareness of that power, from Addie Bundren's quarrel with speech ("words are no good") to the Old General's interpretation of himself as an "articulation." Central also is Faulkner's sense of an unfinished universe, a trope he would employ on public occasions, insisting that the writer's task was to nudge us eternally toward completion. In the Nobel Prize Address, for example, Faulkner made the distinction between writers who "merely" record events and those who provide "one of the props" for readers at large to employ as they construct the future. The flight of the bird in *A Fable* is thus away from representational purposes of literature and toward its cognitive potential, toward the way in which language makes nation, makes reality, by the strength of its imaginative idiom. What Faulkner began his career writing about in the 1920s ("Nowhere today, saving in parts of Ireland, is the English language spoken with the same earthy strength as it is in the United States; though we are, as a nation, still inarticulate"), he returned to in full force in *A Fable*, where the "earthy strength" of the English language confronts the possibilities of humanistic faith in the potential for linguistic creation.

The relation between Faulkner's language and human construction—construction of roads as well as systems of belief—is thought through by Charles A. Peek in " 'A-laying there, right up to my door': As American *As I Lay Dying*." Peek invokes two contexts to know Faulkner's remarkable early novel: The national "good roads movement" of the early twentieth century, particularly the reception of that program in the South and its relation both to taxation and to the growing role of government in the lives of Mississippi farmers, and the culture of the Bible among the peasantry, the way in which Biblical phrases and stories informed their world view and provided metaphoric and allegorical touchstones for understanding and questioning the world of their experience. Anse, for example, is as troubled by "that durn road" as he is by God's mysterious intentions for him. Both seem necessary to his existence but each, in its own way, is inscrutable. Peek extrapolates from the crossing of Lord and road an American duality between the mysticism of the Christian faith and the materialism of capital, between the desire for transcendence and respect for pragmatic methods, between, ultimately, the sacred and the profane. The essay not only explicates but is itself an example of its explication, as Peek grounds a reading of *As I Lay Dying* in the material conditions of its time and place in Mississippi—roadbuilding, subsistence farming, impoverishment—while at the same time linking those conditions to eternities, transcending Mississippi and Bundren and arriving at the desire to acknowledge that there is more to life than roads and wagons, bananas and corpses. American spirituality is as often confused with crass evangelicalism as is its materialism confused with consumption. Peek restores a sense that American spiritualism and American materialism are extremes on a continuum, that, when at the point of crossing, provide human energies unparalleled thoughout most of history. Faulkner, Peek suggests, wrote to this intersection and thus far from being at the margins of American intellectual history, Faulkner, and Mississippi, emerge at its very core.

Core issues in American culture are examined further by Linda Wagner-Martin in "*Go Down, Moses*: Faulkner's Interrogation of the American Dream." Wagner-Martin sees in Isaac McCaslin a conscious shunning of the American Dream, sees in Rider a realization of its emotional vacuity, and finds in Lucas Beauchamp's futile struggle with it a revelation of its exclusions. And not least of all, the novel itself, a culmination of Faulkner's "major period," reveals to the author that his own hard work failed to gain him economic security and the comfort of middle class existence. The essay reads *Go Down, Moses* by retracing the steps of its narrative production. Faulkner began the novel by writing "Pantaloon in Black," which Wagner-Martin calls "Faulkner's most eloquent evocation of human pain," a lament for not only the loss of a spouse, "but for a lost life." Rider had achieved the American Dream: He was head of the timber gang, possessor of his own home and a ritualized, loving, domestic order. Mannie's death guts that life, plunging Rider into the depths of despair and revealing that, as hero, his flaw is "his capacity to be inordinately moved, rather than pacified or dulled, by his grief." Intense emotion transforms the trappings of the American Dream—home, money, possessions—into trivialities. The sheriff's misunderstanding of Rider's grief is thus as class-bound as it is racist. The sheriff cannot comprehend how someone could destroy his class standing because of something as routine as a death. Similar negotiations inform the grieving Worsham/Beauchamp family in "Go Down, Moses" and the suicide of Eunice in "The Bear." In a succession of textual examples, Wagner-Martin examines the way in which Faulkner displays the insufficiency of structures of thought associated with the American Dream to provide significant resources for the contemplation of genuine, emotional loss.

At her hands a fresh, and more contextualized, reading of Isaac McCaslin emerges. Isaac also traded his right to the American Dream in order to pursue a "vision of moral behavior" within the limited resources of its articulation—mostly, that is, in cash. Isaac's twin is Lucas Beauchamp, who, while not through choice, is also compelled to construct his life outside the American Dream. Wagner-Martin's method of reading the text according to its composition process is an intriguing one, a fine example of the confluence of textual scholarship and interpretation. Her strongest challenge is that readers enter the text not through its empowered white male characters, but in those through whom we know Faulkner created the novel as a whole: the black tenant-farmers, Rider, the Beauchamps. "I read this novel as Faulkner's most poignant, most revealing statement of what a man's life is forced to be like in America." Wagner-Martin finds in the text a series of examples of the American Dream as sham, the damage it does to those excluded by birth as well as to those who gain it, only to see it fail to sustain them through times of intense emotional or psychological need. Faulkner wrote so intensely about this because he experienced it, as a worker who felt he worked without just compensation, as a man who was forced to sustain a series of personal crises, loses, and responsibilities.

Charles Reagan Wilson finds that Faulkner's critical engagement with the American Dream continued into the 1950s, when, in his public statements, he grappled with the terms "American Way of Life" and "Southern Way of Life." Wilson traces the varied origins of this peculiar American terminology and reads closely Faulkner's use of it in his essay, "On Privacy: The American Dream: What Happened to It?" Critics have been confused by Faulkner's public statements in this era, seeing his politics as far less complex and sophisticated than his fiction. Wilson offers an important correction to such superficial readings by placing Faulkner's comments historically and elucidating the terminology he employed, terminology which contained distinctions that may escape readers today. For example, Wilson credits Faulkner with detecting a potentially corrosive contradiction between the American Dream, based in individual liberty, and the more collective American Way of Life, which Faulkner saw as based in fear and hysteria and buttressed by corporate and consumer forces. While official, state ideology blandly claimed that the American Dream and the American Way of Life were consistent and seamless, Faulkner insisted repeatedly that they were not. While the American Dream was indigenous to American history and was based on the experience of peoples who settled the nation, the American Way of Life was something fostered by industries, commercial interests, and other profit-based manipulators of public opinion. Wilson suggests that we see Faulkner's warning as similar to President Eisenhower's later in the decade, adding to Eisenhower's military-industrial complex the more intrusive forces of consumer and media manipulation. Wilson recognizes a further distinction drawn by Faulkner between the American Way of Life and the Southern Way of Life, which was coined to defend racial segregation as well as to call into question the industrial values of the American Way. Aligning Faulkner's thinking with the progressive work of activist James McBride Dabbs, Wilson places Faulkner among those Southerners who saw racial integration as more than simple justice but as a social action that should affect the world at large. Faulkner knew that biracial justice in the South would provide a model for world race relations, and thus expand the significance of the American Dream—but only if accomplished by the people themselves, not by the purveyors of the American Way. As a result of the South's success, the American Dream would expand and be accessible to the world's nonwhite peoples.

Faulkner's career did not unfold in a vacuum, of course, and in his relation to female writers of his own time, Faulkner had an uncanny parallel in Nathaniel Hawthorne. Kathryn B. McKee provides evidence in "The Portable Eclipse: Hawthorne, Faulkner, and Scribbling Women," expanding our sense of the similarities between the two writers by drawing our attention to women, contemporaries of Faulkner, whose work, like the "scribbling women" in Hawthorne's famous phrase, paralleled his own. McKee provides detailed analyses of the careers of Evelyn Scott and Frances Newman, and raises troubling issues concerning the way in which the South that Faulkner wrote to national and international prominence was (and is) quite specifically gendered male. By drawing our attention to topical parallels, in particular the subject matter of female sexuality, McKee shows specifically the way in which the absence of Newman and Scott from the canon results in the absence of a female perspective, leaving the realm of "universality" to the male writer. At the same time, McKee examines the ways in which region, and regionalism, may be transcended and ultimately emerge as indispensable to national literature. However, critics often approach regional writers with ideas about how region ought to be treated aesthetically; Hawthorne and Faulkner are our best examples of how a writer confronts a region and its history. For Scott and Newman, region is continuously interrupted by issues relating to gender—in fact, region is as gendered as it is placed. Gender may be known as the physical region through which the author's imagination must traverse, so that any critical concern for the relation between region and nation that fails to account for gender will either flounder, or, what is worse, confuse the masculine for the universal. In drawing our attention to Scott and Newman, McKee accentuates the place of Faulkner in America by compelling us to know that place as very specifically male, and thus to see Faulkner's towering presence as obscuring a fuller, more comprehensive awareness of the South in America.

Joseph R. Urgo
The University of Mississippi
Oxford, Mississippi

NOTES

1. "Verse Old and Nascent: A Pilgrimage," in William Faulkner, *Early Prose and Poetry*, ed. Carvel Collins (London: Jonathan Cape, 1963), 116. Originally published in the *Double Dealer*, January–February 1925.

2. "On Privacy (The American Dream: What Happened to It?)," in William Faulkner, *Essays, Speeches, and Public Letters*, ed. James B. Meriwether (New York: Random House, 1965), 62. Originally published in *Harper's*, 1955.

3. I asked Don Kartiganer how it was that the 1998 conference evolved from "Faulkner and America" to "Faulkner in America." In e-mail correspondence dated December 16, 1999, Don explained, "It was originally *and*, but in putting together the poster, Ann [Abadie] inadvertently changed the *and* to *in*." I am sure that Professor Kartiganer knows better than to believe in inadvertent error, especially by one as thoroughly involved with the Faulkner and Yoknapatawpha Conference as Ann Abadie, whose association goes back to 1974. In a remarkable display of the influence of the graphic arts, Ann replaced *and* with *in* on the conference poster and thus continued her subtle influence on literary history.

4. "On Privacy (The American Dream: What Happened to It?)," 64.

5. "Mississippi," in William Faulkner, *Essays, Speeches, and Public Letters*, 11. Originally published in *Holiday* magazine, April 1954.

6. William Faulkner, *A Fable*, in *Faulkner: Novels 1942–1954* (New York: Library of America, 1994), 931.

7. *Lion in the Garden: Interviews with William Faulkner, 1926–1962*, ed. James B. Meriwether and Michael Millgate (Lincoln: University of Nebraska Press, 1980), 261, 260, 265.

8. William Faulkner, "Books and Things: American Drama: Eugene O'Neill," in William Faulkner, *Early Prose and Poetry*, 89. " Originally published in *The Mississippian*, February 3, 1922.

9. Letter to Malcolm Franklin, December 5, 1942, in *Selected Letters of William Faulkner*, ed. Joseph Blotner (New York: Vintage Books, 1978), 166.

10. William Faulkner, "Books and Things: American Drama: Eugene O'Neill," 89.

11. "Books and Things: American Drama: Inhibitions," in William Faulkner, *Early Prose and Poetry*, 94, 95. Originally published in *The Mississippian*, March 24, 1922.

12. Ibid., 96.

13. William Faulkner, "Verse Old and Nascent: A Pilgrimage," in William Faulkner, *Early Prose and Poetry*, 118.

A Note on the Conference

The Twenty-fifth Annual Faulkner and Yoknapatawpha Conference sponsored by the University of Mississippi in Oxford took place July 27–August 1, 1998, with over two hundred of the author's admirers from around the world in attendance. Ten of the lectures presented at the conference are collected in this volume. Brief mention is made here of other activities that took place during the week.

At the opening session on Sunday afternoon, following a reception at the University Museums, Chancellor Robert C. Khayat welcomed participants. Charles Reagan Wilson, director of the Center for the Study of Southern Culture, presented the twelfth annual Eudora Welty Awards in Creative Writing. First place went to Matt Hedges of Corinth for his poem "My Plight with the Furtive Flight of Light" and second place to Robert Morris of Hattiesburg for his short story "The Sandpiper." Frances Patterson of Tupelo, a member of the Center Advisory Committee, established and endowed the awards, which are selected through a competition held in high schools throughout Mississippi. Next came the presentation of the winner of the ninth annual Faux Faulkner contest, sponsored by the Jack Daniel Distillery, the University of Mississippi, and Yoknapatawpha Press and its *Faulkner Newsletter*. Dr. Robert L. Blake Jr. of Columbia, Missouri, read his prize-winning entry, "Pile On." The program concluded with *Voices from Yoknapatawpha*, which consisted of readings from Faulkner's fiction selected and arranged by Betty Harrington, wife of former conference director Evans Harrington. After a buffet supper, held at the home of Dr. and Mrs. M. B. Howorth Jr., James B. Carothers of the University of Kansas delivered the opening address.

Monday's program included three lectures and the presentation of "Knowing William Faulkner," slides and commentary by the writer's nephew, J. M. Faulkner, and Meg Faulkner DuChaine. Monday's events concluded with award-winning actresses Alcie Berry and Janny Odle dramatizing scenes from the novel *Light in August* and "Twenty Will Not Come Again," a Joan Williams short story about her relationship with William Faulkner.

"Faulkner in Oxford" assembled local residents Mildred Murray Hopkins, Will Lewis Jr., and Patricia Young as panelists for a discussion moderated by M. C. "Chooky" Falkner, another of the writer's nephews. Other highlights of the conference included "Teaching Faulkner" sessions conducted by visiting scholars James B. Carothers, Robert W.

Hamblin, and Charles A. Peek and bus tours of North Mississippi and the Delta, followed by a party at Tyler Place hosted by Charles Noyes, Sarah and Allie Smith, and Colby Kullman. Conference goers also enjoyed exhibitions at the John Davis Williams Library, a walk through Bailey's Woods before the annual picnic at Faulkner's home, Rowan Oak, and a party at Square Books. The week ended with a reception at the home of Diane and "Chooky" Falkner.

The conference planners are grateful to all the individuals and organizations who support the Faulkner and Yoknapatawpha Conference annually. In addition to those mentioned above, we wish to thank Mr. Richard Howorth of Square Books, St. Peter's Episcopal Church, the City of Oxford, and the Oxford Tourism Council.

Faulkner in America

FAULKNER AND YOKNAPATAWPHA

1998

Comparative Idiocy: A Phenomenological Reading of *The Hamlet* as a Rebuke to an American Century

RICHARD GODDEN

1

Central to book 3 of *The Hamlet* (1940) is a liaison between an idiot (Ike Snopes) and a cow (property of Houston). The idiot's name and the cow's owner are misnomers, since each extends its bearer into a social world of tenant families and agricultural markets, whereas Faulkner's style for the encounter limits that extension. Let me give you an example: the idiot has been taught to climb and descend stairs; his teacher, Mrs. Littlejohn, keeps a boarding house in Frenchman's Bend, in which house the idiot sweeps and makes beds: "But at last he learned to negotiate them [the stairs]. Now he merely slowed a little before stepping, not confidently quite but not with alarm, off onto that which at each successive step, was not quite space; was almost nothing but at each advancing instant, not quite was, and hurried on through the lower hall and into the back yard."[1] You and I, for the most part, take the stairs without thought, though as we achieve arthritis we may have to think about how our bodies negotiate descent. Faulkner does not describe the stairs. Nor does he describe thinking about them. Instead, he offers a "step," where step in the phrase "each successive step" is both a noun and a verb. The run of prepositions towards that active entity ("off onto . . . at") indicates that there may be many a slip between lip and lip, where those small words which determine relationships are so determinedly indeterminate. In the phrase "off onto that," "that" does not help either, being a directional imperative which works by pointing towards an absence. If I observe, "This is no time to arrive at a lecture," my audience may suppress a desire to turn towards the entrance at the back, seeking to see the reproved latecomer. There is no one there, but "this," like "that" and indeed "there," has done its work, materializing an absence by gesturing in the direction of what the word's recipient must invent. I dawdle over "that" because that is what Faulkner does: in "off onto that," "that" is deferred, "that which . . . was not quite; was almost . . . but not quite." That "step," either as ambulation or carpentry, is withheld, and consequently Ike reaches the bottom of Mrs. Littlejohn's stairs without appearing to complete a step, and without those stairs gaining depth or perspective, either for him or for the reader. Note how the "lower hall" and "back yard" arrive, as though at a run, out of Ike's hesitation between lip and lip.

I have exacerbated an exacerbating piece of prose in order to exemplify Faulkner's attention to Ike's body as a process. On the stairs and everywhere, Ike engages in the perceptual labor of making himself and of coming apart. Between one step and the next he manages to forget how he made his last step and so cannot anticipate the next. His problem is temporal: because, for Ike on the stairs, any past step is no longer, and any future step is not yet—the present step (both as object and action) cannot be substained.[2] At a loss for memory and anticipation, Ike is unable to configure a single step. He falls down a lot. What is surprising is that he doesn't do so more often, having limited ability (either spatially or temporally) to extend himself into a world through which he may pass with confidence. Yet the effect of his limitations is not primarily one of impairment, at least not for the reader of Faulkner's prose. Because the step down from one stair to the next is stylistically surprising, the gap is neither "space" nor "nothing"; instead it is a small miracle made from prose and characterized by incarnation.[3]

Ike's body, as written, comes to itself, and is incarnate, through its surroundings and only through its surroundings. Ike's surroundings are inaugurated as surroundings precisely as meanings for his body.[4] Put less ponderously, Mrs. Littlejohn's stairs bring Ike's feet into being, even as his footwork displays the condition of the stairs that have made his feet possible. One way of dramatizing the particular condition of openness between subject and object, which is everywhere operative for Ike, would be to have you undertake the following. Place your left hand on the desk. Press down firmly. The skin of your hand experiences "touching" only because of the object touched. The desk calls your hand into being. We might say that our various senses cannot exist in and of themselves; they are neither passive nor causative, instead they are formulated in their responsiveness to the objects which they question. The world is visual in reply to our sense of sight, sonorous in reply to our sense of hearing . . . and so on.

To experience a hand as an aperture into what it is not, rather than as entity or instrument, might be phenomenologically valid, but it renders the hand in question inoperative for labor. Luckily, perhaps, for us (unlike Ike), we reclaim our hands from their experiential dependency upon what is "other" than them, by forgetting the living experience through which they, and the rest of our bodies, are given to us. In effect, we inoculate ourselves against things by way of a body of habits,[5] which allows us to blunt the contribution of perception to consciousness. Safely sedimented within doubles, we descent the stairs, without thought and with minimal perception; after all, we are more concerned with getting where we are going, and with the purpose of our journey in the plot of our day.

For Paul Ricœur, it is exactly our capacity to plot ourselves that rescues us from the dispossessive power of other things as they engage with and incite our perceptions.[6] If a subject is conscious because conscious of things which have primacy,[7] that subject is always liable to be a "self" dispossessed by the engaging otherness of the objects with which it is engaged (and through which it re-engages its "self"). Such phenomenal plenitude or sheer sensory convolution is less available to the subject who must summon sufficient permanence to act. As Ricœur puts it, "the question of identity remains a privileged place of aporias."[8] I take his point to be that since we configure our "identities" through the stories that we tell ourselves, those stories, which may be epic ("He descended into Hell") or minimal ("he went down stairs"), counter the dispersal of the self inherent in subjects who remain purely aprey to the primacy of perception.

I had best explain my somewhat rapid conflation of "habitual body" and "story." To echo Ike on the stairs: imagine standing in the dark in a room that is new to you. To reach for the light switch may seem a reflex, but your reflex has a beginning, a middle, and an end—a story structure. The act of your arm as it reaches for the wall begins in a habit retained from earlier rooms, and moves towards a goal (light at the touch of a switch), whose end can be separated neither from your hand leaving your pocket, nor from its subsequent movement through the air. Arguably, even the most unarticulated and instantaneous occurences—a loud bang, an unexpected extinguishing of the lights—are experienced as "temporally thick"[9] or storied. We may jump at the bang, but in jumping elaborate on the noise in terms of its origin and implication, problem and solution. We blink at the dark, but experience our loss of sight in terms of entry and exit, suspense and resolution. Such terms are often cited as features of narrative; my point is that small plot structures inhere in human phenomena at their inception and are not post hoc constructions laid on top of real things. The loud noise and the unexpected dark make sense prior to our reflecting on them, thanks to the narratives embodied in our habits. Of course, those habits which shape us, leave things out, as Ricœur indicates when he ties "identity" to "aporias." Your hand might not reach so readily for the switch were you to retain the texture of your pocket lining, or the odor of the occupant in the dark air of the room.

Ike is low on both habit and stories; consequently, his "self" (though I find it hard to conceive of his having one) comes apart. His perception, uninformed by much memory or anticipation, cannot edit out that which it perceives, and as a result as soon as it attends to anything that thing becomes legion, with each facet of that thing calling an aspect of his attention into being. To adopt the language of phenomenology: Ike's "self" is realized as "a series of incomplete profiles,"[10] induced by a "synthesis of transitions,"[11] occurring as his senses are called into a "discordant concordance,"[12] with the objects to which they are subject.[13] Having cast Ike, for a time, among phenomenologists, I should perhaps correct the resultant impression. In order to read him, care of Merleau-Ponty, as a device for the generation of minor miracles, I claimed that he lacked habits and stories (the wherewithal of coherence). This is not strictly true: care of Mrs. Littlejohn's "firm gentle . . . hand" (183), Ike can climb stairs because he has learned that they are an habitual element in the plot of housework. Upstairs, he sweeps, but since "the creeping ridge of dust and trash in front of the broom" prompts him to "placid and virgin astonishment" (183) we may assume that should Mrs. Littlejohn's "hold and control" fail of its attentiveness, Ike's "take" on litter could take him anywhere. After all, Faulkner's phrasing, ever acute to Ike's cognitive practice, indicates that Ike makes little sense of sweeping. The litter and the broom happen to him: "*the* broom" is not *his* broom, any more than the trash, granted agency in that it appears to "creep," results (for him) from his work. Unsurprisingly, he is "astonished" and sweeps as though he has never swept before—a virgin among brooms. The hold of habit is scant, so that when, upstairs and sweeping, he sees smoke from Houston's burning woodland, and thinks by association of the cow pastured there, the accessories of housework (broom and stairs), literally vanish. The broom, which must impede his rush to the cow, goes missing in his hands. The stairs, his only route to the hill, cease to exist: "He began to run where he stood, carrying the broom. He ran blundering at the wall, the high small window through which he had seen the smoke, which he could not have passed through even if he could have taken the eighteen-foot drop to the earth" (186). Turned round by the impact of the wall, he sees the corridor and so recovers the stairs; but, as we have noted, shifted from the habitual story of housework to the new narrative of the cow, the stairs will prove adversarial.

I have argued that Ike lacks habits and stories. I should have said, at least for chapter 2 of book 3 of *The Hamlet*, that he is possessed of a single story and some attendant habits, and that in so far as he is conscious he is conscious of one thing, of the cow and of his need to "make one with" (183) the cow. So, phenomenologically prepared, I offer a reading of the one about an idiot and a cow:

> The trunks and the massy foliage were the harps and strings of afternoon; the barred inconstant shadow of the day's retrograde flowed steadily over them as they crossed the ridge and descended into shadow, into the azure bowl of evening, the windless well of night; the portcullis of sunset fell behind them. At first she would not let him touch her bag at all. Even then she kicked him once, but only because the hands were strange and clumsy. Then the milk came down, warm among his fingers and on his hands and wrists, making a thin sharp hissing on the earth.
>
> There was a moon at that time. It waned nightly westward; juxtaposed to it, each dawn the morning star burned in fierce white period to the night, and he would smell the waking's instant as she would rise, hindquarters first, backing upward out of invisibility, attenuating then disseminating out of the nest-form of sleep, the smell of milk. Then he would rise too and tie the rope-end to a swinging branch and seek and find the basket by the smell of the feed which it contained last night, and depart. From the edge of the woods he would look back. She would be still invisible, but he could hear her; it is as though he can see her—the warm breath visible among the tearing roots of grass, the warm reek of the urgent milk a cohered shape amid the fluid and abstract earth (198–99).

The passage takes its pattern from the primacy of Ike's perceptions. For example: prepositions set their subject (often Ike) in a transitive relation, not of governance but of supplication, to their objects (often bovine); with the result that Ike, a disassemblage of perceiving parts who is rarely an entity, experiences milk "on his hands and wrists" but "among his fingers." Had the sensory list run "warm on his fingers and on his hands and wrists," as, removed from Ike's perceptual provenance, it so easily might, much would have been lost. "Among" is phenomenally generous: acting to slow and subdivide the moments of lactation, it allows milk to draw the elements of Ike's hands out of darkness and into a coherence that is less manual than oral. The idiot does not so much milk the cow as suck her manually: the suckling mouth would seem to be the ground, "the milk came down . . . making a thin sharp hissing on the earth."

To draw back, for a moment, from the prepositional dynamic of the passage: Ike is a Snopes, and we should remember that some among his kin are noted for knowing the price of each thing and for reducing every thing to a price. They are accordingly reduced. Flem and I. O., like their cousin, have difficulty keeping body and soul together, but where his body comes apart from perceptual excess, theirs shrink to bits. Flem is a chewing jaw, famously extracting the "suption" from a nickel (26). Note the contraction from chewing tobacco to coin, and from coin as a measure of value (a nickel) to coin as liquidity (suption) existing to ease the flow of commodities. I. O.'s garments give "no indication whatever of what the body within them might be doing—indeed, if it were still inside them at all" (70). His physique, "a furious already dissipating concentration of energy," is the instrument of his intention, and as such it "vanishe[es] the instant after the intention [takes] shape" (71). Most typically, I. O. intends a profit. Flem and I. O.'s names nominate their reduction, Flem to a bit of human waste,[14] and I. O. to a credit note, an I.O.U. signed Initials Only.[15] Ike, who pronounces his name "Ike H-mope," may, as Jack Matthews suggests, be "Ike who mopes" (at a loss for his love[16]), but I feel justified, given a context where he possesses the cow, in suggesting that we attend to his phrasing of the letters of his name. Asked to "Say it," by Flem, he articulates "hoarsely," "Ike H-mope" (95). The H, capitalized, is stressed. The m, hyphenated, is uttered separately but as a demoted phoneme, shadowed both by the H and the missing S. To "say it," to enact and annotate the enunciation of the phonemes, is to be made aware of the surfaces of the throat. To "say it" is to sense the passage of air over interior muscles ("Ike H-mope") ("H-mope"), and is finally to foreground the H as a phenomenological experience. Ike "Hopes" exactly because of his perceptual excess: for him "a hand's breadth of contact shapes her solid and whole out of the infinity of hope" (201). Hope mopes only when the cow, which gives plot to his excess, is taken from him.

To return to Ike possessing the cow, and to a second promiscuous pronoun—to "in," loose prefix to "invisibility": "she would rise, hindquarters first, backing upward out of invisibility." The phrasing recalls Ike's earlier emergence during a "false dawn" from Mrs. Littlejohn's barn, at which point: "he could already see and know himself to be an entity solid and cohered in visibility instead of the uncohered all-sentience of fluid and nerve-springing terror alone and terribly free in the primal sightless inimicality" (182). Since the dawn is "false," and he can barely if at all see, "in" and "visibility" (hard to keep apart at the level of enunciation), slide together; at which point, the various hyphens and hyphenate words slip their ties. At a loss for the sight, which his longing for the cow had caused him to anticipate, Ike is "all" "sentience," which is to say that he is dispossessed by the excess of his senses. "Less" "sight," he becomes "all" "one" with the dark, into which his "nerves" "spring," leaving him not just "un" "cohered" but "in" "imicality." Of course, one cannot be "in" "imicality"; there's no such place or word. However, to say "inimicality," thanks to the preponderance of "i" ("in" "im" "ic" "it"), is to be aware of the word as a tense compression of phonemes waiting to burst apart. Faulkner prompts separation by way of rhythm and rhyme. The rhythm of his sentence draws "inimicality" (an iambic trimeter), rhyming on "ee", towards "terribly free" (an iambic dimeter). Rhyme, rhythm, and latinate strangeness combine to take "inimicality" (that which is adverse, hostile, wounding) apart, producing the neologism, "imicality." I am close to nonsense, but to a nonsense, achieved through dissolution, whose oddity may take us towards the sense of Ike's body distended on the dark.

All of which may seem a tiresomely long route to the extraction of "in" from "invisibility" (on the grounds that elsewhere and earlier there is a reversed precedent for such activity). Exasperating and exasperated, I can only hope my peregrinations among prepositions have served to alert and not numb you to Faulkner's prepositional preoccupation as regards Ike. Prepositions, marking relations between words and their referents, put things into position. Ike is "terribly free" because incapable of positioning himself, either perceptually or socially, within predicated relations.

Having primed "in," I can return to the cow as she rises with the dawn, "hindquarters first, backing upwards out of invisibility." Given the "in visibility" of another and recent dawn, we may question just how the cow enters Ike's visual field. Ike, lying next to her, watches by smell: "he could smell the waking instant as she would rise." To see by smell is not to see by sight. The cow is not at this point visible. At the close of the paragraph, with Ike at the edge of the woods looking back, "she would be *still* invisible but he could hear her, it is *as though* he can see her—the warm breath visible among the tearing roots of grass, the warm reek of the urgent milk a cohered shape amid the fluid and abstract earth" (199, my emphasis). Ike's instances first of olfactory and then of aural vision depend on milk. He has slept "where the milk came down . . . on the earth." The cow, grazing that milky ground, exists "invisibly" in the field of Ike's visibility on condition that she makes milk. The passage is filled with the conditional, "would." "Could hear" becomes "can see," at the sound of chewed cud.

Arguably, the pervasive emission of milk obscures an equally important emission of semen. The cow "attenuate[s]" and "disseminate[s]" from "the smell of milk." "Attenuate"—to make thin or weaken by dilution. "Disseminate"—to scatter abroad, as in sowing seeds. Neither word refers in any simple way to the outline of the cow, since that outline is sensed by Ike as extending from an odor. The smell, in which he sleeps and from which she rises, has thinned but retains (care of "disseminating") a seminal residue. Clues to insemination are elusive and marked by omission. Between the "hissing" of milk "on the earth" at nightfall and the smell of milk at dawn falls a paragraph space. I would suggest that the break contains the emission. Traces of evidence may be extracted from "hissing," "moon," and "that time." The directional imperative "that" gestures indexically towards a missing moment which readers must reconstruct. Since "that time" is moonlit, it is unlikely to occur within its own paragraph, during which the moon wanes. Nor can the time in question fall during the previous paragraph which is moonless. The moon, in *The Hamlet*, is twice directly associated with insemination and fertility: Houston moves his marital bed so that the full moon of April will fall across his union (238); Mrs. Varner, already pregnant with Eula, "show[s] her belly to the full moon" in April to ensure the gender of the child (339). Ike takes Houston's cow in April. "Moon" contains more clues: linked by color to milk and semen, its sound, activated by "hiss," yields a faint bovine cry. Evidence for Ike's act remains circumstantial, a matter of subsemantic whispering across a marked gap. Clearly, the presence of sperm is unstated; instead, and in accordance with Ike's perceptual habits, semen and milk mingle. As fluids expressive of a sometimes erotic transitivity,[17] occurring between subject and object (through which Ike lives), they pervade the amatory space.

I have traced the copresence of both fluids as that out of which the figures and their landscape are constituted, in order to establish that Ike penetrates the cow as a prelude to a second penetration of the earth, and of that which the earth sustains. Put crudely, the cow is a hole by way of which Ike becomes intimate with the soil. The pattern of the episode with which I have been concerned typifies Ike's nights with the cow. In each instance, through her he delves into the earth and turns autochthonic. An autochthon is one who springs from the soil which he inhabits: Adam formed from dirt, and limping Oedipus, tagged by his name (meaning "swollen foot") to that from which he came, are noted carriers of autochthony. Symptomatically, while still at the prepenetrative stage, Ike would watch his love while prone on the ground and subject to an erotics made mainly from mud (183). "Drenched" and sunk in "water-heavy grasses," Ike attends to "the plopping suck of each deliberate cloven mud-spreading hoof." "Suck[ed]" by sound he "wallow[s] . . . from thigh to thigh": necessarily, in the context of so much grass, the sounds he makes are "hoarse." His punning declension towards herbivore is incomplete in that he cannot yet catch the cow, and so lacks a point of entry to the "earth's teeming minute life" that actively excites him. The damp ground exudes mist, rhetorically cast as a third-party to the scene: the mist has "malleate hands" that "palp" Ike's "flanks" and the cow's "barrel." The liaison is triangular and interrupted: the cow is untouched, the mist filled with "hymeneal" bird song, and Ike's "wallow" autoerotic. But it is difficult to escape the suggestion that the ground, and not the idiot or the cow, is the dominant sexual partner.

The three parties are copresent and have the same hierarchy in Faulkner's only other extended account of a night between Ike and the cow. Once again Ike passes through the cow and into the earth, although the autochthonous scenario is varied in that the two figures drink at a spring, which spring displaces the cow as the earth's orifice. Darkness falls. Milk falls. The figures both drink at "the well of days, the still and insatiable aperture of earth" (205), otherwise described as a "tender mouth" (206). The earth's "mouth" is doubly "insatiable": first, because it draws into itself "the complete all of light" (206) from the sun's passage during the day; and second, because when Ike drinks, his image is kissed by a liquid "aperture" into which it passes and drowns, "he breaks with drinking the reversed drinking of his drowned and fading image" (205). The prose is vertiginously vague: glossed, it might read—the image of Ike's head, mirrored in the water and broken by his drinking, returns as he lifts his head. A return which ensures that the watery "aperture" retains, though "drowned and fading," the image of Ike's sucking mouth. One mouth (the earth's) contains another (Ike's).

The earth's orifice is capacious. Faulkner moves directly from describing its absorption of Ike's image to detailing its absorption of all the light of day; indeed, the two (Ike and light), fuse in a piece of luminous innuendo: "until at last the morning, noon, and afternoon flow back, drain the sky and creep leaf by voiceless leaf and twig and branch and trunk, descending, gathering frond by frond among the grass, still creeping downward in drowsy insect murmurs, until at last the complete all of light gathers about that still and tender mouth in one last expiring inhalation. He rises. The swale is constant with random and erratic fireflies" (205–6). The "mouth" which inhales the "expiring day" inescapably sucks. Since that mouth is "insatiable," fringed and damp, its metamorphosis into vagina is imminent, and affirmed by Ike's reaction. "He rises," physically from the pool and phallically into its "aperture." "Swale," prompted by "rise," doubles as "moist and marshy depression" and pudendum. The "fireflies," caught in the logic of the innuendo, may be translated as semen. Ike turns from the spring to the cow who acts as the spring's structural analogue. Both draw light into themselves, the cow being "Blond too in that gathered last of light" (206). Faulkner closes the paragraph and the chapter with a Biblical echo, "They lie down together," a phrasing which recalls "to lie with" and so summons any number of Old Testament couplings. The second account of a night with the cow is consequently structured like the first, both containing breaks in which omission implies emission.

The purpose of all my interpretative fiddle is to establish how absolutely yet covertly Ike cohabits with the soil; in which case, the cow becomes something of a stalking horse, existing primarily to obscure a secret autochthony. Moreover, Ike's milky inseminations are productive. We are assured that the earth into which he passes is packed with progeny: the list is various, "Troy's Helen," bishops, kings, victims, nymphs, and "graceless seraphim" (200, 206). We may doubt his paternity, yet it remains the case that Frenchman's Bend is, by declaration, haunted ground—and I have established that traces of Ike's semen are to be found in that place. The question of paternity is further compounded once we realize that we as readers have been a party to the generation of ghosts. My case is that only by exactingly close reading can we trace Faulkner's stylistic sensitivity to those perceptual practices whereby an idiot constructs himself within movements from subject to object. We, the tracers, are therefore complicit in Ike's passage into the earth and the earth's objects. Ergo, if the Bend is haunted, and Ike did it, we are his accomplices.

2

Before establishing a motive for the secret crime of autochthony, I would stress that Faulkner tends to reach for an idiot when he has something precious to hide—witness Benjamin Compson. At various interviews and with varying emphasis, Faulkner insisted that Caddy was "too beautiful . . . to reduce her to telling."[18] In what better place might he preserve her, untold, than in the linguistically impaired consciousness of a silent simpleton? Benjy's verbal limitations are the commonplace of Faulkner scholarship; what is not so frequently recognized is that Benjy is as rich in small sisters as he is poor in linguistic resources. Having no question or exclamation mark, he sets Caddy beyond inquiry or outrage. A basic sentence format denies complication. He has few negatives with which to exclude his sister, no causal words to explain her, and limited adjectives with which to modify her. I should perhaps add that prior to the image from which the novel sprang (Caddy with stained drawers up a tree in 1898), Benjy is quite literally a blank. He was born in April 1895, but no word in his section antedates 1898. Moreover, since he is temporally inclined to regress to that point (of the some one hundred and six pieces that make up his day, April 7th 1928, the majority occur before 1910), it is possible to argue that Benjy's consciousness is geared to restoring Caddy to a blank space, synonymous with innocence and silence. Prior to 1898 Benjy had no words and Caddy was unmarked by sex and death. If Benjy can retain Caddy, ideally as she was before her subversive tree climbing (to look into the room where her grandmother's corpse was laid), or at best prior to 1910 (in 1909 she loses her virginity, in 1910 she is married), he can keep to himself a more or less virginal sister.[19]

Such claims require multiple readings and laborious decipherment. Even then, they may not add up to answering Sartre's still resonant question, "why is the first window that opens on this fictional world the consciousness of an idiot?"[20] To hazard a simple answer (and I have space only for simplification): Benjy allows Faulkner to hide a hymeneal sister in the mazey space of a simple mind. That a hymen should matter enough to generate a guardian at its edge is the stuff of ethnic fear and class closure—it is not, however, the stuff of my current lecture. Enough to say that Benjy, like Ike, is an idiot in whom a secret of elusive value is stored.

Despite sharing Benjy's habit of staring at fetish objects (Ike's toy cow surely derives from Benjy's slipper, cushion, mirror box, and flower), Ike has closer and more companionable idiots. In terms of the run of the novels, Jim Bond (from *Absalom, Absalom!* [1936]) and another Ike from *Go Down, Moses* (1942) are more revealing of Faulkner's covert purposes in the matter of idiots and earth, circa the late '30s. Although Ike McCaslin is less an idiot than a fool, who in turning away from history (as represented by the commissary) and towards nature (embodied in the great woods) would recast himself as a natural, he, nonetheless, shares a key structural imperative with his namesake. Both Ikes look through the body of an animal into the ground.

Revisiting Sam Father's burial plot, where Lion's bones and Old Ben's paw intermingle with the corpse, "not in earth, but of earth . . . myriad, one," Ike almost treads on a snake, "more than six feet of it . . . and old."[21] He experiences double vision, so that the snake exists in two times: in the early 1940s and in a prehistorical space marked by spectral evidence of rudimentary limbs: "The elevation of the head did not change as it began to glide away from him, moving erect yet off the perpendicular as if the head and that elevated third were complete and all: an entity walking on two feet and free of all laws of mass and balance and should have been because even now he could not quite believe that all that shift and flow of shadow behind that walking head could have been one snake" (314). Ike, "without premeditation," addresses the monster as "Chief . . . Grandfather." His attribution is genealogically interesting, and open to at least three interpretations. Strictly speaking, if Ike is addressing a serpentine grandfather, and since Theopholus McCaslin or Uncle Buck is his biological father, we must assume that he casts his grandfather, Lucius Quintus Carothers McCaslin, as the snake that, historically speaking, he very much was. The bestial name fits, but its Chickasaw form, tone, and unfallen accessories suggest that Ike has a different grandfather in mind. Let us assume that, given Sam Fathers as an adopted father, Ike looks through the vegetative reptile (with its "smell of rotting cucumbers") to Sam's father, Ikkemotubbe, also known as Du Homme/The Man. But this option is not without problems. Ikkemotubbe was indeed known for his poisonous behavior, falling from the grace of his Indian title to be called Doom: in which case, he too is just too reptilian to warrant prelapsarian markers. A third genealogy can be traced from the name: let us suppose that Ike, "speaking the old tongue which Sam had spoken" (314), speaks for, or as though he were his mentor, Sam. If so, the line would run from Sam to Ikkemotubbe, The Man/Doom. Since the most doomed man is Adam, and Adam's father is God, Ike in addressing his grandfather (through Sam) is talking to God. There is, however, an ancillary option: Sam's Chickasaw name means Had-Two-Fathers, one Indian, the other a quadroon slave. It follows that, in order to talk to God, via a divine snake, Ike revises Genesis and suppresses an alternative lineage (with its attendant history). Ike's projections and omissions are complex: he becomes an ethnically cleansed Sam so that he may project, through the mulch where Sam lies with animals, a revisionist reptile. The snake contains post- and prelapsarian times; but Ike's "Oleh" renders the earth rife with Eden, into which Ike, by way of Sam's word, all but degenerates. His archaic usage allows him to regress along a genealogical line to its fount—an alternative grandfather and original autochthonist, happy to make men from prelapsarian mud. With luck, my genealogical exercise has established a structural similarity between the two Ikes, both of whom would secrete themselves in the earth by way of an animal.

However, within the context of *Go Down, Moses*, rather than the intertext it forms with *The Hamlet*, Ike's earthing is linked to another and more morbid autochthony. A cursory reading of "Pantaloon in Black" reveals Rider and Ike as secret sharers, both being drawn earthwards by spectres; in each case, their progress is attended by animals. Rider's wife Mannie dies (her name should be noted as consisting of a male term and a potential play on the first person pronoun). Rider's grief is explicitly and repeatedly presented as a compulsion to rejoin his wife. Mannie's ghost appears, vampirically absorbing his air, and convincing him that his body is the "insuperable barrier" (136–37) to their reunion. The trajectory of Rider's desire is clear: he must move from the animate to the inanimate. His method is only apparently murky: he kills a white gambler for cheating, though Birdsong's crooked dice have been recognized for years. Rider is lynched by Birdsongs. Again, the names resonate. Rider is a synonym for sexual athlete.[22] Birdsong is but one among a sequence of animal references, Rider being a "horse" (138), given to "wolfing" food (139), who spends time in the "bull pen" (153) and who when drunk claims to be "snakebit" (147). He is attended by a large hound. That the Birdsongs should effect Rider's movement into the earth is in keeping with the wider and emergent structural imperative that those enamoured of autochthony should pass earthward by way of animals. Just as Ike is linked to Sam through bear, dog, and snake (and Boon sleeps with Lion), so Rider (half man/half animal) recovers his identity (man → I) via a penetration of the soil.

The recognition that "The Bear" and "Pantaloon in Black" are structurally analogous in the matter of grieving autochthony effectively puts the black back into the ethnically cleansed ground. Stated reductively, Ike goes "natural" so that he can forget the commissary ledgers, with their evidence of McCaslin land as the land the slaves made. However, Sam may only operate as Ike's "aperture" to the earth because Ike represses Sam's enslaved quadroon father, burying his adopted shadow family among the impacted genealogical narratives latent in "Oleh." Structurally speaking, Rider won't let us forget Ike's selective memory, because Rider's pathological autochthony emphatically locates the soil as the extended body of the black worker. Rider, it will be remembered, is, among other things, a giant in the work place. Moreover, by entering the earth he enters Mannie, in a conceit which casts the soil both as a black signature and as a black vagina containing a black phallus.[23] Whether or not the Birdsongs emasculate their victim seems secondary to a deep plot that has Rider earn his name (as man and as sexual athlete) via a drift (attended by animals) into the body of the earth.

If the soil of the big woods, though ethnically cleansed, is residually marked "black" in 1942, then perhaps one is justified in reconsidering the soil of Frenchman's Bend, marked "milky" in 1940? Intertextually speaking, because the two Ikes are structurally similar, and because Ike McCaslin and Rider share an approach to the ground, there may or perhaps should be traceable links between Ike Snopes and Rider, both of whom (pushing it) might be said to inseminate the earth. I am aware that in my hunt for a deep narrative informing several texts and turning on hidden autochthony, I am straining your patience once again. I can only ask you to bear with me as I seek to establish a missing link, whose presence may finally allow me to address Faulkner's motive for telling the one about the idiot and the cow, in the way that he does, in *The Hamlet*.

My argument has involved assembling a series of secretive idiots, mainly white—Benjamin Compson, Ike Snopes, Ike McCaslin. The tangential appearance of Rider would suggest that Jim Bond be admitted to the comparative frame. Jim Bond is unlike Benjy and the Ikes, not simply because he is black, but because Faulkner does not attend to how he thinks, but rather deploys him as something Quentin Compson (at the end of *Absalom, Absalom!*) thinks *with*. Crucially, however, like Rider and the white fools, Jim Bond is bound to the earth, and more particularly to one place. If Quentin is to imagine Sutpen's Hundred, and to close his account with it, he must think through Jim Bond.

I run ahead of myself. Jim Bond is the idiot child of Charles Etienne de Saint Valery Bon and "a full-blood negress."[24] He is the grandson of Charles Bon. Probable janitor and putative incendiary to Sutpen's Hundred, he keeps the gate when Quentin visits in 1909, and will not be driven from the "ashes" and the "gutted chimneys" (301). He howls, and for his listeners he becomes little more than a howl with a name attached. The acoustic of the sound is tricky: to listen too long is to lose any sense of the direction from which the noise comes; but the noise remains constant and all pervasive. If Jim Bond is "wraithlike and insubstantial" (300) it may be because he haunts a sound, which sound so haunts a place as to become inseparable from that place—the howl which is the Hundred's signatory ground. As with Ike Snopes's "hoarse" articulation of his name, so with Jim Bond's barely human "howl," Faulkner's prose warrants attention as it attends to the experiential process involved in uttering and receiving a sound: "the howling did not diminish nor even seem to get any further away. . . . But they couldn't catch him. They could hear him; he didn't seem to ever get any further away but they couldn't get any nearer and maybe in time they could not even locate the direction of the howling anymore. . . . the house collapsed and roared away, and there was only the sound of the idiot negro left" (300–1). The idiot's "sound" is residual in several senses. After and out of the "roar" comes the "howl." Jim Bond burns the once white house down, and therefore his howl (albeit unintentionally) not only *re*places but *dis*places the plantation. Moreover, Faulkner attaches the howl to "the scion, the last of his race" (300). "Scion" used twice, first by Quentin (296) and then by the narrator, means "heir" or "descendant," but has an earlier, and in this context relevant, horticultural meaning, being also a "shoot, twig or graft." So, Jim Bond's sound is variously grafted to the earth.

My case for Jim Bond as yet another more or less idiotic autochthonist is also evidenced by his name. You may recall that on the last page of *Absalom, Absalom!*, Quentin admits to Shreve that he "still hear[s] him at night sometimes" (302). Jim Bond may have vanished from the Hundred, "Whereabouts unknown" some time during 1910, as the Genealogy suggests (309), but his howl persists in Quentin's head as he lies on his Harvard bed, "rigid" and silently quoting from "The Raven," "Nevermore of peace. Nevermore of peace. Nevermore. Nevermore. Nevermore" (298–99). His choice is fitting, since Poe's poem features a talking bird that settles on "the pallid busts of Pallas"[25] to torment the poem's already disturbed narrator. Poe's selection of perch (referred to three times) is doubtless color-led—an "ebony" bird on a white head. Pallas euphonically yields "pallid" but is also another name for Minerva, goddess of wisdom, who, it is popularly supposed, sprang from the split skull of her father, Jupiter. Poe's black bird is an obscurely wise headache, and in quoting it Quentin may well be attending, through its choric word, "Nevermore," to the choric cry of another obscure blackbird. "Jim Bond," in the context of "The Raven," euphoniously yields "Jim Crow" because the semantics of the pun, "bond," have it so. "Bond," whether as "shackle" or "binding agreement," contains the idea of constrains. The name was presumably given at birth (1882), and although the network of Jim Crow laws, disenfranchising Southern blacks, was not fully in place as a legal system until the 1890s, one of the first instances of such legislation was adopted by the Tennessee legislature in 1881.[26] Jim Bond is birdlike in another sense: as noted, he is that which cannot be caught. His sound (part animal) and his name (part bird) provide Shreve with the pattern for his final and infamous joke: "I think that in time the Jim Bonds are going to conquer the western hemisphere. Of course it wont quite be in our time and of course as they spread toward the poles they will bleach out again like the rabbits and the birds do, so they wont show up so sharp against the snow. But it will still be Jim Bond; and so in a few thousand years, I who regard you will also have sprung from the loins of African kings" (302–3). Just as Minerva, who was eaten in foetal form along with her mother, by Jupiter, her father, sprang black and birdlike from the paternal skull. So too Jim Bond, constrained to be little more than a loud thing, will prove seminal, once it is recognized that his blackness gives substance to white bodies insofar as it provides them with their true patronym. Shreve's joke exhibits a metamorphic logic, deriving from his and Quentin's sense of Jim Bond as bound to and bodying forth white landed property (a black "animal" in a white "wig," pressed close to snowy ground). Bond's bleached-out bird, under pressure from "snow," transforms into semen, becoming a flutter in the "rabbit" loins of an African king. By means of innuendo and contortion Shreve suggests that his and Quentin's heirs (like Bon's before them) will eventually descend from a great black father.

Shreve's is a joke against white paternalism. But the name Jim Bond, turned Jim Crow to proffer the joke's ultimate associative source, holds a last and more disturbing laugh. "Bond" contains "Bon." In the Genealogy, Faulkner underlines the point by referring to the character as "JIM BOND (BON)" (309). I have annotated the name "Bon" at length elsewhere:[27] here, I shall merely gloss that argument in order to point its relevance to Ike Snopes's encrypted and spectral insemination of Frenchman's Bend. Quentin Compson, citing his father and his father's father on the subject of naming, notes: "Father said he [Sutpen] probably named him himself. Charles Bon. Charles Good . . . Grandfather believed, just as he named them all—the Charles Goods and the Clytemnestras" (213–14). Bon: Good: Goods—the pun is cruelly obvious yet it remains largely unheard. That single syllable retains the novel: retains rather than contains, because "Bon" makes its subterranean narratives available by withholding them. We are told little about why Sutpen repudiated his first born, beyond a reference to a first wife's "Spanish blood" (203) in its capacity to "mock" his "design" (212). If "Spanish" is a euphemism for "African," as seems likely on Haiti, then Bon is black, and would technically and in antebellum Mississippi be a slave. Hence his repudiation, on grounds of an initial and unwitting miscegenation, later compounded by witting and incestuous miscegenation—or so, as we all know, the occluded, disputed, and combined argument of the five narrators, as revised by Shreve and Quentin, runs. Except that Sutpen's transmission of the name "Bon" suggests that at some level blood, whether Spanish or African, is a false clue, and that the planter set his son aside (in the last instance) for proprietorial reasons; because in him he recognized his own white property (that substantive "good" which makes him a master) as black "goods." The recognition that white owners are blacks in whiteface is, of course, unhearable to those who own, and must be put aside—but must return (as does Bon), being inherent in the labor structure of the planter's substance. Put another way, should the Southern planter absolutely deny that which makes him what he is (his "good" in the form of his "goods"), he will cease to be Southern, and ceasing to be what he is—he will die. Witness what happens when Henry Sutpen kills Bon at the gates to the Hundred in 1865. Since Henry is his father's heir, and the murderer of his father's (and of his own) substance (Bon), he must die. Having killed that which makes him, he does indeed vanish—much to the consternation of the narrators—returning, all but a corpse, to the ruined shell of the Hundred to die in 1909.

Generically speaking, Sutpen shares the conundrum of a Southern owning class which founds itself on constrained labor. Again, the conundrum runs, if the white "good" of the owning class depends on the "goods" that the black makes, the owning class must deny it, while retaining that "good" (that Bon) in which their very substance resides. I would point out that the narrators of Sutpen's story (with the honorable exception of the Canadian, Shreve) are all inheritors of planter property. (Quentin's Harvard place is paid for by the sale of land deriving from plantation wealth.) They, like their subject, are caught in a class contradiction: their substance, whether as body, property, land, or language is haunted by black labor, a shade that must be repressed *and* embraced. Their solution is stylistic—a way of talking which buries the bound man alive in the language of those who own. Dead and buried, the boundman conceals the master's means to mastery. Alive and acknowledged, he troubles the master's independent consciousness. As a linguistic presence (a revenant *in language*), operating at the lower levels of the narrator's consciousness, and consequently at the outer reaches of his or her language, the bound man's trace (*almost* readable) ensures that the consciousness of the class (and of its narrators) will retain its peculiar substance. The word "Bon" is just such a revenant in language: keeping the "goods" hidden in the "good" and obscuring both by translation. Similarly, Jim "Bond" encrypts a raven and crow to ensure that an elusive "howl" will issue from Quentin's head, when he seeks to close with the ur-property on which his Harvard place and his Southerness are grounded.

3

Economically, between 1936 (*Absalom, Absalom!*) and 1940 (*The Hamlet*), the regional form of labor, which in binding the black to the land bound him to the land's lord, was transformed. A labor revolution, driven by federal funds, effectively exorcised black from white. To read sociological commentators in the 1930s, addressing Southern agriculture, is to hear black tenants described as "virtual slaves,"[28] held "in thrall,"[29] subjected to "almost complete dependence"[30] and "incapable of ever achieving but a modicum of self direction,"[31] or, as one Arkansas sharecropper put it in 1939, "De landlord is landlord, de policeman is landlord, de shurf is landlord, ever'body is landlord, en we ain't got nothin."[32]

Although the Civil War freed the slave, it did so only for Southern landowners to bind him again in an alternative form of "dependency": for chattel-slavery read debt-peonage. The postbellum agricultural worker most typically lived under forms of constraint. In the words of the economic historian Jay Mandle, he was "not slave: not free."[33] Mandle's fine distinction remains true until the second half of the 1930s, when New Deal agricultural programs finally unbind black laborer and white owner. Masters were freed from "mastery" to become employers who paid a wage. The unfree were freed to be un- or underemployed. Between 1933 and 1938 the influx of Federal funds into the South produced systematic eviction, enclosure, and drastically increased cropper mobility. Between 1933 and 1940 the Southern tenantry declined by more than 25 percent.[34] All of these trends occurred as Faulkner wrote

Absalom, Absalom! Economically, black and white were forced apart, one consequence of which was that white need never be as black again.

This historical interlude may go some way to explain Faulkner's observation at the end of only his third paragraph in *The Hamlet*, "there was not one negro landowner in the entire section. Strange Negroes would absolutely refuse to pass through it after dark" (5). Although the novel is set during the 1890s,[35] at time of writing and publication (1940),[36] the Southern soil was progressively less likely to be owned, tenanted, or cropped by blacks—all of which bears heavily on Ike Snopes's cohabitation with that soil. In 1936, and while writing *Absalom, Absalom!*, Faulkner may still sense the unbearable passage of black into white by way of, and necessary to, a residual and resistant form of labor. Perhaps because he writes *as* that archaic regime is restructured, he needs must whisper about the *dis*figured black figure encrypted in the white body. By 1940, at least structurally, the black is no longer buried in the white. The whited ground is not, or perhaps should not, be haunted: which returns me to Ike's seminal ghosts, most of them white, a few Jewish, but none black. It would seem that, in the historical absence of black spectres, any spectres will do. My point is serious and simple: confronting a structurally emptied and un-Southern earth, Faulkner seeds the ground with false ghosts. As I argued earlier, the residency of "Troy's Helen . . . nymphs . . . snoring mitred bishops" et al. in the Bend's "silt and . . . refuse" (200) is saved from perverse anomaly by the stylistic labor of readers who, in working to trace Ike's passage into the earth, may well find themselves partially committed to whatever he puts there. What Ike puts there is, in several senses, white.

However, James Snead notes crucially that, from the outset of *The Hamlet*, the Bend itself rests on quite other buried and contradictory work. The land left by the founding Frenchman, now "parcelled out" into the "small shiftless mortgaged farms" (4) that are the Bend, is only habitable because the Frenchman's slaves had straightened a ten-mile river bend, "to keep his land from flooding" (4). Snead, properly makes much of this,[37] indicating an ethnic fraud at the point of origin—the Bend depends on the removal of a bend, and since that straightening results from black labor it is only inappropriately referred to as the Frenchman's. I would simply add an intertextual dimension to Snead's insight. In the context of my roster of autochthonists, the African Americans, whose work lies obscurely buried in Frenchman's Bend, join Rider and Jim Bond as exemplars of the disfigured black encrypted by name in the earths of *Absalom, Absalom!* and *Go Down, Moses*.

Although blacks dig themselves into the earth of *The Hamlet* on its first page, their labor (both foundational and nominal) goes unnoticed by most readers, and is all but forgotten by the inhabitants of the Bend—displaced by shifts in regimes of accumulation and, perhaps, by Ike's alternative revenants. Faulkner's need for alternative "presences" in the earth can be glossed by reference to his return to digging at the novel's close. Famously, *The Hamlet* ends with Flem's "Come up" (406), a terse summation of his rise, enunciated as he leaves both Bend and Frenchman's Place, having taken a detour to the latter, en route for Jefferson, in order to witness Armstid digging for fool's gold in the ruined garden of the once great house. Armstid is a double autochthonist; he drags a twice broken and "stiffened leg" (404), most typically into a trench, where "waist-deep" in the ground, he "dug himself back into that earth which had produced him" (399). When resting in his pit, he is "immobile as the lumps of earth he had thrown out of it" (395). The analogy between earth and Armstid is emphatic, and begs the question, "Why does he dig, rendering himself lumpen?" The conventional critical line is that, having been tricked by Flem's salting of the ground, Armstid along with Ratliff and Bookwright digs because Flem dug before them, and because they believe that he would not work at anything that did not have a considerable profit in it. Ergo, Armstid digs in mechanistic celebration of Flem's discovery that land (like everything else) is "real" only insofar as it contains, somewhere about it, a price. Joseph Urgo exemplifies the position, arguing forcefully that the Frenchman's Place (like any place) has no "intrinsic value," and that its "monetary value" derives from Flem's skill in restoring a story to the land. Flem, he says, converts a "forgotten property" into "a site of desire"[38] by silently performing the one about the buried gold of the plantocracy, allied in his person to the other one about Flem Snopes the infallible speculator.

All of which may be true of Flem and perhaps for Ratliff,[39] but there are other and less "American" options latent in Armstid's work and in the earth he works. The real estate line cannot accommodate the series of foolish autochthons hovering intra- and intertextually over Armstid's self-burial. Their earthy persistence should, perhaps, inhibit a reading of *The Hamlet* which overprivileges the viewpoint of exchange. As the annales historian Fernand Braudel observes, the market has a brief and "modern" history which remains less than ubiquitous: he proposes that beneath any market-money economy lies "the lowest stratum of the non-economy, the soil into which capitalism thrusts its roots, but which it can never really penetrate. The lowest layer remains an enormous one."[40] Arguably, the presence of a nonmarket remainder, with its residual non-money modes of exchange, is more likely in a soil which, until recently, has been worked towards meaning through a premodern regime of accumulation. Recently, here, maybe 1890 shadowed by chattel slavery, or even 1940, shadowed by debt peonage. Either date allows that the Bend retains practices of exchange which should not be simply assimilated to market terms. Braudel's lowest layer persists variously among Faulkner's "peasants" as subsistence production for use rather than sale; simple barter where desires are unmediated by price,[41] and libation—the gratuitous outpouring of milk and sperm entailing no obligation. Such strands of exchange may remain only at levels of memory and hope, but their presence at least impedes the explanatory currency of coin.

When Armstid digs (therefore), though he digs for coin, he releases uncoinable company. As a crazed autochthon he cannot escape resemanticization by way of Ike and his host of fools (both black and white). Read through the stencil of Ike and company, Armstid puts back more than he extracts, returning to the earth the secret of his inseparability from it.[42] That inseparability is cemented through the enforced practice of subsistence as an economy of "use values,"[43] that is, of things made to satisfy immediate wants or to fulfil immediate purposes. Money, on entering such an economy, ceases to be money; losing its abstract value and its metamorphic capacity to represent a certain quantity of any and all things, it takes on the specificity of the labor that went into it. So, Mrs. Armstid says of her five dollars, given by her husband to Buck Hipps in payment for a painted pony: "I would know them five dollars. I earned them myself, weaving at night after Henry and the chaps was asleep. Some of the ladies in Jefferson would save up string and such and give it to me and I would weave things and sell them. I earned that money a little at a time and I would know it when I saw it because I would take the can outen the chimney and count it now and then. . . . I would know it if I was to see it again" (360). Armstid's digging, like his wife's coins, is a summation—expressive of his life's work on and in the land; a labor dedicated to the assumption that it had to be worth something. Part of Armstid may dig for the Frenchman's coin as reminted by Flem, but another part of him digs for his own sweat; that is, to recover from the ground the lifetime's practice that he has put into it. Faulkner's account of the hill farmer, from whose barn Ike Snopes steals grain, might stand as the type of life-work informing Armstid's excavation: "the constant and unflagging round of repetitive nerve-and-flesh wearing labor by which alone that piece of earth which was his mortal enemy could fight him with, which he had performed yesterday and must perform again today and again tomorrow and tomorrow . . .—this until the day came when (he knew this too) he would stumble and plunge, his eyes still open and his empty hands stiffening into the shape of the plow-handles, into the furrow behind the plow, or topple into the weedy ditch, still clutching the brush-hook or the axe" (212). Having worked so hard, Armstid foolishly believes that there must be something in what he has done and what he has done it to. For that treasure, different from Flem's or the Frenchman's, he digs.

Of course, as I have already suggested, Armstid's covert autochthony (like Ike's before it) secretes a deeper and less aboriginal secret—that by 1890, as seen from 1940, the Frenchman's place occupies desecrated because unrevenanted ground. Bereft of the labor of the bound black which gave to it (and to its owners) a peculiar and un-American substance, the house and its hamlet are liable to market conversion. Ike's activities, related to and yet revising the displaced labor of the Frenchman's slaves, haunt the earth; and haunted ground is hard to move in real estate terms. Armstid, at least in part and all unknowingly, is of Ike's party. That company, a series of comparative idiots each of whom informs the others, renders Ike and his cow at least as economically focal to an understanding of the hamlet as Flem and his nickel.

NOTES

1. William Faulkner, *The Hamlet* (New York: Vintage, 1991), 188. Hereafter, page references will appear in parentheses, following citation.

2. For insight into "the threefold present," less as a "point" than as a liaison between the residual, the perceptual, and the anticipatory, see Paul Ricœur, *Time and Narrative*, volume 1 (Chicago: University of Chicago Press, 1984), particularly 5–30.

3. My use of the term "incarnation" derives from Maurice Merleau-Ponty's recognition that the "mind/body" division abstracts from the more experiential sense in which, since the body brings existence into being, perceiver and thing perceived are incarnate in one another. Ponty notes: "the body expresses total existence, not because it is an external accompaniment to that existence, but because existence comes into its own in the body. This incarnate significance is the central phenomenon of which body and mind, sign and significance are abstract moments. . . . Neither body *nor existence* can be regarded as the original of the human being, since they presuppose each other, and because the body is solidified or generalized existence, and existence a perpetual incarnation." *Phenomenology of Perception* (London: Routledge and Kegan Paul, 1962), 166.

4. I am indebted, here, to an unpublished essay by John Wiles, "The Dialectic and the Adventures of Merleau-Ponty." See also, William J. Mistichelli, "Perception Is a Sacred Cow: The Narrator and Ike Snopes in William Faulkner's *The Hamlet,*" *Faulkner Journal*, 5:2 (Spring 1990): 15–35; and Richard Gray, *The Life of William Faulkner* (Oxford: Blackwell, 1996), 262.

5. See Merleau-Ponty's account of the "habit-body," *Phenomenology of Perception*, 82–83.

6. Paul Ricœur, *Oneself as Another* (Chicago: University of Chicago Press, 1992), particularly, "Sixth Study: The Self and Narrative Identity," 140–68.

7. See Theodor W. Adorno, "Subject and Object," in *The Essential Frankfurt School Reader*, ed. Andrew Arato and Eike Gebhardt (Oxford: Blackwell, 1978), 497–511.

8. Ricœur, *Oneself as Another*, 134.

9. David Carr, *Time, Narrative, and History* (Bloomington: Indiana University Press, 1986), 47. My arguments concerning the narrative structure of experience rely heavily on Carr's work.

10. Cited by Merleau-Ponty, *The Primacy of Perception* (Northwestern University Press, 1964), 52.

11. Merleau-Ponty, *Phenomenology of Perception*, 30.

12. Ricœur, *Oneself as Another*, 148.

13. "Approaching knowledge of the object is the act in which the subject rends the veil it is weaving around the object. It can do this only where, fearlessly passive, it entrusts itself to its own experience. In places where subjective reason scents subjective contingency, the primacy of the object is shimmering through—whatever in the object is not a subjective admixture. The subject is the object's agent, not its constituent." Adorno, "Subject and Object," in *The Essential Frankfurt School Reader*, 506.

14. Frederick J. Hoffman notes the pun in Flem's name. See his *William Faulkner* (New Haven, Conn.: Twayne Publishers Inc., 1961), 87.

15. I am indebted for the Initials Only point to a conversation with James Hinkle. The phrase is of military derivation (for use in roll calls).

16. John T. Matthews, *The Play of Faulkner's Language* (Ithaca: Cornell University Press, 1982), 206.

17. Departing from Merleau-Ponty's observation that "language is meaningful when, instead of copying the thought, it allows itself to be broken up and reconstituted by the thought," Wolfgang Iser makes a case for the significance of "blanks" and breaks within a text. His case runs, "the [reader] is drawn into the events and made to supply what is meant from what is not said. What is said only appears to take on significance as a reference to what is not said. But as the unsaid comes to life in the reader's imagination, so the said expands to take on greater significance than might have been supposed." A text high on "constitutive blanks" (one as broken and interrupted as Faulkner's text for Ike) requires much "interaction" from its reader, whose "communicative labor" (filling in the hidden side of the perceived object) involves both a hunt for a manageable meaning, and the tense recognition that such an achievement forecloses the very multiplicity that prompted it. Iser presumes that readers who read among the "blanks" experience reading as a constant process of "ideation" and "reformulation." Whether or not this is the case for reading *per se*, I would suggest that it has resonance for how we make Ike mean, and for our commitment to that meaning as *de* and *re*formation. See Iser, *The Act of Reading: A Theory of Aesthetic Response* (London: Routledge, 1978), particularly 168, 180–98.

18. William Faulkner, *Faulkner in the University*, ed. Frederick L. Gwynn and Joseph L. Blotner (New York: Random House, 1959), 1.

19. For a more sustained version of this argument, see my "Quentin Compson: Tyrrhenian Vase or Crucible of Race," in *New Essays on "The Sound and the Fury,"* ed. Noel Polk (Cambridge: Cambridge University Press, 1993), 99–137.

20. Jean-Paul Sartre, "On *The Sound and the Fury*: Time in the Work of Faulkner," in David Minter's edition of *The Sound and the Fury* (New York: Norton, 1987), 253.

21. William Faulkner, *Go Down, Moses* (New York: Vintage, 1991), 313–14. Hereafter, page references will appear in parentheses, following citation.

22. In *If I Forget Thee, Jerusalem* Faulkner has Charlotte say to her unwilling abortionist and "husband," "What was it you told me nigger women say? Ride me down, Harry." Faulkner, *Novels: 1936–1940* (New York: Library of America, 1990), 645.

23. Where "Pantaloon in Black" ethnically darkens the worked earth, Ike's perspective on the diminished big woods whitens the hunted ground and renders it hymenial: "He had watched it, not being conquered, destroyed, so much as retreating since its purpose was served now and its time an outmoded time, retreating southward through this inverted-apex this ∇-shaped section of earth between hills and River until what was left of it seemed now to be gathered and for the time arrested in one tremendous density of brooding and inscrutable impenetrability at the ultimate funnelling tip" (*Go Down, Moses*, 326–27). For elaboration see, "Iconic Narratives: Or, How Three Southerners Fought the Second Civil War," in my *Fictions of Capital* (Cambridge: Cambridge University Press, 1990), 139–69.

24. William Faulkner, *Absalom, Absalom!: The Corrected Text* (New York: Random House, 1990), 309. Hereafter, page references will appear in parenthesis, following citation.

25. Edgar Allan Poe, *Selected Writings* (Harmondsworth: Penguin, 1974), 80.

26. C. Vann Woodward, *The Strange Career of Jim Crow* (New York: Oxford University Press, 1959), xvi.

27. See my *Fictions of Labor: William Faulkner and the South's Long Revolution* (Cambridge: Cambridge University Press, 1997), 69–79.

28. Norman Thomas, in a letter to Senator Robert F. Wagner, quoted in Vera Rony, "The Organization of Black and White Farm Workers in the South," in Thomas R. Frazier, ed., *The Underside of American History: Other Readings,* vol. 2: *Since 1865* (New York: Hardcourt and Brace, 1971), 165.

29. Charles S. Johnson, Edwin R. Embree, and W. W. Alexander, *The Collapse of Cotton Tenancy: Summary of Field Studies and Statistical Surveys, 1933–35* (Freeport, New York: Books for Libraries Press, 1972), 11.

30. Charles S. Johnson, *Shadow of the Plantation* (Chicago: University of Chicago Press, 1960), 4. Originally published 1934.

31. Hoffsommer, in his study "The AAA and the Cropper," based on interviews undertaken in 1934, and quoted in *The Collapse of Cotton Tenancy*, 58.

32. Quoted by Jack Temple Kirby, *Rural Worlds Lost: The American South, 1920–1960* (Baton Rouge: Louisiana State University Press, 1987), 239.

33. See Jay Mandle, *Not Slave, Not Free: The African American Experience since the Civil War* (Durham: Duke University Press, 1992), particularly chapter 3, 33–43.

34. Kirby, *Rural Worlds Lost*, 64. See also, Gilbert Fite, *Cotton Fields No More: Southern Agriculture, 1865–1980* (Lexington: University Press of Kentucky, 1984), 120–62, and Harold D. Woodman, "Class, Race, Politics, and the Modernization of the Postbellum South," *Journal of Southern History* 63:1 (February 1997), 3–22.

35. Writing to Saxe Commins (October 1939), Faulkner notes, "Book Four happens in 1890, approximately. Hence Civil War ended 25 years ago. Have recollection of dating War somewhere in script as 40 years ago. Please watch for it. I will catch it in galley if you h'ave not." *Selected Letters*, ed. Joseph Blotner (New York: Random House, 1978), 115. Assuming 1890 as the date of authorial choice, one must discount Bookwright's finding of coins minted in 1901 (and later), among Flem's "fool's gold" (361), as an error missed both by Faulkner and by his editors.

36. In 1926 Faulkner worked on the unfinished story *Father Abraham,* in which Flem Snopes's rise to the presidency of a Jefferson bank is detailed. From the mid '20s to the late '30s he borrowed, extended, and revised the Snopes material, much of it appearing in modified form in *The Hamlet*. See Richard Gray, *The Life of William Faulkner,* 253–54.

37. James Snead, *Figures of Division: William Faulkner's Major Novels* (New York: Methuen, 1986), 144–47.

38. Joseph Urgo, "Faulkner's Real State: Land and Literary Speculation in *The Hamlet*," *Mississippi Quarterly* 48:3 (1995), 443–57.

39. What Ratliff buys is precious to him in a double and contradictory sense: he buys for speculative profit and to defeat a speculator, but he also buys Eula's dowry or marriage portion. Eula, it should be recalled, in childhood and puberty was a trainee autochthon. According to anecdote, unwilling to move from wherever she sat, her bovine inertia, allied to a conspicuous mouth, rendered her (like Ike's cow) an "aperture" to the earth. Ratliff purchases, at one level, the landed body of Eula.

40. Fernand Braudel, *Civilization and Capitalism, 15th–18th Century,* vol. 2: *The Wheels of Commerce* (London: Collins, 1982), 229.

41. For the manner in which barter differs from other modes of exchange, see Caroline Humphrey and Stephen Hugh-Jones, introduction to *Barter, Exchange, and Value: An Anthropological Approach*, ed. Humphrey and Jones (Cambridge: Cambridge University Press, 1992), 1–20. See also John Forrester, *Truth Games: Lies, Money, and Psychoanalysis* (Cambridge: Harvard University Press, 1997), particularly "Gift, Money, and Debt," 111–71.

42. For a Chodorowian account of inseparability as the complex "pull of the maternal," see Karen R. Sass, "Rejection of the Maternal and the Polarization of Gender in *The Hamlet*," *Faulkner Journal* 4:2 (Fall 1988/Spring 1989), 127–38.

43. For the "use value"/"exchange value" distinction, see Karl Marx, *Capital,* vol. 1 (Harmondsworth: Penguin, 1976), 125–31.

Faulkner Adds Up: Reading *Absalom, Absalom!* and *The Sound and the Fury*

Hortense J. Spillers

In the midst of the 1998 Faulkner Conference, to which I had been invited as a guest speaker, it occurred to me—rather stunningly, I should add, because it was too late to alter course—that I had actually misconstrued my assignment: my remarks should have been based on the thematics of Faulkner's writings and the implications for a conceptualizing "America." But I had been captivated by something else altogether different, it seemed—quite simply, the awesome repetitive schemes inherent in Faulknerian address and how the former help shape and sustain the readerly response. After years of teaching Faulkner to undergraduate constituencies, literally up and down the length of the country, I am still amazed (a good Faulkner word) that this work remains news and provocation for me and as importantly, that out of this ever-newness some aspect of reading emerges to draw the attention that had missed it before. I should acknowledge, however, that it was the work of Gertrude Stein, especially *The Autobiography of Alice B. Toklas* and *The Making of Americans*,[1] that raised the problematics of repetition to the forefront of my interest, and while I have not even come close to solving, or dissipating the puzzle that this epiphenomenon of writing occupies in my imagination, I must express profound thanks to my host and convenor of the Faulkner Conference, Professor Donald Kartiganer, for providing me the occasion to have a few first thoughts on the subject in a "rich and strange" (and welcoming) public forum. (What a sense of humor he and that Tuesday night audience must have had to pretend not to notice that the name "America" did not escape my lips more than once that evening!)

In the fourth chapter of *Absalom, Absalom!*[2] Jason Compson III is speaking to his Harvard-bound, much-put-upon son, Quentin III, when he expresses what I would regard as one of the driving metacritical motions that subtend the work. Quentin, tapped by Rosa Coldfield to be the chosen auditory in the next generation of her forty-three years' worth of impressive outrage, might be thought of as a kind of punctuality—an omniscient narrator calls him a "commonwealth": "[H]is very body was an empty hall echoing with sonorous defeated names; he was not a being, an entity, he was a commonwealth" (7). The moment of convergence of numerous vectors, Quentin is not entirely unlike an epical proper name or instrumentality, insofar as the space of a proper name conforms to a geopolitical and generational denomination; nearly all of the *personae* of *The Odyssey*, for instance, are identified as the "son/or daughter of," the ineluctable apposition and repetition in which case the law of the phallus is not only "photographed," as it were, but assumes an obligatory appeal in the poetics. (Could it be said that the Appendix of *The Sound and the Fury* and the Chronology of *Absalom, Absalom!*, both added after the respective facts of publication, parody epical, even Biblical, design by staging the ambition of the "genome"?) Quentin, of course, comes to us far removed from the mandates and practices of epic genre in any sense, even as it is fairly clear that he has no text, no *word/verbe*[3] that he could call his ownmost. Along the course of the narrative, Quentin keeps thinking that he will never hear anything else his whole life, will never have to hear anything else, cannot *but* hear and have heard through his sinews, his muscle-build, on the pulse of the nerve, what his elders obsessively repeat about the South. Perhaps that intense concentration of narrative energy, even an "investment" of it, finds an analogy in Benjy's howling that lines *The Sound and the Fury*[4] with its irresistible madness and in its disembodied match that presides over the conflagration of Sutpen's Hundred and its aftermath in *Absalom, Absalom!* In any case Quentin, ringing like a commonwealth, is loaded with discursive and narrative registers, foisted on him by his elders, which Rosa Coldfield believes might well have a market equivalent, and which his father explains this way: "We have a few old mouth-to-mouth tales; we exhume from old trunks and boxes and drawers letters without salutation or signature, in which men and women who once lived and breathed are now merely initials or nicknames out of some now incomprehensible affection which sound to us like Sanskrit or Chocktaw" (80).

These tales of mouth-to-mouth resuscitation, as it were, are nevertheless stripped by Compson of their mystical valence—another way to put it would be to say that "being" has been subtracted from the objects—as they translate into sign-vehicles, whose messages are no longer transparent, if they ever were, or any more meaningful than marks on a page of foreign language; in this case, the foreignness skips several beats, leaps over the modern, and looks toward some passage or doorway even more inaccessible, even though we imagine that Compson, one of Faulkner's most cynical and voluble speakers, is here "putting on the dog" of impressing the troubled young man poised before him by signaling what would be, to his mind, the outlandish and the romantic—*Sanskrit*, the mother-tongue of the Indo-European families of language, and *Chocktaw*, the language of the Chocktaw and Chicasaw peoples,[5] once installed, ages ago, in what is now Mississippi, Alabama, and Louisiana of the American New World. (And for all that, perhaps no strangeness to "Ikemotubbe," which invocation inaugurates the Compson line of the "sons and daughters of.") What these buried, now exhumed, objects-monuments, proferred like so many tokens of historical and semantic trust and brought to the half-light of Faulknerian narrative, require, then, is a speculative instrument, an interpretive and heuristic device of which the novel itself, in its unrelenting narrative pressures, is prime suspect and motive. I would go further: Faulknerian narratologies appear to have sprung into this world for the express purpose of breaking the reader's heart (say nothing of Quentin's in the particular case in question), to make her lose sleep, and to doubt the intuitive "logic" of reading as a forward and progressive momentum in time which takes us steadily along a trajectory initiated in ignorance and brought to closure on knowledge and certainty. But in reading Faulkner, one cancels all the bets, holds all torn tickets, as we enter the realm of the stochastic; as we learn, in fact, to shake loose the time-honored faith of the "English major" that reading, if you just stick to it long enough, will bring you to a successful end. On this ground of interrogation, reading becomes the quintessential human stake, if not folly: "[Y]ou re-read," Compson muses, "tedious and intent, poring, making sure that you have forgotten nothing, made no miscalculation; you bring them together again and again nothing happens: just the words, the symbols, the shapes themselves, shadowy, inscrutable and serene" (80).

These signatures of a dead past, which claims and marks the body of Quentin Compson in *symptomaticity*, account for one kind of repetitive enterprise at work in *Absalom, Absalom!* At the level of the line (in the semantic and lexical folds of the novel), as well as in the larger temporal units that we would demarcate as "narrative" (in the *diegesis*,[6] the would-be trajectory of plot, here stalled and subverted and we could even say "bereaved" by Faulknerian recurrence and delay, and in the narrative duration of the plot device), we are confronted with the truth of sheer accumulation as a "return" with a difference, sometimes marked, and an "addition," which compounds the puzzle rather than dissolve it. The problem that I am attempting to track, then, is twofold, separated by neighboring territories of discursive organization: (1) those of prose stylistics, on the one hand, and that of the (2) "function and field of speech in psychoanalysis," on the other; it seems that in both *The Sound and the Fury* and *Absalom, Absalom!* these "neighbors," we might call them, experience *detente* on a new frontier of fictive persuasions, wherein stylistic repetition, to put the matter another way, sounds the depths of an itinerary of the "one," whose conceptual career is mapped in the Lacanian project.[7] In neither field is the matter of repetition new and therefore, a cause for anxiety—at least in *theory*—but to speak them together, as I believe Faulkner's writings urge, is not automatic: whereas repetition—the same word for orders of the socius that differ in both degree and kind—is regarded in the poetics sphere as a positive trait and may be said to conduce to pleasurable feeling,[8] the appearance of the phenomenon in everyday life, or in the experential sphere (routine, boring activity that *must* be repeated) generates ambiguous value; the latter, when taken over by the discourses of psychoanalysis, becomes the high water-mark of a special category of "psychic material," if not that of a symptom of trauma and neurosis.[9] What Faulkner's writings manage to achieve—with quite stunning success—is an economy of praxis that relies on both attitudes or postures and postulates to engender *style*. In what ways might we think of *style*, however, as a *symptom*?

What I hope to do here, then, is to gain a bit of ground on understanding a deepened dialogism between these discursive terrains, straddled by an American writer, who, for the longest time, I suspect, was quite probably thought of as "quaint" and merely "Southern," as though the latter were a flat surface, by portions of an American readership. As one blurber puts it, regarding a Faulkner reading from his own work, "he conjures up many vivid, picturesque images for his listening audience."[10] In my view, never "quaint," Faulkner, the Southerner, "told" us a great deal about the workings of language and discursive regimes long before the protocols of structuralism and poststructuralism had given us names for them. In fact, I think of this canon, especially the two novels examined here, in addition to *Light in August*, *As I Lay Dying*, part 4 of "The Bear," spates of *The Mansion*, and *A Fable*, through and through, as the site of a radical discursivity and in that regard well ahead of the modernist language game, which Faulkner himself was likely *not* very interested in playing, *per se*. Of course, I am suggesting that whatever Faulkner's project might have been *for him* is not everywhere consonant with what it is for us, the epigone, if related at all. I cannot even remotely imagine what the world of everyday readers, beyond the ken of official notice and review must have thought in 1929, when *The Sound and the Fury* appeared (along with the Great Depression), and in 1936, when *Absalom, Absalom!* was published (toward the end of FDR's initial term of office). It is also useful to keep in mind that Faulkner did not exactly fit the mythical fashion mode by which we read his generation's avant-garde—the sexy, glamorous, "lost," young American male in exile, while hanging about the premises of 27 rue de Fleurus, lamenting the decline and fall of Western Civilization, or acting out the alter-ego of Nick Carraway and Jake Barnes. William Faulkner's consumer packaging, let's call it, was somewhat different, it seems to me *because* he was Southern, at the time he was Southern, and as the "South"/ "New South" was, until fairly recently, always cast as the nation's backward "other," who, in turn, engendered, in fear and trembling and terror, its own "others." Might it be that this "South," through William Faulkner, is liberating the word of its truth and the truth of its word on the nation-ground?

If Compson's lines might be taken as an apt metaphor for reading *Absalom, Absalom!* (or other Faulkner, for that matter) and as an adequate précis of what its various speakers enact, each with his/her own "hermeneutic demand" concerning the "self-life-writing" of Thomas Sutpen and the mystery of his children, then they point to the actual crisis that readers face in the onslaught of a *tsunami* of prose, or perhaps more locally, going through a high-powered car wash *without* your car—that getting the world down between a cap and a period.[11] Our readerly position imitates Quentin and roommate Shreve's, desperate to solve the riddle which the pair, in some sense, have invented. In the iron grip of a New England winter bearing down on Harvard yard, as the radiators lose heat over the course of the night, that small enclosed space resembles a crypt, if anything at all, which would render the task of creation quite a lot closer to a small death: "Wait," either of them and both of them think(s), "For God's sake wait!" And what is it that they are *waiting* for? It is certainly for no lack of a pregnant narrative generation—it has no rival in U.S. letters this century, to my mind, and to match it, even approach it, we would have to drop back to Melville in the nineteenth—that they are on pins, at pains, no semantic or lexical impoverishment that needs fleshing out, but, rather, a discursive drowning, more precisely, that requires reading a Faulkner novel as we would a poem, line by line, as Ezra Pound claimed the basic unit of composition should be. In the modernist project, the line would be replicated as signature for Faulkner and his fellow visionaries. But Faulkner seems to achieve striking emotional intensity and affect by accumulation in repetition, analogy, and correspondence or correlation in lines and scenes that do not always "go" somewhere, although they stir up quite a commotion. We should take a minute to try to explain how it happens.

Because Quentin Compson in both *The Sound and the Fury* and *Absalom, Absalom!* plays out his career in obsession with a kind of strident commitment, objects stick to him like a second skin: meandering toward the bake shop in Italian Boston, where he first "picks up" the "little sister," Quentin remembers, back along a memory trace through centers of attention that always include "Caddy" and other home-related phantastical material, this: "The buggy was drawn by a white horse, his feet clopping in the thin dust; spidery wheels chattering thin and dry, moving uphill beneath a rippling shawl of leaves" (76). In the same stream of thought, lines later: "The wheels were spidery. Beneath the sag of the buggy the hooves neatly rapid like the motions of a lady doing embroidery, diminishing without progress like a figure on a treadmill being drawn rapidly offstage." Then, finally, after he has entered the bake shop and purchased two buns from the "neat gray face lady," who "looked like a librarian," the scene washes back over his thoughts: "A buggy, the one with the white horse it was. Only Doc Peabody is fat. Three hundred pounds" (78). Repetition here is simple recurrence, with grace notes, as we see it choreographed in the three movements, but it also creates a coherence of mental disarray that lifts the mundanity of his psychic wounding to a level of powerful poetic ritual and achievement. Quentin's madness, in other words, exhibits a perfection and precision of logic that now relentlessly looks ahead to a syntax that not only repeats the textual grooves in which consciousness is stuck (as he also does in *Absalom*), but repeats as if compelled by law, and it is the law of a missed encounter with reality[12] that repetition is said to commemorate.

The character shows fidelity, then, to the poetics of style that circumvents him—a sentence structure with the ellipses and points of transition that ought to draw blanks and spaces soldered to contents broken and parcelled out over highly disparate spatio-temporal occurrences—this would mean that the character is never other than *beside* himself, is never other than *other than* himself; colloquially speaking, the lights are on, but nobody's home. In strict complementarity with modes of psychic behavior to which Quentin remains captive, his syntax proffers all the earmarks of puzzle and halting that competing claims of attention would reenforce: we are at once both in the moment with him and all the capital elsewheres that overtake him with immeasurable speed on this, his last day's odyssey.

In *Talking Voices*,[13] Deborah Tannen investigates the phenomenon of repetition and image-making in conversational discourse and suggests that it lies at the heart of particular and general discursive production; modalities of "prepatterning" in language—"formulaicity" and "idiomaticity," for example—would support the view that " 'the actual apriori of any language event—the real deep structure—is an accumulation of remembered prior texts.' "[14] To that extent, "languaging," the sociolinguists call it, involves a competence that has gained access, by way of memory, to this horde of linguistic treasure—Jakobson speaks of it as " 'the filing cabinet of *prefabricated* representations' "[15]— delimited by a code. Each "message," or new use context, witnesses the efficacy of the code. While Tannen's study has to do primarily with instances of speech, her work on figures of style, examined in the opening chapter of *Talking Voices*, is complementary to studies in rhetoric that have long occupied an honored place in the general fields of literary criticism and stylistics. I find especially suggestive for my purposes here her view on the interactional aspects of "languaging": "[S]eeing language as relatively imitative or prepatterned rather than freely generated seems to push us toward automatism rather than autonomy—make each of us more 'it' and less 'I.' But a view of language as relatively prepatterned does not have to be seen this way. Rather, we may see it as making of us more interactional 'I's.' "[16]

It seems that this reading accords well with the notion that I am advancing here of the Faulknerian character as the subject of *other* address. If Quentin, the "commonwealth," bears the symptoms of a cultural and historical wounding, then the repetitive and obsessive onrush that grinds him down offers monumental tribute to that past. What the latter induces as pathological figures of character yields, remarkably, in the hands of the "writing writer" to narrative space as temporal plasticity, in which event a point in time is saturated with entirely disparate elements. Related Quentin passages from *The Sound and the Fury* demonstrate a similar duplicity of motives which seem to make it difficult to determine how to evaluate the auspices of a scene, or where to apportion responsibility for it; recognizing Quentin's obsessive gaze as a mode of signature, would we attribute what I would call the "objective" world of his narrative to his own inventiveness, or is it the work of an objective narrative device, e.g., the types of street cars out of Cambridge and back, the Charles River and landscape on which Gerald Bland's long-handled oars appear? And what about that "gull on an invisible wire attached through space dragged" (64), or variations on it—"a gull motionless in midair, like on an invisible wire between the masts," or "with three gulls hovering above the stern like toys on invisible wires"? (55). Because the gulls, on the one hand, are juxtaposed here with inanimate or automistic referents, which make them appear to be parodic instances of flight, we may tend to say that they are products of Quentin's perversely keen vision, while, on the other, the excerpts, appropriate to poetic machinery, draw the attention for *that* reason. If that is so, then Quentin Compson, as well as Darl Bundren (*As I Lay Dying*), plausibly demarcates a common ground between the workings of insanity and the discourses of fictive and poetic invention. The idea is hardly new, but in Faulkner's case, the puzzle is woven into the thematic fabric of discourse.

Another such moment invites attention: on the way to the bake shop—a serendipitous destination for Quentin—he comes upon three boys, each with a fishing pole, busying themselves in child's play of an early summer afternoon, 1910. Apparently a small footbridge, suspended over a pond, or reservoir, the fishing spot seems to be a favorite rendezvous of the trio, primarily because of the trout, a neighborhood character in its own right, that makes its home there and refuses to be reeled in. Quentin only later notices the boys themselves, but is, at first, hooked—like the three lads—by the elegant geometry unfolding before him: "and then I saw a shadow hanging like a fat arrow stemming into the current. . . . The arrow increased without motion, then in a quick swirl, the trout lipped a fly beneath the surface with that sort of gigantic delicacy of an elephant picking up a peanut" (71).

The humorous simile that draws this nimble filip to a close relies on sharp contrast, distributed over the law of couples ("gigantic . . . elephant"; "delicacy . . . peanut"), to drive the play of oppositions at the lexical and dramatic levels—as severe as Quentin's situation may be, the eruption of wry humor and detachment withdraws it from the wasted energy of the lachrymose and melodramatic. In other words, one must pay attention to Quentin, as Quentin does the trout, than feel pity for him; in fact, the survey of mental activity expressed in Quentin's narrative is so exercised by fastidious detail that we nearly forget the fatalism in which he is suspended and that we are effectually spending the day with an anal, meticulous, drowning man. The seagulls, the trout, and the fishing poles all belong to a carefully crafted repertory of inflections which suggest that "action" in this narrative is not defined by movement through a material scene, but across an intrapsychic space of the most refined neurotic order. *The Sound and the Fury* and *Absalom, Absalom!* may both be regarded as quintessential fictions of the mental theatre. In that regard, repetition is experienced as one of the enabling postulates of both novels.

A kind of extended conceit, the fishing poles, borne by the trio, migrate through objects and textures of the near-at-hand, as well as angles of sunlight. Schematizing the instances might be useful. At first, the boys "leaned on the rail, looking down into the water, the three poles like *three slanting threads of yellow fire in the sun*." Shortly thereafter, nearly all the elements in this paradigmatic syntactical pattern recur in a dazzling circuitry of transposition and exchange:

The shadows on the road were as still as if they had been put there with a *stencil, with slanting pencils of sunlight*. . . .

Their voices came over the hill, and *the three slender poles like balanced threads of running fire*. . . .

> The third boy slowed and halted. The first went on, *flecks of sunlight slipping along the pole across his shoulder and* down the back of his shirt. . . .
>
> *Sunlight slanted into* it [an orchard buzzing with bees], sparse and eager. *Yellow butterflies flickered along the shade like flecks of sun*. . . .
>
> *Sunlight slid patchily across his walking shoulders, glinting along the pole like yellow ants*. . . .
>
> They turned into the lane and went on, the *yellow butterflies slanting about them along the shade*. . . .
>
> . . . and the *dappled sun motionless* at last upon his *white shirt*. (73–75; emphasis mine)

The intense focus on aspects of landscape may be thought of as instances of the "objective correlative," or a kind of synecdochic close-up, but it would be difficult to imagine how a cinematographer could demonstrate or capture *nuance* in this case; a picture here would *not* be worth a thousand words, as impact is carried by purely textual and linguistic means. Though the latter induces image-making, it seems that its effects are not translatable into a literal economy of signs or messages. These verbal crosscuttings of angles of light and texture convey, for only an instant, the rare playfulness, even "lightness of being," that works against the mournful quality of Quentin's suicidal day. Perhaps these discrete moments of perception—not "seen" before and not ever again—are the sort of thing, in their perfections of the harmonious, that one carries to the grave.

After so long and patient a time, one should be able to say what repetition is without further ado. But somehow the problem seems harder to solve than that: is it the exact or approximate replication of lexical, syntactical, semantic, and scenic elements, as we have seen in numerous examples from the two Faulkner novels? And is the sign of repeating just the replicative? Is it an *interval* that works a seed planted at some prior time in the consciousness of the "reading reader," who then bears out the second and subsequent instances *as instances*, as the fruit of the first, whether or not the words are the same? If the latter is so, then what factors must be present in order for the reader to posit a kind of "pronoun/antecedent" relationship in the first place? Is "theme," then, the built-up impact of these resemblances over narrative intervals so that the whole narrative structure is nothing but the repetition of itself? Enough questions of the kind I have just posed would pulverize the problem into a "not there," or a "there there" by some other name. And certainly the problem appears quite a lot easier to dispose of when we are dealing with smaller units of measure than fictive temporality. In short, the problem of repetition leads us into an examination of the "philosophy of literary form,"[17] the just treatment of which is a subject for volumes. At the same time, we do not forget, either, that seismic shifts in the critical topography that reconfigure the very concept of "literary form"—today, one of several semiotic ranges on the landscape, ever vulnerable to the wrecking crews of deconstructive acts—have not only changed the topic and altered the status of the object, but dissolved object-positionality itself as a *figment*, or *shadow* of subject/subjectivity. From that angle, repetition is only in "me," where it might not have been in 1941, when Kenneth Burke first published an astonishing piece called *The Philosophy of Literary Form*. We are dropping back, then, to claim an anachronism in order to hear what it might "say" now.

A gathering of "thirty-minded" essays, *The Philosophy of Literary Form* is both brilliantly speculative and doggedly quirky and peculiar. Not a standard academic work—as the author himself was not standardly academic—this study of "symbolic action" carries only two entries on the subject of "repetition," one of them encompassed within Burke's review of Adolf Hitler's *Mein Kampf*,[18] the other, in a reading of Erskine Caldwell's *Tobacco Road* and *God's Little Acre*.[19] On both counts, repetition for him holds negative value, and in the case of Caldwell, conduces to trivial pursuit—"Sometimes when reading Caldwell, I feel as though I were playing with my toes" because Caldwell "seems as contented as a savage to say the same thing again and again."[20] That is hardly what one expected (even needed) Burke to say! But at least it signals that the quality of repetitiousness has built into it a negative charge, as well as a pleasurable one.

Studies in classical rhetoric often discuss repetition as one of the inherited figures of speech—with neither "good" nor "bad" energy—that takes the form of the foreshortened space, usually at the level of the sentence or the line. Winifred Horner's *Rhetoric in the Classical Tradition*,[21] for example, disposes of the question as one of *utility*: "Repetition of words or patterns of words can be used for good stylistic effect, for reinforcement of meaning, and for emphasis."[22] She then demonstrates examples of it by way of three figures, starting with *anadiplosis* (also the chiasmatic figure)—the "doubling back," wherein "the last word of one clause or phrase is used as the beginning word in the following clause or phrase." The beautiful "twirling" effect of "people are trapped in history, and history is trapped in them"[23] is shared by instances of *polyptoton* and *anaphora*: in the former, "the same root word is used in different parts of speech," as in, "I agree if agreement is required."[24] In the latter, the "carrying back" of *anaphora*—"the regular repetition of the same word or phrase at the beginning of successive phrases or clauses"[25]—behaves rather like *alliteration*, even though it seems that the alliterative explodes the sound *intra*syntactically and over a shorter distance, while the anaphoric is summoned to handle longer units of recurrence. Horner's example of the latter from Martin Luther King's well-known 1963 Address at the "March on Washington" rally, "I Have a Dream," perfectly illustrates the idea, with added value—the nervous rush of sound over the same footage, so to speak, builds the climax. The ear can hear it coming on like a jet engine, roaring in the distance, and stronger, unbearably, as it comes in for the landing. But on paper, the effect appears to be quite the same, as in King's "Letter from Birmingham Jail,"[26] which text, as far as I am aware, was never spoken. We could multiply examples of this very effective rhetorical resource, but suffice it to say that *anaphora* seems to have been made for the exhortative/persuasive/comminatory task, as the entire era of the Civil Rights movement in the United States, for instance, became, among other considerations, a prime stage for the use and display of rhetorical power turned toward quintessentially democratic goals.

Richard A. Lanham's *Analyzing Prose*[27] carries a description of a repetitive function in the figure of *plocé*: "repetition of a word with a different meaning after the interval of another word or words." The example that he provides is a delightful one: "On the walls were pictured groups of early Americans signing things and still earlier Americans shooting arrows at things. But all over the immaculate mushroom-coloured carpet . . . stood groups of present-day Americans drinking things."[28]

In both Horner's and Lanham's work, terror has been stricken from the heart of the rhetorical in the sense that what they and other rhetors describe as process has been delivered from the strict uncertainties of the free fall—the encounter with a "wild man," like Faulkner, who apparently suspended all the rules. There is significant repetitiousness in his order of the case, but it seems to defy any attempt at classification and to carry right over, for that precise reason, into the translation of an *affect*. The haunting mournful tenor of Benjy's narrative in *The Sound and the Fury* offers a good example because it asserts the same thing "over and over again," Burke's bane of syntactic existence. But it is the "over again," which totality strikes my ear as a dirge; if this "thing" of Benjy's were ever scored, it would have to be thought of as an American version of the classical mass—a subterranean *hum*—in the mass, the *drone* of the organ—beneath all that howling and yelling. It doesn't even make sense that my ear registers in Benjy's narrative a profound and steady *silence*, when, as one of my fellow Faulkner readers once keenly observed, Benjy must howl throughout the novel. But it is also the unanswering noise of the silence that *isolates* it that I mark as well. If, as critics have argued, *Sound and Fury* offers formal incoherence as "the form that is the consequence of contingent being,"[29] as Donald Kartiganer rightly contends, then the belated reader is still confronted with something of a paradox: how the "remainder" of the text, the discourses of it that flicker in the mind's awareness as a completely finished, even self-sufficient project, "becomes" the novel.

What remains for me in an aftermath of reading here is an unmistakable sense of loss and mourning, when it is fairly undeniable that such a thematics does not "announce" itself as such. Kartiganer explains that Benjy's narrative, for example, does not yield an interpretation, but that, rather, "his succession of lived images passes over into our interpretation, becomes a temporal fiction of Compson history that is so clear it is unbelievable."[30] The sense of mourning that I am referring to, then, is related both to our understanding of what we posit in the *affectual* dispositions of the characters and also in that "passing over" of its mournful affects into the reading reader, who receives them, in turn, in a mimesis of grief—not *as*, but *in* the reading reader's *felt* grief. It is in this "passing over" into our interpretation and responses that incoherence is undermined, perhaps we could even say *redeemed* and accepted, as a different fictive logic.

As we have pointed out before, Faulknerian narrative space is frequently redefined as temporal porosity—the overlay, the superimposition of "times," whereby a single space is filled up with discontinuous properties, in some cases, triggered by associative devices, in some others, an opening, or cleavage along the seams of memory, in still others, simple juxtaposition. In any case, we are confronting alignments that are both *contiguous* (juxtaposition that would define an interval) and *continuous* (the wreck and ruin of the same). The sign-vehicle "Caddy"/ "caddie" appears in all three cases: as a proper name, with its paronomastic figure in the homonym of "caddie," it is both juxtapositional and associational in Benjy's narrative; it performs a juxtapositional, or contiguous, function, as well as an associational one, in Quentin's, albeit for quite different reasons. A visual, or graphic sign, "Caddy" operates like a sight-gag, but on the ear, except that on the page, it also works like an eye rhyme. A brilliant find for the writing writer, "Caddy" is chief among several saturated elements. (Its recurrence in both Benjy's and Quentin's narratives is so frequent that it is no longer even repetition, perhaps, since the latter is recognizable because it is generated around a gap, or an interval, or how else would we perceive it? We need another name, then, for this aural image that appears in so great a quantity of replication that it obtains to a different *quality* and valence of the repeated.)

We should also include "hush" in this repertory, which sound belongs, most often, to Dilsey Gibson, the Compsons' black matriarch *and* mama, who must worry—as was the traditional circumstance—about both her family and that of her charges. Dilsey's admonitions to the children to keep quiet on eschatological occasions seem to accompany nearly every utterance by the powerful fact that Benjy's narrative marks no fewer than three Compson deaths in its duration and because the register of dying does not appear *in seriatum* (as it must have happened over the years), but as a complicated steady state of sonal markers (words and noises): (1) his grandmother Damuddy's death, which occurs when Benjy is approximately three years old and still named "Maury"; (2) Quentin's death by suicide, which we deduce must have taken place when Benjy was about fifteen years old; (3) Jason III's death, which seems to have occurred about three years later, approximate to Benjy's eighteenth birthday. All the deaths, then, are "blocked," or punctuated by Dilsey's "hush," which also plays another important dramatic role, insofar as Caroline Compson, who *ought* to be mama, is dysfunctional—hypochrondriac and infantalized, in short, a veritable mess. "Miss Kahline" might be thought of as the *fifth* Compson child. Any child's play disturbs her already disturbed mind, which renders Dilsey's tasks all the more onerous. But as the only one capable of managing this pathological nucleated family, Dilsey assumes the good offices of an angel of mercy.

Is "hush" a word, or is it a signal? If that is an interesting problem, we add to it its onomatapoetic translation in "shhh," as well as Benjy's materialized howling, which noise we can only imagine. These "agitated layers of air," I think Marx called it, reverberate across the text so that its walking and talking "knock" against the ear like echoes. If grief makes a noise, then I would say that Faulkner not only found it, but discovered a way to represent it by the manipulation of marks on the page. Much of the magic here is conveyed by the labor of repetition.

What I would like to propose, then, is that repetition in Faulkner's work is an act of rhetorical *regression*, demarcated by various periodicities; a breach that is distinct from its environment, it is represented by a clustering or isolating that would identify a common ground between territories of the symbolic: In Kenneth Burke's view, the Freudian theories, while not designed for literary criticism at all, developed a perspective that "was able (by reason of its scope) to migrate into the aesthetic field."[31] For him, the "margin of overlap" is captured in the behavior of a symbolic sphere, broadly defined: "The acts of the neurotic are symbolic acts. Hence insofar as both the neurotic act and the poetic act share this property in common, they may share a terminological chart in common. But insofar as they deviate, terminology likewise must deviate."[32] It seems to me that *regression*, a term borrowed from the nosological chart, may be applied, in a suggestive way, to the literary criticotheoretical one without violating either its psychoanalytical properties or the rhetorical ones that I mean. With the work of structuralists and poststructuralists, however, particularly the Lacanian project, bent on a Freudian revision in a specific historical juncture, the territories are brought into closer alignment by way of the operations of the *linguistic*. The latter gives the hinge that swings between two doors.

It is useful to our purposes here that the classical etymology that names certain figures of speech—the "doubling back" of *chiasmus*, the "carrying back" of *anaphora*, for example—are, technically speaking, a kind of regressive move, insofar as they execute the word's doubling back on itself. In the case of Faulknerian repetition, words do "double back" and "come back," which processes may or may not entail replication, since *synonymity* may occur instead. In either case, we lay hold of an analogy on the metaphoric operations as one of "two aspects of language" and language disturbance as Roman Jakobson described them.[33] The play between the "concurrence of simultaneous entities and the concatenation of successive entities" becomes not only "the two ways in which we speakers combine linguistic constituents,"[34] but also the ways by which the literary surface is created and sustained as a *generative* (progression) and *regenerative* (repetition/regression) field of signifying.

This "return," more or less demarcated, to a discursive condition, or circumstance that Burke referred to as a "causal ancestor" reveals itself in all forms of similarity—doubling[35] and replication, synonymity and reverberation. These phenomena of the same would benefit, however, from a strategy of naming that could distinguish between their role and status in the expression of a truly multiple order of cases. Interestingly, a "first" appearance on a given literary surface cannot be finessed away by scare quotes, but must be naively and "really" registered as the "first" time that a mark or series of them appears on it, which would be, by definition, *a repeat*. Since we have here to do with the business of the "res," some future itinerary of theoretical alignments might pursue repetition on the literary surface against the problems of reproduction in a no-longer mechanical age[36] and the dizzying duplicities of cyberspace.

If we accept the notion that psychoanalytic readings might be analogously applied, only where fitting, to an engagement with literary texts, then we are less inclined to commit the procrustean error. But the difficulties that the literary critic experiences, even by way of analogy, or even especially by way of it, must be squared with the originations and the destinations of psychoanalytic practices in the first place. The lures are significant and far too attractive: For one thing, psychoanalytic researches were forwarded in the interest of biohistorical subjects, not made-up ones, even though both, given the narrative genre of the case history, are immersed in fictions. One of the important differentials here is outcome and orientation—one repertory of subjects can go only in one direction—straight ahead toward a future—except under very special, strictly limited, and decisively circumscribed conditions, called "analysis," in the one case, and/ or, more commonly, the circumference of the dream; whereas, the other repertory of subjects earns the future only insofar as a community of readers reenacts and reengages the printed page. The "times" of the literary character, then, are not actually its own, but persist in temporalities borrowed from its biohistorical constituents. There is, moreover, an inbuilt salvific dimension to psychoanalytic practices and theories, critiqued from its inception and mockingly disparaged in certain quarters today, that literary ones most usually do not sustain. While they have induced much talk about their ties to the project of upliftment, such talk is sometimes regarded as the equivalent of the sirens' call, some public, or institutional misprision. The psychoanalytic, on its side, was, on occasion, at least, thought to be fitted to the vocation of the *ecclesia super cloacam*. Burke described this "church over a sewer" and the arts of "haruspicy" this way: "over the course of [Freud's] work, it is the matter of human rescue that he is concerned with . . . the very essence of his studies, even at their most forbidding moments (in fact, precisely at those moments), is its charitableness, its concern with salvation."[37] This "charitableness," he goes on, is approached in terms of " 'secular hospitalization,' " as opposed to, " 'religious hospitality,' " and it was "the spirit of Freud; it [was] what Freud's courage [was] for."[38]

Translating the verbs of the passage into the past tense robs it of its felt historical immediacy, given that Burke was writing these essays contemporaneously with the nightmare blossoming over Europe and the final days in exile of Sigmund Freud. Was it any wonder, then, that *rhetoric/symbolic action* (as a route to a just "attitude") were felt to be essential instruments in the "battle" against a massive and global psychosis—"let us try to discover what kind of 'medicine' this medicine-man [Hitler] has concocted, that we may know, with greater accuracy, exactly, what to guard against, if we are to forestall the concocting of similar medicine in America"?[39] Few literary texts are accorded such direct efficacy as Burke here attributes to dialectical reading; which leads to the last catch: having in common with the psychoanalytic reading the paying attention to the slope and play of signs, the literary critic/theorist is engaged with the *word* so that his/her work makes a kind of mimesis to the analyst's.

We can only mean the repetition compulsion and the complex of regression, then, in a shadow dance to the psychoanalytic sphere. Faulknerian repetition/regression must be entertained at that level. But insofar as it becomes a mode of *representation* of the speaking subject entangled in the symbolic order, as one's membership in it remains captive to the imaginary,[40] it bristles with all the borrowed thrust and vitality of the biohistorical subject. If the unconscious is "*structured like a language*,"[41] as Lacan contended, and if "linguistic structure gives its status to the unconscious,"[42] furthermore, then where are we placing the repetitive/ regressive moment? Whose "unconscious" does this fictive speaking subject show? If we locate the compulsion in the character, then how do we explain its appearance otherwise? And is there a way to account for such recurrences "beyond" in the *rhetoric* of the structure, without appeal to biographical claims? I cannot answer these questions any more directly now than I have already attempted to suggest in the course of this essay. But it seems to me that we must eventually get there since *that* place constitutes our sole license to "practice."

My own responses to Faulkner are shaped, primarily, by the monumental sense of loss and mourning, scored in these novels, that the encounter with modernity has installed. But we will find such routings only indirectly, or should we say that some ghastly demarcations leave their traces there? I am suggesting that *grief* in Faulkner is not simply limited to an American region—the South of the United States—but that the sketch of a configuration of it in his work, the excruciating care to ferret it out, render it a gift to the national culture. That loss, without content, on the one hand, and full of it, on the other, is as close as I can come to naming "it," which begins to explain, I think, the powerful import of repetition in the canon. It is the repetition of loss, as Jacqueline Rose describes it,[43] that can never be satisfied in a subject with an answer to a demand: "That loss will persist over and above anything which [the mother, say] can possibly give, or say, in reply."[44] A demand, or what cannot be named, actually exceeds what is called for, Rose argues, "and each time the demand of the child is answered by the satisfaction of its needs . . . this 'something other' is relegated to the place of its original possibility."[45] In reference to the Lacanian synthesis, Rose interrogates the protocol of the remainder of the subject, which is called "desire."

It would be incorrect, I think, to try to boil these novels down to a capital promise, but I would read both the scopic and invocatory initiations of the small Compson boys beneath the death tree (at Damuddy's death) and the utter terror that Quentin feels in that dorm room later on, forestalling the lures of death with *stories*, by the lights of desire—its misses and the mourning that ensues.

In closing, I want to try a *glissando*: We are reminded now of the little girl's "dirty drawers," as if a sacred object, but certainly something that looks like, behaves like, the Lacanian "petit objet," which the brothers saw at a distance and probably recognized even then the moment of loss that it portended. Having no idea what it meant, although the moment is forever linked in Benjy's mind with the *smell* of death, and in Quentin's, with the rage to obsessive focus on *anything*, and perhaps in Jason, the younger's money-craze, the adult brothers have each "forgotten" where it all started. It reappears for Quentin as the near-at-hand summer wedding—a beautiful young woman, running out of a bank of flowers in a shining veil—and in the fear of carnal knowledge, registered in all those "doors" in *Absalom*, and it will likely repeat in his brother Jason as a tendency to migraine, camphor rags, and a near-scatological vileness of speech. Its substitutions, detours, and reroutings will re-appear in Harvard Quentin's stutterings and puzzlements as the anguish to recover the forgotten. But the words are not his; they are someone else's—all the someone elses that fall under the Father's law and the generative order, which he wishes to reverse. If Quentin and company have been "mugged by a metaphor," as Wahneema Lubiano puts it,[46] then the language of return that captures them is forever the grand tautology, forever the round and round. As the subject of speech, *as if* they were biohistorical subjects, they would be subject to the processes of symbolization which begin "when the child gets its first sense that something could be missing; words stand for objects, because they have only to be spoken at the moment when the first object is lost."[47] In the child's mind, the words *stand for*, the words *are*, the absent thing: "For Lacan, the subject can only operate within language by constantly repeating that moment of fundamental and irreducible division. The subject is therefore constituted in language as this division or splitting."[48] But in the case of Faulkner's character, this "moment" can only be posited, remains abstract, and must be regarded as the absolute *irrecoverable*: cantilevered over the desiring, the words keep trying to say over and over; the only problem is that what they are saying they don't say!

Mrs. Ramsay reported that Mr. Ramsay had gotten all the way up to "R," I believe it was. We are still abecedarian with this "R," but it is a good place to end by promising to work on it.

[The full text of this essay will appear in the author's essay collection, *Peter's Pans: Essays on Literature and Culture*.]

NOTES

1. Gertrude Stein, *The Autobiography of Alice B. Toklas* (New York: Vintage Books, 1960); excerpts from *The Making of Americans* in *Selected Writings of Gertrude Stein*, ed. Carl Van Vechten (New York: Vintage Books, 1962); all quotations from *The Making of Americans* come from this edition, page numbers noted in the text. The entire work was

republished in 1995, with a foreword by William Gass (Normal, Illinois: Dalkey Archive Press, Illinois State University).

2. William Faulkner, *Absalom, Absalom!* The Corrected Text (New York: Vintage Library, 1990). All quotations from the novel come from this edition, page numbers noted in the text.

3. The psychoanalytic method that Jacques Lacan was devoted to inaugurating was based on a revision and correction of Freudian theory and practice. Incorporated in Anthony Wilden's text, Lacan's "Rome Report," delivered to an international forum of psychoanalysts after a split within the French circle during the 1950s, elaborated what Wilden has called "the new terminology"—which sought to integrate the Levi-Straussian hypothesis about the interrelatedness of linguistic and social structures with psychoanalysis. Jacques Lacan, *Speech and Language in Psychoanalysis*, trans. Anthony Wilden (Baltimore: Johns Hopkins University Press, 1981), xiv. In "The Empty Word and the Full Word," which appears in Wilden's translation, Lacan speaks of the subject's verbalizing of the event as the way by which the latter passes into the *verbe* "or more precisely into the epos," when the subject "brings back into present time the origins of his own person" (16).

Wilden points out that the *verbe*—"more or less synonymous with *mot*, *parole*, *logos*, and the *Logos*"—maintains a flavor of its own. In its early acceptations, the term was "reserved for religious and ecclesiastical contexts" (n. 41, 104). In reference to Faulkner's character, I am taking it to mean the Word, "insofar as the Word confers a meaning on the functions of the individual; its domain is that of the concrete discourse; insofar as this is the field of the transindividual reality of the subject; its operations are those of history, insofar as history constitutes the emergence of Truth in the Real" (19). "Ownmost" is borrowed from the Heideggerian canon, as Lacan's work is braided from philosophical elements that trace back to Hegel and the influential teachings of Alexandre Kojève: *Introduction to the Reading of Hegel: Lectures on the Phenomenology of Spirit*, assembled by Raymond Queneau, ed. Alan Bloom, trans. James H. Nichols, Jr. (Ithaca: Cornell University Press, 1980).

4. William Faulkner, *The Sound and the Fury*, Norton Critical Edition, ed. David Minter (New York: W.W. Norton, 1987). All quotations from the novel come from this edition, page numbers noted in the text.

5. In his magisterial study of Faulkner's life and work, Joseph Blotner points out that only the southern third of the state of Mississippi was inhabited by whites when the state was admitted to the Union in 1817. The remainder of the state was occupied by the Choctaw and Chickasaw communities; by way of the Treaty of Dancing Rabbit Creek, "a large part of North Mississippi running eastward from the Mississippi Delta" was ceded to the United States in 1830. Joseph Blotner, *Faulkner: A Biography*, 2 vols. (New York: Random House, 1974), 1:11. Belonging to the era of President Andrew Jackson's coercive policies toward Native Americans and the notorious "Trail of Tears," the Treaty of Dancing Rabbit Creek, as well as others, was little short of unilateral surrender. Jeffrey P. Brain and Frank W. Porter III, *The Tunica-Biloxi*, Indians of North America Series (New York: Chelsea House Publishers, 1990), 10. The guilt that ensued left its fictive trail through Faulkner's work, particularly in the instance of Ike McCaslin and the repudiation of the land.

6. For a full discussion of "diegesis," from its platonic origins, to its career in the hands of modern writers, see Gérard Genette, *Figures of Literary Discourse*, trans. Alan Sheridan (New York: Columbia University Press, 1982); "Frontiers of Narrative," 127–44. Migrating into film theory, "diegesis" is defined by one pair of cinéastes as the film's "recounted story," "the total world of the story action," over and against its plot: David Bordwell and Kristin Thompson, *Film Art: An Introduction*, 3rd ed. (New York: McGraw-Hill Publishing Company, 1990); 56–57.

7. The "one" of the Lacanian project runs parallel to the "individual" of liberal property, but is far more complicated, insofar as his/her subjectivity arises elsewhere, not only in the sense of other subjects who precede him on his own stage, but also regarding the subject's relationship to his "unconscious." If the particular aim of psychoanalysis is "historically defined by an elaboration of the notion of the subject," then the "Ich"—"the complete, total locus of the network of signifiers, that is to say, the subject, *where it was*, where it has always been, the dream"—must be mapped. And "*[w]here it was*, the *Ich*—the sub-

ject, not psychology—the subject must come into existence." Jacques Lacan, *The Four Fundamental Concepts of Psychoanalysis*, ed. Jacques-Alain Miller, trans. Alan Sheridan (New York: W.W. Norton, 1981), 44–45; 77.

8. The paradigm of repetition in the poetics field rests in poetry itself. When such strategies appear, as they inevitably do, in works of prose fiction, we usually recognize them as image clusters, or other configurations of figures that add up to kinds of patterning, more or less predictable. But the repetitive in Stein's work, for example, does not produce an image or a visual field. From *The Making of Americans*, the following passage, among others, seems to defy traditional repetitive practices and expectations: "It is a very difficult thing to know it of any one the being in them, it is a very difficult thing to tell it of any one what they are feeling, whether they are enjoying, whether they are knowing that they are hurting some one, whether they had been planning doing that thing. It is a very difficult thing to know these things in anyone, it is a difficult thing if that one is telling everything they can be telling, if that one is telling nothing" (287; cf. n.1). The effect of the repetitive here might be described as *tickling*, though I can detect no humor in it. The self-conscious manipulation of signs, however, is somehow pleasurable at the same time that it makes the reader *herself* self-consciously engaged in the act of reading.

Soren Kierkegaard's 1843 novel *Repetition* bears the subtitle "An Essay in Experimental Psychology" and is narrated under a "symbolic pseudonym"—"Constantine Constantius." An excerpt from it appears in *A Kierkegaard Anthology*, ed. Robert Brettal, trans. Walter Lowrie (New York: Modern Library, 1946), 134–52. The entire novel, alongside *Fear and Trembling*, appears in *Fear and Trembling; Repetition: Kierkegaard's Writings*, 6, ed. and trans. Howard V. Hong and Edna H. Hong (Princeton: Princeton University Press, 1983). In flight to Berlin after disappointment in love, Kierkegaard remained captive to his desire to marry one Regine Schlegel. The possibility of a "repetition" of this affair, as well as the theme of repetition from other experiences in his life, is said to have suggested the plot of Kierkegaard's novel (Brettal, 135). Constantine's pursuit of repetition on aesthetic grounds is supposed to be a failure "just because it is an *attempt* and because it is *pursued*" (136; emphasis added). In this case, repetition consists in an action—the return on a scene in four dimensional space; but perhaps it has in common with repetition on a literary surface the idea of *fixation*, and "in so far as fixation is to be understood as an 'inscription' . . . regression might be interpreted as the bringing back into play of what has been inscribed." "Regression," *The Language of Psychoanalysis*, ed. J. Laplanche and J.-B. Pontalis, trans. Donald Nicholson-Smith (New York: W.W. Norton, 1973), 386–88.

9. Freud offers the paradigmatic model of repetition in "Remembering, Repeating, and Working Through," *The Standard Edition of the Complete Psychological Works of Sigmund Freud*, 24 vols., trans. James Strachey (London: Hogarth Press, 1958), 12:147–56. Contrasted with "remembering," repetition, or the compulsion to repeat, becomes a major aspect of the transference; not only a transfer onto the person of the doctor, but "also on to all the other aspects of the current situation," repetition "now replaces [in the patient] the impulsion to remember." The patient "repeats under the conditions of resistance" (151).

10. Citation appears on the dusk jacket of *William Faulkner Reads*: The Nobel Prize Acceptance Speech, *As I Lay Dying* (excerpts), *A Fable* (excerpt), and "The Old Man" (excerpt), Classic Literature. Caedmon Audio (New York: HarperCollins Publishers, Inc., 1998).

11. David Krause, "Reading Bon's Letter and Faulkner's *Absalom, Absalom!*," *PMLA* 99:2 (March 1984), 225–41. Krause, quoting from Joseph Blotner's *Selected Letters of William Faulkner*, points out that the author, in response to a question posed by Malcolm Cowley about *Absalom, Absalom!*, wrote the following, in November 1944: "I am telling the same story over and over, which is myself and the world. Tom Wolfe was trying to say everything, get everything, the world plus 'I' or filtered through 'I' or the effort of 'I' to embrace the world in which he was born and walked a little while and then lay down, again into one volume. I am trying to go a step further. . . . I'm trying to say it all in one sentence, between one Cap and one period. I'm still trying to put it all, if possible, on one pinhead."

12. Jacques Lacan, *The Four Fundamental Concepts of Psychoanalysis*. In "Tuché and Automaton," Lacan takes up the problematic of repetition by focusing on the startling

dream of a father, who loses his sick child by fire; assigned the responsibility of watching over the child while its father took a rest, the attendant fell asleep, upsetting a candle at the child's bedside, setting the bed aflame. The father dreams the child's saying to him: " 'I'm burning . . . Father, don't you see?' " (cited from Sigmund Freud, *The Interpretation of Dreams,* Standard Edition, 5:509–10; in this case, the burning child is running a fever—Lacan asks whether or not the father's remarkable dream of the situation is "an act of homage to the missed reality—the reality that can no longer produce itself except by repeating itself endlessly, in some never attained awakening?" (58). If, as Freud argued, the dream fulfills a wish, then the father's dream would appear to directly contradict such a conclusion. But as Lacan reads it from Freud, the dream signals that the father wants to continue sleeping, in which case his son, the dream's coprotagonist, is still alive.

13. Deborah Tannen, *Talking Voices: Repetition, Dialogue, and Imagery in Conversational Discourse,* Studies in Interactional Linguistics 6 (Cambridge: Cambridge University Press, 1989).

14. Ibid., 37.

15. Roman Jakobson and Morris Halle, *Fundamentals of Language* (The Hague; Mouton, 1975); "The Twofold Character of Language," 72–76; emphasis in original.

16. Tannen, 95.

17. Kenneth Burke, *The Philosophy of Literary Form: Studies in Symbolic Action,* 3rd ed. (Berkeley: University of California Press, 1973).

18. Ibid., 191–220.

19. Ibid., 350–60.

20. Ibid., 360.

21. Winifred Bryan Horner, *Rhetoric in the Classical Tradition* (New York: St. Martin's Press, 1988).

22. Ibid., 316.

23. Ibid., 317.

24. Ibid.

25. Ibid.

26. Martin Luther King, "Letter from Birmingham Jail," *Why We Can't Wait* (New York: Signet, 1964), 76–96.

27. Richard A. Lanham, *Analyzing Prose* (New York: Charles Scribner's Sons, 1983); "A Brief Glossary of Rhetorical Terms," 254.

28. Ibid.

29. Donald Kartiganer, *The Fragile Thread: The Meaning of Form in Faulkner's Novels* (Amherst: University of Massachusetts Press 1979), 22.

30. Ibid., 9.

31. Burke, *The Philosophy of Literary Form,* 261.

32. Ibid.

33. Jakobson, "The Metaphoric and Metonymic Poles," *Fundamentals of Language,* 90–96.

34. Ibid., "The Twofold Character of Language," 73.

35. Reading Faulkner against Nietzsche and Freud, John Irwin provides a seminal study of the novels by way of the "Quentin Compson" configuration. Irwin places the double and the theme of the uncanny at the center of the oscillations of his argument between texts. *Doubling and Incest/Repetition and Revenge: A Speculative Reading of Faulkner* (Baltimore: Johns Hopkins University Press, 1975).

Other important psychoanalytic inquiries into aspects of the Faulknerian canon include Carolyn Porter, "Symbolic Fathers and Dead Mothers: A Feminist Approach to Faulkner," and Jay Watson, "Faulkner's Forensic Fiction and the Question of Authorial Neurosis," in *Faulkner and Psychology,* ed. Donald M. Kartiganer and Ann J. Abadie (Jackson: University Press of Mississippi, 1994); 78–123; 165–89; Doreen Fowler, *Faulkner: The Return of the Repressed* (Charlottesville: University Press of Virginia, 1997).

36. Walter Benjamin, "The Work of Art in the Age of Mechanical Reproduction," *Illuminations: Essays and Reflections,* ed. Hannah Arendt, trans. Harry Zohn (New York: Schocken Books, 1968), 217–53. Benjamin suggests that in the age of mechanical reproduc-

tion the aura of the art work withers, as "the technique of reproduction detaches the reproduced object from the domain of tradition. By making many reproductions it substitutes a plurality of copies for a unique existence" (221).

37. Kenneth Burke, *The Philosophy of Literary Form*, 260.

38. Ibid.

39. Ibid., 191.

40. Though Lacan's triangulation of the psychic web is foundational to his own vast contributions to the psychoanalytic field and is, therefore, woven throughout his work, a concise definition of the imaginary/symbolic/real concatenation is offered in the "Translator's note" to *Écrits: A Selection*, trans. Alan Sheridan (New York: W.W. Norton and Company, 1977), vii–xii.

41. Lacan, *The Four Fundamental Concepts of Psychoanalysis*, 20.

42. Ibid., 21.

43. Jacqueline Rose, *Sexuality in the Field of Vision* (London: Verso, 1986), 55. Elements of this work appear in Jacqueline Rose's introduction to *Feminine Sexuality: Jacques Lacan and the école freudienne*, ed. Juliet Mitchell and Jacqueline Rose, trans. Jacqueline Rose (New York: W.W. Norton and Company, 1982), 27–59; the "moment of fundamental and irreducible division" initiates, in Lacan, entry into the "order of language," or the symbolic sphere, whereas "that of the ego and its identifications" belong to the "imaginary (the stress, therefore, is quite deliberately on symbol and image, the idea of something which 'stands in.')" The real is Lacan's term "for the moment of impossibility onto which both are grafted, the point of that moment's endless return" (*Feminine Sexuality*, 31).

44. Rose, *Sexuality in the Field of Vision*, 55.

45. Ibid.

46. This powerful concept is introduced and elaborated by Wahneema Lubiano, "Like Being Mugged By a Metaphor: Multiculturalism and State Narratives," in *Mapping Multiculturalism*, ed. Avery F. Gordon and Christopher Newfield (Minneapolis: University of Minnesota Press, 1996), 64–75.

47. Rose, *Sexuality in the Field of Vision*, 54.

48. Ibid., 55.

"The Force that through the Green Fuse Drives": Faulkner and the Greening of American History

NOEL POLK

My title is a wee bit shy of my paper, in that it offers something more wide-ranging and cleverer by half than the two novels I am really here to speak about. I cling to it, however, for a couple of reasons. I hoped that the line from Dylan Thomas would provide me with a workable metaphor for discussing Faulkner and history. To a certain extent, it does just that: it suggests the direction and power of a Biblical or at least puritan *telos*, the primal urge of Schopenhauer's Will, the uncontainable energy of Goethe's nature at its most fecund, and the absolute randomness of a world governed by chance and accident. As metaphor it offers me both the unpredictable predictableness of fractals and chaos theory and the butterfly theory, which holds that the flapping of a butterfly's wings in Mississippi can start a chain reaction that will eventually cause a monsoon in China. The metaphor offers a sense of history's absolute and unstoppable motion and energy both in its singularity and in its complex and wonderfully inventive variations.

It does all this, most importantly, I think, by allowing us to think of all this motion as a *forward*, not *backward*, energy. We are far less concerned with the rose's origins than with the resulting bud in front of our eyes. Unlike human beings, nature constructs itself forward, rapaciously and rambunctiously, with little regard for where it comes from or how it got to where it happens to be, and without any concern whatsoever for hierarchy: in its profusion it cares not a whit whether it is a Jungfrau or the most finite and historically disposable of snail darters. What the metaphor does *not* do, alas, is give us much scope, outside the botanist's, to talk about that backward look toward origins, which we seek precisely to understand the forces that have made some Alps, politically and economically speaking, and others snail darters. Or rather, if we are Alps, we write a history that justifies the hierarchy that makes Alps more important than snail darters. If we are snail darters, of course, we write histories that try to explain what went wrong, why we are not Alps too. A good deal of Southern history, even its fiction, is precisely that: snail darter history: we *were* God's people. Why did God let this happen to us? Thus Southern myth and history prefer to memorialize beautiful houses in Natchez rather than the black backs whose forced labor built them. You can visit Natchez, you can visit Beauvoir, Jefferson Davis's final home, in Biloxi, and get almost no hint, unless you ask, that slavery ever existed. And some of the most influential voices out of Nashville have held quite openly the opinion that the prebellum South was the last manifestation of order in human history. Order? For whom?

But history, natural history, is not about order; order is for museums and monuments. Left to itself nature would run amok in its disorderly profusion. History, the history of human nature, is about *disruptions* to the flow of that force-through-the-green-fuse. History disrupts by its commodification of nature, its sale and despoliation of the forest, long understood, and misunderstood, to be a, perhaps the, central operating metaphor in Faulkner's work.

The site of that disruption is very much like Frederick Jackson Turner's American frontier, which he describes as a rolling edge of aggression where the past meets the unknown and each struggles to meld and alter the other: a fuzzy unbounded expanse in whose constant flux boundaries, identities, appear and disappear, where the past and the unknown meet and alter each other and wage a constant battle for dominance over a shifting and unstable present. Time is a fluid medium in which the present moment exists as a nexus of contingency between the past and the future, as a constantly destabilizing landing which we try to stabilize by bringing past and future together in a seamless conjunction. History for Faulkner is precisely this self-same disruption: an *event*, a motion *against* the motion, a reaction *against* that registers some kind of resistance to the force that through the green fuse drives. Event, disruption, marks the physical world with a scratch or a monument to mark the resistance, whether it be despoiling a forest or defacing paper with little squiggles that try to say. That monument or scratch, the Mont St. Michel or letter home from the front, then, stops flux; it becomes a site, a point, around which time and space organize themselves and to which, especially in the historical imagination, they yield dominion, as the Tennessee woods organize themselves around and yield dominion to Wallace Stevens's jar.

Not for nothing does Faulkner, in *Requiem for a Nun,* describe the earth itself, the "confluent continental swale," as a "broad blank . . . page for the first scratch of orderly recording."[1] He connects the alteration of the natural world with writing, with narrative, and he makes, as so many of us have noted, the disappearance and appropriation of north Mississippi's Big Woods the backbone narrative of his Yoknapatawpha books.

We live our lives forward, of course, but we write about them backward, so that what we know as Turner's frontier, a chaos of contingency and possibilities, becomes, as we write about it backward, not a mere succession of moments but rather a succession of causes and their inevitable effects. We make of the past a lean mean clean narration which pares contingency away and which clarifies, simplifies, and explains how, for better or for worse, things got to be the way they are, who is to *blame* for how things are, and so whose responsibility it is to *fix* things.

Critics have valued Faulkner as a chronicler of Southern history, especially that history handed to him by his family and his region, but not that part of it that he witnessed and tried to participate in during the last decade or so of his life, those post-War, Cold War, and early Civil Rights years, because of his controversial and problematic participation in the nation's debate on civil rights. And, of course, being a Mississippian, he could not understand the complexities of the twentieth century.

Yet he was keenly interested in the contemporary scene. I do not believe that Faulkner himself was obsessed by the past, although of course many of his characters are. Even so, his characters nearly always mark their obsessions with the past in Faulkner's own world; most of his works take place contemporaneously with their writing. Especially in his later work, as the twentieth century became more and more complex and terrifying, he tended to depict his little postage stamp of native soil not as a region isolated out of time and space from the rest of the world, but as intimately inseparable from it.

But I am not here to discuss Faulkner as a *chronicler* of American history. In fact he was, I think, less interested in history as a chronicle, as a seamless narrative, than he was in any individual's temporary footing on that constantly destabilizing moment we call the present. What I would like to do is to talk about Thomas Sutpen's and Isaac McCaslin's confrontations with their own histories, which are reverse mirror images of each other, and their attempts to create rupture in their histories. Several questions hover, without hope of resolution, just above my comments. They are not, to be sure, original questions. But as Hayden White and many others have insisted, the kinds of assumptions one makes about how history operates determines the kind of history one writes: Does history exist outside its narration? If so, does it therefore exist as a Grand Narrative that stands outside of human telling and so subsumes all smaller, local and individual, narratives? If so, is it therefore teleological? Is history an inevitable movement toward conclusion, a destiny manifesting itself, or is it, as Faulkner puts it in *Requiem for a Nun*, "litter from the celestial experimental Work Bench"? (540). Is there a guiding hand presiding benignly or not over human history, directing it, us, toward a preforeordestinated end, as Huck Finn might put it? If, on the other hand, history exists only in its narration, how can we ever hope to experience or understand it outside the political and cultural agendas of the narrator or outside the inevitable cultural mythmaking that is history's twin sibling, or, finally, outside the problematic of our own frail, often traumatized, memories? Does Gavin Stevens's famous assertion that "The past is never dead. It's not even past" mean that we are creatures of history who cannot escape the point in time or circumstance in which our heredity and environment have placed us? If so, what is the point or meaning of human striving? If are we victims of our history, how are we, how can we be, morally responsible *to* it? If we are *not* victims of history, how can we act against those very circumstances? Can we act morally, that is, as free moral agents, within history, to change what is evil or unjust, to promote what is good? Indeed can we in fact *act* at all, or is what we take to be a single act merely one small cog in the wheel of that larger Grand Narrative, put into place long ago, and over which individuals have no more control than do robots over their programmers?

The animating spirit of America, of course, is precisely the belief that people can indeed opt out of history, can indeed start over, change things, take control of and then micromanage their own destinies. To be sure, our Puritan forebears opted out under the perceived direction of God, so that in coming to this country they were merely playing their part in God's Grander Narrative of redemption. Even so, from its discovery and exploration, the American continent became identified as a land where indeed one might step aside from the long miserable chronicle of European history—where God's people, at any rate, could recover the historyless innocence from which our original Mother and Father had so ignominiously fallen into time. But that dream, the dream of starting over, brought its own inescapable and self-canceling dark twin to these shores, the Calvinistic burden of predestination or, to put it more generously, the general burden of the human condition. Our Puritan forebears brought with them, even as they came to discover and to own the new Eden, both a history and a vision of the future, rank with the odor of purpose, which they then attempted to impose upon the new world Eden, a world they considered without form and void, a world without its own history and therefore malleable to their designs upon it, designs handed down, they claimed, from God Himself.

The Puritans' "errand into the wilderness" is the thematic jumping-off point of American history, at least that version of American history told by novelists and poets who found themselves constantly testing the promises of the new world against its realities. Our predecessors came here looking for Eden, they noted. What did they find? And what did they bring with them? That Edenic wilderness—or WILDerness—found its own inevitable trope in America's formidable natural world, and a good deal of America's most important literature engaged itself in one way or another with Nature and with the question of Nature's significance in the American moral landscape. For such writers as Emerson and Thoreau, Nature was generous, expansive, and lifegiving, and human beings were inextricable from it; others, like Bradford, Hawthorne, and Melville, understood it rather as dark, troublesome, and chaotic, filled with visions and demons that danced in the night to trouble such Puritans as Young Goodman Brown.

For Faulkner in the twentieth century, however, forests were inherent with neither positive nor negative moral value. He understood that people rather imposed such value on forests by the uses to which they put them. He noted how the forces of modernity used nature up to build houses and towns for a multiplying population to live in and so found in the disappearance of the wilderness an irresistible metaphor for both American history and a history peculiarly Southern. He did *not*, however, like many of his characters and traditionalist critics, see modernity as an absolute evil that was therefore opposed to the value-laden past. For him the wilderness was *both* Eden *and* raw material for moral and commercial appropriation. He understood perfectly and sympathized with those of his characters who see it as the repository of humanity's fading memory of ease and plenitude, the mysterious original site where we experienced oneness, wholeness—what theologians and psychologists might call innocence—, before falling into history; but he also understood, more completely, that nature is the raw material from which progress, the urban, is constructed. It is thus the very stuff of modern urbanization and fragmentation. Nature is the matrix of history. Whether "history" is teleological or a chaos of the possible, it must move forward. History, the marker *of* time, is also subject *to* time.

Faulkner's signal contribution to the developing cultural narration of American history is to place the problem of slavery squarely at the center of the narration of the wilderness. According to Sam Fathers's indoctrination of Isaac McCaslin in *Go Down, Moses*, the wilderness disappears not just because of humanity's fall from Edenic splendor, but because of the corruption of the land by ownership: the first man that thought he owned a piece of land sufficiently to sell it or trade it corrupted it. Slavery, the foul byproduct of land ownership, tainted not only the land but the people who owned and sold it, and then tainted as well the history of those transactions, and of those who made them.

Isaac uses this version of history, a highly moralistic and sentimental vision, as his stated reason for renouncing both his family's heritage of land- and slave-ownership and what he takes to be his grandfather's incestuous inbreeding with his own mulatto daughter. We shall return to that renunciation shortly. For the moment, however, I merely note that the version of history Isaac acts upon is his own, and not necessarily Faulkner's. Until very recently it has been taken to be Faulkner's, partly because Isaac's heart seems to be in the right place—certainly his rhetoric is—and we want to admire one who is so completely horrified by America's racial history and by his own family's complicity in it that he wants to put a stop to it. He wants, like the Puritans, to opt out of his own history.

Faulkner describes the intimate connections between the Big Woods of North Mississippi and American history in *Requiem for a Nun*, in which he pulls together in one almost seamless narrative the history of his little postage stamp. As he recounts it, the very circumstances under which Jefferson and Yoknapatawpha County were founded become both a general fable of the founding of Western Civilization[2] and also, and more particularly, a fable of the founding, rape, and refounding of America. Like the Puritans, Jefferson's first settlers come to the North Mississippi wilderness precisely to escape the old world corruption of the east coast and the Natchez Trace. No more than those original Puritans can they escape that past, however, and they very soon have to deal with anarchy's invasion of their neat, ordered little Eden. As you recall, they reclaim themselves from the chaos of that invasion by confederating first with one another and then, as they become overwhelmed with the symbolism of the courthouse they have built, with the United States of America, crowning that symbol by naming their new town Jefferson—even if they do arrive at that name through the complicated interventions of the misnamed irascible mail rider, Thomas Jefferson Pettigrew.

The complications that lead to the founding of Jefferson are not important here; you have all read the novel. What *is* important is the metaphorical chemistry that energizes the telling. First of all, as noted, the settlers come to north Mississippi precisely to escape the corruption of the Natchez Trace on one side of them, and the Mississippi River on the other. They want to step outside the corrupting history of the east coast and the western frontier, and they discover that they cannot do so. Second, Faulkner depicts these events as occurring not by any logic of design but strictly by chance and accident: there is no telos here, only the gargantuan and terrifying workings of chance.

Third, we should remark Faulkner the Hawthornian: in *The Scarlet Letter*'s second paragraph, Hawthorne observes that the "founders of a new colony, whatever Utopia of human virtue and happiness they might originally project, have invariably recognized it among their earliest practical necessities to allot a portion of the virgin soil as a cemetery, and another portion as the site of a prison."[3] It may or may not be significant that Faulkner's settlers begin with a jail and a tavern instead of a jail and a cemetery, but it is certainly significant, I think, that Faulkner positions the jail as coeval with the only other significant building in the community. Both Hawthorne and Faulkner understand that order is the first, the essential, and the defining requisite for society; thus civilizaton must recognize, at its inception, the human condition in sin—or if not in sin in any theological sense, then at least in the human impulse toward freedom that acts against whatever laws there are. Jails in Hawthorne and Faulkner symbolize civilization's understanding of the human condition, whether in sin or in rebellion. They also symbolize historical continuity, a continuity in this Edenic case that reaches all the way back to creation.[4] The settlers *claim* that history, indeed *impose* it upon their brand new courthouse and jail by placing atop it, as its crowning and ultimate point, a four-faced clock, which hourly reminds them of the "dingdong of time and doom" (*Requiem* 505).

Finally, it is profoundly significant that the settlers build the new Jefferson courthouse as an adjunct, almost as an afterthought, to the jail. The courthouse and jail, thus paired, represent the need for security and order and inspiration on the one hand, and the human condition in rebellion on the other. Civilization thus counters the human condition in anarchy by an appeal to something higher, nobler; it recognizes the continuity in sin of the human past and inspires humanity to refocus its restless, rebellious energy into channels that operate for the common good. Civilization, then, with its necessary adjunct ownership, possession, its necessary division of the landscape into buildings and streets, is thus one form of that rupture in historical process I spoke of a moment ago, an ordered resistance to humanity's inevitable movement toward disorder. The towns, jails, and courthouses are the marking monuments that organize the landscape into usable portions and then dominate it. Civilization wants to alter the course of that historical continuity, to create a better people for a better world, by controlling the internal and external chaos in which people, without order, without laws, would perforce live.[5] For Faulkner *this combination* of baser impulses and nobler aspirations *is* the human condition: for him it is not a condition in sin so much as a condition in history. The symbiotic relationship between base impulse and noble aspiration, between the desire for order and the opposing desire for absolute freedom, provides the specific energy, the creative matrix, of much of Faulkner's fiction.

I want now to talk about two of Faulkner's major explorations of the workings of history, *Absalom, Absalom!*, published in 1936, and *Go*

Down, Moses, published in 1942, though both spring from common sources in his work of the mid-thirties. In *Absalom*, Faulkner resurrects Quentin Compson to help narrate that novel's reconstruction of Thomas Sutpen's story. *Go Down, Moses* grew out of a story he wrote in 1935, while he was writing *Absalom*, called "Lion," which features that same resurrected Quentin Compson as its central character, later to metamorphose into Isaac McCaslin. For now I'm less interested in the Quentin Compson third of this triangulation than in the base line that connects Isaac and Sutpen, but I do want to note Quentin Compson's centrality to Faulkner's treatment of time and history in his work. In *The Sound and the Fury* Quentin and his brother Benjy experience time as a series of fragmentations which occlude traditional narrative; though family and Southern history are a part of *The Sound and the Fury*, they are marginalized into the background, giving way to the Compson brothers' individual histories. By the time of *Absalom, Absalom!*, Faulkner has become more interested in that regional background, and so foregrounds it as a major component of Quentin's historical consciousness. In *Absalom, Absalom!* and *Go Down, Moses*, then, Faulkner allows Quentin to try yet again to make sense out of an incomplete history, to force coherence upon fragments which perhaps have no necessary relationship to each other. In effect, Quentin cannot, as Southerner or as Compson, figure out where he has come from, what forces are working to shape him, because for him the past is a scattering of fragments that may well admit of no coherence. Quentin is one of several narrators of *Absalom* who try to reconstruct Thomas Sutpen's story on scant and highly problematic evidence: *Absalom*'s narrators have almost none of the evidence a historian would require, certainly none of the requisite documents, but only what the novel calls the "rag-tag and bob-ends of old tales and talking." In *Go Down, Moses* on the other hand, Isaac McCaslin has a document, a cryptic chronicle, which demands interpretation.

The heroes of these two chronicles of the American South, Thomas Sutpen and Isaac McCaslin, are thematic siblings in Faulkner's work. To oversimplify, Sutpen desperately wants to have what Isaac just as desperately wants to give away: that peculiarly Southern way of life built upon the exploitation of land and people. That is, they are both looking at the same thing, but from entirely opposing and mutually exclusive perspectives. Like Quentin, like the founders of America, like the founders of Jefferson, both of them want to step outside of their histories in order to start things over.

Indeed, Thomas Sutpen abrupts into the north Mississippi wilderness as a savage creator. As Rosa Coldfield recounts it to Quentin, in *Absalom*'s opening paragraphs, "Out of quiet thunderclap he would abrupt (man-horse-demon) upon a scene peaceful and decorous as a schoolprize water color, faint sulphur-reek still in hair clothes and beard, with grouped behind him his band of wild niggers like beasts half tamed to walk upright like men, in attitudes wild and reposed, and manacled among them the French architect with his air grim, haggard, and tatter-ran. Immobile, bearded and hand palm-lifted the horseman sat; behind him the wild blacks and the captive architect huddled quietly, carrying in bloodless paradox the shovels and picks and axes of peaceful conquest. Then in the long unamaze Quentin seemed to watch them overrun suddenly the hundred square miles of tranquil and astonished earth and drag house and formal gardens violently out of the soundless Nothing and clap them down like cards upon a table beneath the up-palm immobile and pontific, creating the Sutpen's Hundred, the *Be Sutpen's Hundred* like the oldentime *Be Light*."[6] Though Rosa's imagery paints Sutpen as demonic, however, clearly this is a Creation metaphor, in which Sutpen acts as the creator God, sitting majestic and serene on his horse, palm uplifted, and *willing* Sutpen's Hundred into being in language specifically Biblical. In subsequent pages Sutpen does more than *will* it into being: he works hard, right along with the wild blacks that he has brought with him to do his will, to raise his mansion out of the "absolute mud" of the North Mississippi wilderness. They work naked to save their clothes and wrap themselves in the "croaching and pervading mud" to ward off mosquitoes. Thus Sutpen-God creates himself as God had created Adam, out of the primal mud of that primal Eden, but shaping himself rather in the combined images of his predecessor, the man he is trying to supplant, the owner of the plantation whose Negro servant had turned the boy Sutpen away from the door, and of that wonderful Paris architect, without whom he could not have built his dream.

You'll recall the scene in which the stunned and puzzled boy retreats from that repudiation into a maternal cave to reflect upon his experience. Without having a language to understand it, Sutpen has discovered class differences, discovered that there are people who are rich and own other people who look down on him because he isn't rich and doesn't own them. He is smart enough, even at that young age, to deduce that simple revenge won't work because *they*, the plantation system, *the system*, are too powerful to be beaten by a single person. He comes to understand that in order to beat the system he must join it. He is thus the American Dream embodied; his *Be Sutpen's Hundred* in the north Mississippi wilderness precisely marks his successful re-creation of himself out of his poor white trash origins into the sort of respectability that the plantation manor house represents, his transfiguration from one level of historical process into another.

As a boy, and as a young man, Sutpen has no historical sense. He knows nothing of the historical processes that have separated people by class and race, divided people and earth into ownable chunks. He does not know that to succeed he has to overcome all of American and Southern history—indeed, all of Western history too—and that his strength lies precisely in *not* knowing. At first his ignorance of history serves him well, for a historical sense might have locked him in to the life into which he was born, overwhelmed and victimized him into immobility. Lacking the historical sense, he does in fact, for a brief shining Camelotian moment, overcome that history. But his lack of historical consciousness finally brings about his downfall. That is, he never learns that in the act of living he creates a history that *will* hold him responsible, that will catch up with him, in the form of Charles Bon, who may be his son from an earlier marriage. He does indeed start over once, opting out of the history he had been handed; but he cannot opt out of the history that he himself creates. He offers General Compson a narrative in which he tries to deny responsibility for his own history by admitting to mistakes that he had tried to rectify, as though history could be ameliorated through the recognition of error, or an apology for it.

Even as the Puritans brought to the American continent the very human condition that they hoped to escape, so does Thomas Sutpen bring with him to north Mississippi a human condition in history both personal and cultural. He thinks he has left behind the problematic son in Haiti, of course, and discovers too late that he has not. And in bringing the Haitian Negroes with him, he brings with him all the baggage of slavery. Finally, in bringing the French architect with him, he symbolically loads his own history down with all the vast accumulated sophistication and corruption of Western Civilization: the same corrupt civilization that the Puritans thought they escaped but in fact brought with them, too.

Sutpen's much-discussed "innocence," then, from this point of view, is his ignorance of history and of the historical process. A huge part of his innocence lies in his investment in the other direction, in his belief in the future. With only a minimal sense of history, he believes not only that he can escape his past but that he can control his future. Thus, his also much-discussed "design" is very much a part of his innocence. As General Compson passes the story down to his son and grandson, Sutpen's innocence and his design are directly connected, and that design is just as directly connected to his need to control the future: "His trouble was innocence. All of a sudden he discovered, not what he wanted to do but what he just had to do, had to do it whether he wanted to or not, because if he did not do it he knew that he could never live with himself for the rest of his life, never live with what all the men and women that had died to make him had left inside of him for him to pass on, with all the dead ones waiting and watching to see if he was going to do it right, fix things right so that he would be able to look in the face *not only the old dead ones but all the living ones that would come after him when he would be one of the dead*" (178; italics added).

Scholars and critics, thinking of Horatio Alger and Jay Gatsby and too simplistically of the "American Dream," have nearly always taken Sutpen's design to be a plan whereby he would overcome hardship and lowly origins by working hard and make of himself a rich planter in the grand Southern tradition. As it seems to me, however, *that* plan is merely the vehicle for a design both more and less grand or complex or compelling than a rags to riches romance. Sutpen's "design" is, in a larger sense, just that: a design, a plan, a desperate need to impose order on his life. We have only to look at the formlessness, the absolute chaos, that he came from in order to understand this. Quentin tells us that Sutpen was born at the top of a mountain in West Virginia; Shreve's factual objection that there was no West Virginia until well after Sutpen could have been born there places Sutpen's origins outside of recorded time and space, outside of history and geography, in a world as much without form and as void as the original chaos. He spends his formative years in a place where he "never even heard of, never imagined, a place, a land divided neatly up and actually owned by men who did nothing but ride over it on fine horses or sit in fine clothes on the galleries of big houses while other people worked for them; he did not even imagine then that there was any such way to live or want to live, or that there existed all the objects to be wanted which there were. . . . Because where he lived the land belonged to anybody and everybody and so the man who would go to the trouble and work to fence off a piece of it and say 'This is mine' was crazy. . . . So he didn't even know there was a country all divided and fixed and neat with a people living on it all divided and fixed and neat because of what color their skins happened to be" (179).

Sutpen's formative world is thus defined as the opposite of the order that design, that class and race and fences and roads, enforce upon the world. His life as a child is anything but orderly. He and his slovenly family "fall" (Faulkner's word) into history by coming down the mountain from that boundaryless and timeless and historyless chaos, descending, as General Compson puts it, "perpendicularly through temperature and climate—a (you couldn't call it a period because . . . it didn't have either a definite beginning or a definite ending . . .)—an attenuation from a kind of furious inertness and patient immobility while they sat in the cart outside the doors of doggeries and taverns and waited for the father to drink himself insensible, to a sort of dreamy and destinationless locomotion after they had got the old man out of whatever shed or outhouse or barn or ditch and loaded him into the cart again and during which they did not seem to progress at all but just to hang suspended while the earth itself altered, flattened and broadened out of the mountain cove" into a world increasingly ordered and sufficient, where "doggeries and taverns now become hamlets, hamlets now become villages, villages now towns and the country flattened out now with good roads and fields and niggers working in the fields" (182). It is a completely chaotic childhood. "That's the way he got [his education]," Quentin suggests. "He had learned the difference not only between white men and black ones, but he was learning that there was a difference between white men and white men not to be measured by lifting anvils or gouging eyes or how much whiskey you could drink then get up and walk out of the room" (183).

Confronting the boundaried demarcations of roads, fences, and property, Sutpen also confronts, again without understanding it, historical privilege, symbolized by the plantation house from which he is turned away, though he does not understand this, ever; even so, he is not stupid, and he deals quite rationally with his rejection by the established order. He teaches himself that the Negro butler who turned him away was not the problem, that the problem was with something beyond and above the Negro, a problem and a solution as vague and amorphous as history itself: how to understand *and so fix* the injustice inherent in the way things are—or, rather, in the way things have come to be? One of the crucial episodes of his confrontation with privilege occurs when Sutpen and his sister, walking along a dusty road, are nearly run down by a black coachman driving two white women who glare down at his sister. Sutpen's response is to throw "vain clods of dirt after the dust as it spun on, knowing now, while the monkey-dressed nigger butler kept the door barred with his body while he spoke, that it had not been the nigger coachman that he threw at at all, that it was the actual dust raised by the proud delicate wheels, and just that vain" (187). The passage irresistibly evokes a later scene when, under siege in Haiti, he fires "at no enemy but at the Haitian night itself, lancing their little vain and puny flashes into the brooding and blood-weary and throbbing darkness" (204). The dust and the night, then, represent a chaotic history that has put him on the bottom of the pile. The rock and the bullet represent that innocence: his impotent belief that he can dominate history.

Sutpen teaches himself that throwing rocks at dust and shooting into the night are ineffective ways to deal with the formlessness of his life. Order and control are his design: the plantation and the dynasty are secondary to it. His mistake as an adult is that, having made himself invulnerable to the cultural past that made him white trash, he believes that he is invulnerable to his own history. He allows himself to believe that he can control the future in the same way he believes he has tamed and overcome the past. Very much like Jefferson's settlers in *Requiem*, he enters his own history without any knowledge of it, and, when it catches up with him in the person of the son he has apparently denied, he is, "taken . . . by surprise, unawares, without warning to prepare and fend off" (*Requiem* 477). Such is innocence indeed. That he cannot even escape his past, much less control his future, is suggested by his own disgraceful end, in which he simply reverts to type and becomes the same drunken white trash his father was, and repeating, as so many have observed, the sin of turning the boy away from his door.

In *Go Down, Moses* Isaac McCaslin has a diametrically opposed relationship to history. Isaac is in some ways far more interesting, from this perspective, than Sutpen. If Sutpen is a figure out of Greek tragedy, one consumed with a passion that sees only itself, Isaac is a far more philosophical sort, a contemplative whose meditations on his familial and his cultural histories, whose long conversations with his cousin Cass Edmonds, and whose investigations into those histories form the narrative, philosophical, moral, and thematic backbone of the novel. Isaac is born directly into the historical privilege that Sutpen covets and takes for himself; Isaac wants nothing to do with it.

History begins for Isaac with the words of Sam Fathers, his mentor-in-the-Big-Woods, who fills his head with the wisdom of the old people, who remembers an Eden-like wilderness, a land owned by nobody and so owned equally by everybody. He thus is sympathetic to the Puritan's indictment of what he calls the "old world's corrupt and worthless twilight"[7] and their escape from it. As we understand from his unwillingness to shoot the bear, Isaac wants to preserve Eden, to continue in the prelapsarian innocence of a world before history. More: he wants to reverse history, to restore the wilderness to that state before it was corrupted by ownership and by commerce in human beings.

In the long philosophical debate with Cass that constitutes a good deal of part 4 of "The Bear," Isaac casts himself as a pivotal figure not just in American and Southern but also in human history, a crucial figure upon whom history will turn. He constitutes himself as a self-appointed Moses, or Christ, who will intervene in history to free a people long in bondage, and change the course of the future by breaking the chain of causality that history has imposed upon slaves and owners alike. But unlike Moses and Christ, he believes that a simple act of renunciation of his region's history will suffice. To justify his renunciation, however, Isaac must first establish the telos, the cosmic chain of causality, that brought him to this point.

I give you a heavily truncated version of Isaac's rendering of world history, since we hardly have time for the whole complicated rigmarole. God, Isaac argues to Cass, "saw the land already accursed even as Ikkemotubbe and Ikkemotubbe's father old Issetibbeha and old Issetibbeha's fathers too held it, already tainted even before any white man owned it by what Grandfather and his kind, his fathers, had brought into the new land which He had vouchsafed them out of pity and sufferance, on condition of pity and humility and sufferance and endurance, from that old world's corrupt and worthless twilight . . . and no hope for the land anywhere so long as Ikkemotubbe and Ikkemotubbe's descendants held it in unbroken succession." Maybe, Isaac continues, the Civil War itself was God's way of purging the land to accomplish His purposes, just as Rosa Coldfield believes that God made the Civil War only to kill Thomas Sutpen, and failed: "Maybe He saw that only by voiding the land for a time of Ikkemotubbe's blood and substituting for it another blood, could He accomplish His purpose. Maybe He knew already what that other blood would be, maybe it was more than justice that only the white man's blood was available and capable to raise the white man's curse, more than vengeance . . . when He used the blood which had brought in the evil to destroy the evil as doctors use fever to burn up fever, poison to slay poison." God had his eye on me all the time, Isaac continues, though he humbly qualifies his narrative with a series of "Maybes": "Maybe He chose Grandfather out of all of them He might have picked. Maybe He knew that Grandfather himself would not serve His purpose because Grandfather was born too soon too, but that Grandfather would have descendants, the right descendants; maybe he had foreseen already the descendants Grandfather would have, maybe He saw already in Grandfather the seed progenitive of the three generations He saw it would take to set at least some of His lowly people free" (191–92). Inevitably, Isaac claims, God saw *me*.

Isaac argues history as a teleological force, of which he is both victim and agent. But the novel problematizes his claim on design in a couple of significant ways. First, Isaac helps that teleology along a bit by attributing to God some things that God didn't say, at least in earshot of any of the writers of the Bible, and by his interpretation, perhaps misinterpretation, of the faded, almost illiterate ledgers which record his family's commerce in human flesh. You will remember the crude entries that Isaac convinces himself record the incestuous relationship of his grandfather with his own half-white, half-black, slave daughter, and her mother's suicide upon learning of that incest. The ledgers, of course, don't actually *say* why Eunice committed suicide, much less record his grandfather's incest. But Isaac interprets them that way; to justify his renunciation he needs to forge a direct connection between his own family history and the worst excrescences of racial history. The ledgers do not endorse his reading, but they do not need to, because, as Faulkner tells us, Isaac "knew what he was going to find before he found it" (198); Isaac, like Sutpen's telling to General Compson, interprets the evidence from his own need to have history serve his purposes.

The second serious problematization of Isaac's argument from teleology is the novel's opening chapter, entitled "Was," but originally entitled "Almost." "Was" recounts an episode, ritualized and doubtless often repeated, in what can only charitably be called the courtship of his parents-to-be. Never was there a less likely match than these two. In "Was" his homosexual father-to-be, Buck McCaslin, is "almost" trapped by his supercilious Southern belle of a mother-to-be, Sophonsiba Beauchamp. Buck is saved from marriage this time only by the intervention of his twin brother's reputation as a poker player. Both parents-to-be become ante in a poker game set up to resolve the bets that Hubert and Buck have made earlier in the day. Several lives and several futures, black and white, turn on a poker game, on Uncle Buddy's bluff of Mr. Hubert.

We don't know how Miss Sophonsiba and Uncle Buck finally get together to engender Isaac, but "Was" entitles us to suppose that at some point Uncle Buddy's bluff didn't work, that the cards fell another way, or at least that some other contrivance by Miss Sophonsiba or Mr. Hubert finally worked against history and Nature—Buck's homosexuality—to trap him into marriage. One of the points of "Was," then, is to establish, early in the novel, how completely improbable it is that Isaac was conceived at all, *much less* that all of history since the beginning of time should have been aimed at, pointed toward, should have culminated in, him and his renunciation of that history.

To be sure, Calvinists, Baptists have no trouble believing that God can work His will even through such a bewildering array of what seems to be chance and contingency. I expect that Faulkner did not believe this, but he does not here take sides. In reading Faulkner, one always has to be aware of the discrepancy between what his characters *say* and what they *do*. Isaac's case is especially difficult for us because we so much like what he *says* about Southern and American history, and we can only speculate whether his renunciation is a selfless, altruistic act, or consummately self-serving; whether he is an humble agent of that telos he claims, a hero-martyr like Christ or Moses acting against an oppressive history, or simply a man afraid of responsibility; maybe he is all three, and more. But it *is* fair, I think, to ask what are the practical effects of his attempts to intervene in the history of his time, to stop slavery: does his renunciation work? Plainly, no; no more than does Sutpen's appropriation of history. Sadly in "Delta Autumn" Isaac becomes the very agent of that selfsame history he had repudiated and hoped to sidestep. Like Sutpen, he too turns the beggar away from the plantation door. When he hands Roth Edmonds's money and the hunting horn to Roth's cousin and mulatto mistress, he replicates the very sin of which he had accused his grandfather, the prime and proximate cause of his renunciation. In passing on the money, Isaac denies the moral foundation upon which he has lived his life, repeating with a vengeance the history he has renounced. Faulkner's point could not be clearer: Isaac might have done more to change history. Had he accepted and not repudiated the burden, engaged his history, he would have assumed, along with the guilt and the shame, the power and privilege that history wanted to hand him, and he might indeed, from such a position of privilege and power, have come nearer to effecting change.

The novel's most telling irony, however, is that after choosing to intervene in American history by opting out of it, Isaac wraps himself in a mantel of humility: he decides he will support himself by carpentering, invoking the example of Jesus in doing so: "because if the Nazarene had found carpentering good for the life and ends He had assumed and elected to serve, it would be all right too for Isaac McCaslin" (229). He forgets, of course, that to accomplish his ends, Jesus *left* carpentering in order to engage the world; he did not assume carpentering in order to escape it.

Faulkner lived twenty years after *Go Down, Moses*—twenty years that saw catastrophic change in the Southern and the American old order: World War II, the Holocaust, the Cold War, and, not least, the beginnings of the Civil Rights movement. Prior to 1950, when he won the Nobel Prize, he mostly busied himself, as a good anti-bourgeois high modernist was supposed to, with his art and with the nitty-gritty details of feeding his family. After 1950 he began to involve himself in his nation's and region's political turmoil. He spoke and wrote often and publicly to criticize Mississippi's racial institutions, to the consternation of many of his fellow Southerners and Mississippians. Scholars, even his most loyal fans, have more often than not been embarrassed by his political activity, patronizing him and his statements on race for reasons I am not sure I understand. His political engagement in the fifties seems to me a thoroughly admirable, courageous, and direct response to the racial and historical morality of his own fiction—perhaps to Isaac McCaslin—which perhaps forced him to see himself as an artist passively isolating himself from the history of his own time, a history in which he as a citizen should be involved. We might say, scholars have said, that his intervention, like Isaac's, accomplished nothing, though how can we ever know how things might have happened, for better or for worse, if he had kept silent? He made enemies of both white and black groups and did nothing discernible to forestall the bloodshed and the federal intervention that he feared and abhorred; and after a lustrum or so of slugging it out to no avail in the public arena, he retired again to the aerie of his high art.

Maybe all Faulkner's example as a public man proves is that history is inexorable, that it operates independently of human agency, and that no one can intervene to change it; maybe destiny operates in its own way, in its own good time. I doubt that Faulkner, finally, believed this; certainly he did not believe that "destiny" or "fate" were unchallengeable, and he certainly believed in the human capacity to want to be better than we are capable of being, as he so often put it. At the very least he believed that we have to continue to believe that we can change things, else we yield to the diffusions of entropy.

At the very least, perhaps his retreat in his last years from engaged citizen to artist-observer put him in the place he ought to have been, observing and writing, not warning folks, as he had done in his public statements, but himself casting back over the events of his own life and ruminating, meditating about them. In *Requiem for a Nun* he had written that the earliest settlers of Jefferson had come to North Mississippi to escape the underworld of the Natchez Trace and the Mississippi River, and when that underworld pressed itself into their Edenic solitude, as it was bound to, they were, he writes, "taken as it were by surprise, unawares, without warning to prepare and fend off" (477). Thus he implicitly accuses them of the same sort of innocence, both of human nature and of history, that render both Thomas Sutpen and Isaac McCaslin impotent to deal with the present and the future. We cannot, Faulkner implicitly holds, afford the sort of innocence that makes the past any more fixed, immutable, monumental or controllable than the future. History is best when, like Faulkner's fiction, it reminds us of the fragmentations and contingencies of life in the present moment, no matter in which century it occurs.

What he preached from his public pulpits in the 1950s was that no matter where we are in time, we can't go back to another time, we have to deal with the world as we find it: "I don't hold to the idea of a return," he told interviewers: ". . . once the advancement stops . . . it dies. It's got to go forward and we have got to take along with us all the rubbish of our mistakes and our errors. We must cure them; we mustn't go back to a condition, an idyllic condition, in which the dream [made us think] we were happy, we were free of trouble and sin. We must take the trouble and sin along with us, and we must cure that trouble and sin as we go. We can't go back to a condition in which there were no wars, in which there was no bomb. We got to accept that bomb and do something about it, eliminate that bomb, eliminate the war, not retrograde to a condition before it exists, because then if time is a [forward] and continuous thing which is a part of motion, then we have to run into that bomb again sooner or later and go through it again."[8]

In one of the most moving and significant and oft-misunderstood episodes of "The Bear," Isaac as a boy hopes to be vouchsafed a vision of Old Ben, but cannot succeed. Sam Fathers advises him first to leave his gun behind, and then, when that does not work, to leave behind his watch and compass too. He hangs them across the limbs of a bush and, divested of time and space, begins wandering through the wilderness looking for Old Ben, until he is completely lost in the universe. He sits on a log, as Sam had instructed him to do, and as he does he sees not Ben himself, but Ben's footprints disappearing as the water from the wet ground fills and overflows the paws' indentations. Isaac follows the fading prints through the wilderness right back to the glade where he had left his watch and compass; that is, Old Ben himself leads Isaac right back into time and space, right back into history, before allowing Isaac that vision. His lesson seems clear: Ben is no mythological bear but a mortal creature, even as Isaac is, engaged in the mutable present moment, as Isaac is not. It is not a lesson Isaac, with his fixation on the past, seems capable of learning.

"Once the advancement stops," Faulkner said, "then it dies." Perhaps it worse than dies; perhaps it repeats itself endlessly into diffusion. *Was* is the saddest word of all, Mr. Compson tells his suicidal son. No, Quentin argues, not *was* but *again*. They are both sad words, the saddest of all, because they lock our eyes and minds backward toward a world fixed and containable. The vital force that through the green fuse drives, drives us forward, not into was or again but into possibility, the most terrifying and exhilirating of frontiers.

NOTES

1. William Faulkner, *Requiem for a Nun*, in *Faulkner: Novels 1942–1954*, ed. Joseph Blotner and Noel Polk (New York: Library of America, 1994), 541. Subsequent references to this text are parenthetical.

2. Noel Polk, *Faulkner's "Requiem for a Nun": A Textual and Critical Study* (Bloomington: Indiana University Press, 1981).

3. Nathaniel Hawthorne, *The Scarlet Letter*, in *Hawthorne: Novels*, ed. Millicent Bell (New York: Library of America, 1983), 158.

4. ". . . indeed, as Gavin Stevens, the town lawyer and the county amateur Cincinnatus, was wont to say, if you would peruse in unbroken—ay, overlapping—continuity the history

of a community, look not in the church registers and the courthouse records, but beneath the successive layers of calsomine and creosote and whitewash on the walls of the jail" (*Requiem*, 616–17).

5. See my *Faulkner's "Requiem for a Nun."*

6. *Absalom, Absalom!* The Corrected Text (New York: Random House, 1986), 4. Subsequent references to this text are parenthetical.

7. *Go Down, Moses*, in *Faulkner: Novels 1942–1954*, ed. Joseph Blotner and Noel Polk (New York: Library of America, 1994), 191. Subsequent references to this text are parenthetical.

8. *Lion in the Garden*, ed. James B. Meriwether and Michael Millgate (New York: Random House, 1968), 131.

William Faulkner's Dialogue with Thomas Jefferson

PETER NICOLAISEN

The story Faulkner tells in *Requiem for a Nun* about the naming of the town of Jefferson has all the elements of a tall tale. It contains a number of bizarre and highly unlikely incidents, it's funny, and it has a victim. Its salient point is that it is not really Thomas Jefferson who served as the patron saint of the settlement that was to become the hub of Faulkner's fictional universe. Instead, we learn that the citizens used Jefferson's name in order to bribe the mail carrier Pettigrew, whose mother had named her son after the famous Virginian, so that he "would have some of his luck."[1] According to *Requiem for a Nun*, in other words, the town of Jefferson received its name through an act of deceit; those who chose the name did so in order to extricate themselves from a quandary into which they had gotten partly through their own fault. If at the same time they meant to pay tribute to the third president of the United States and the principles he stood for, they did so in a most indirect and circuitous way.[2]

Faulkner first mentioned the town of Jefferson in the fragment "Father Abraham," on which he worked in 1926 and which he then abandoned for a number of years in order to pursue other projects. The name "Jefferson" stuck; the author used it again in *Flags in the Dust*, and then retained it throughout all his later fiction set in Yoknapatawpha County. But not until *Requiem for a Nun* did he ever comment on his possible reasons for his particular choice of a name. It is tempting to think that it involved an element of irony from the very beginning. For early on in "Father Abraham" Flem Snopes is introduced as "a living example of the astonishing byblows of man's utopian dreams actually functioning; in this case the dream is Democracy."[3] Democracy, that is to say, produces the Flem Snopes's of this world. Nineteen twenty-six was the year of the sesquicentennial of the Declaration of Independence and the centenary of its author's death, representing, as Merrill Peterson has said, "the high point thus far in the patriotic commemoration of Jefferson."[4] It was the year also of the dedication of Monticello, Jefferson's home on the mountain top, as a national shrine. Claude G. Bowers's *Jefferson and Hamilton: The Struggle for Democracy in America* had been published in the previous year and received lavish praise from scholars and politicians alike. It was "an eventful book," to quote Merrill Peterson once more, "because it related itself to conditions. In the postwar reaction against hyperbolic nationalism, both foreign and domestic, many Americans of a liberal persuasion found in Jefferson just that range of ideas that most needed reemphasis. The intellectual wind was strongly blowing in Jefferson's favor."[5] In 1926, then, the association of Flem Snopes as a representative of "the utopian dream" of democracy come true, with Thomas Jefferson, "one of the foremost democrats of all times," as Bowers had called him, must have come almost naturally.[6] To name the town in which Flem Snopes will later find his apotheosis after Thomas Jefferson surely must have appealed to the young author's sense of humor.

But perhaps we should not put too much weight on a mere name. When he decided to keep Jefferson's name, Faulkner may well have thought of his choice as a realistic one; many towns, after all, bear the famous Founding Father's name. Many years later, when, during one of the interviews at the University of Virginia, he was asked why he had chosen Jefferson's name for the seat of Yoknapatawpha County, Faulkner did not even quite remember the story he had told in *Requiem for a Nun*. Pettigrew, the mail carrier, he now said, "had been a *tenant* on Mr. Jefferson's place, one of Mr. Jefferson's places here in Albemarle County."[7]

For all we know, Faulkner took little interest in the statesman from Virginia. Only once, and then only briefly, did he refer to Jefferson's "principles of order within the human condition and the relationship of man with man."[8] In all likelihood he did not even pay his respects to the "Sage of Monticello" when, late in his life, he was staying in Charlottesville, Virginia. How then can we justify a comparison between the two men? Taking my cue from the topic of the conference—"Faulkner in America"—I want to hold Faulkner against what during his lifetime was, and to an extent still is, considered a Jeffersonian vision of the United States. "In principle [Faulkner] seems to have endorsed Jeffersonian values," writes Myra Jehlen; Cleanth Brooks would have agreed.[9] Did Faulkner indeed endorse "Jeffersonian values" and if so, where did he agree with Jefferson, where did he part company with him? To answer these questions I will focus on three areas which figure prominently both in Faulkner's fictional universe and in the thought of Thomas Jefferson—the concept of an agrarian order, the issue of slavery and race, and the idea of liberty and the rights of the individual. If the second topic was probably less closely linked with Jefferson's name in Faulkner's days than it is in ours, it still had enough currency to be considered one on which Jefferson had taken a stand, both in his role as a slaveholder and in his pronouncements in his *Notes on the State of Virginia*. The "agrarian" Jefferson had been revived in the writings of the Vanderbilt Agrarians, while Jefferson as the "apostle of liberty and democracy" was very much the focus of the biography by Claude Bowers I have just mentioned.

To this can be added another suggestion. Even though temperamentally few men could have been further apart than these two, Faulkner is remarkably like Jefferson in the kind of controversial discussion he evokes. Was he a conservative, or was he a progressive and a liberal? Myra Jehlen has argued that his "tragic vision of the South" was inspired by his inability to choose sides between "the lords" and "the peasants"; a similar claim can easily be made for Jefferson. Jefferson, to be sure, did not have a "tragic vision" of the South, or of America, but he, too, at times waivered between the "peasants," the people, that is, and those in power, the aristocracy. In his taste, it has often been said, he was on the side of the latter; in the ideology he professed, he was a democrat.[10] Many readers have felt a similar tension to be at work in Faulkner. Like Jefferson, he was an advocate of change—"life is motion," he said on more than one occasion—but at the same time Faulkner had a conservative streak that would align him with the principles of "classical republicanism" recent historians have attributed to Jefferson.[11] As we know, he felt very much at home in the Farmington Hunt Club just below Monticello. Did he see eye to eye with Jefferson on "the dream of democracy," or did he continue to think of it as "utopian"?

* * *

"Aint no benefit in farming," Flem Snopes says in *The Hamlet*.[12] Faulkner, who had bought Greenfield Farm a few years before *The Hamlet* was published, would probably have disagreed, even though he was not making any money with his crops. But then, as Andrew Lytle had quipped in *I'll Take My Stand*, "a farm is not a place to grow wealthy; it is a place to grow corn."[13] Is there an agrarian sentiment that informs Faulkner's fictional realm? And, by extension, is the rural world that functions as the backdrop of so much of his fiction one Thomas Jefferson would have recognized as an environment fit for "those who labour in the earth" and who are, in his famous phrase, "the chosen people of God . . . whose breasts he has made his peculiar deposit for substantial and genuine virtue"?[14]

None of the characters working the land in novels like *Flags in the Dust, As I Lay Dying*, or *The Hamlet* is either particularly virtuous or happy. On the contrary, the anonymous farmer in *The Hamlet* who actually owns the land he lives on and therefore would come closest to Jefferson's independent yeoman, is portrayed as a madman, linked to his "small neat farm" by "unflagging mutual hatred and resistance" (908). The lot of tenant farmers like Ab and Mink Snopes or Henry Armstid is no better. The land is felt to be stifling and constricting man's freedom to move; the nourishment it yields in return for the farmer's "nerve-and-flesh wearing labor" (908) is meager enough. The moral qualities of "the peasants," as Faulkner calls them in *The Hamlet*, possibly alluding to an even older source of pastoral, bucolic thinking than Jefferson's, is anything but admirable—witness the scenes of communal voyeurism in Mrs. Littlejohn's lot or the silence greeting Lump Snopes's perjury before the Justice of the Peace.[15] Much the same can be said of the farmers we encounter in *As I Lay Dying*. Anse Bundren, too, owns the land he and his family live on, yet their existence is primarily one of drudgery and, especially in Anse's case, complaint.

Faulkner's overall vision of rural Yoknapatawpha County, in short, is a far cry from the agrarian order either Thomas Jefferson or his latter day disciples at Vanderbilt contemplated. When his country folk assert their independence, this often ends in violence or death. Education, by which Jefferson set such great store, is an ambivalent undertaking at best, as Addie Bundren in *As I Lay Dying* or the teacher Labove in *The Hamlet* demonstrate. Most importantly, the economics of Frenchman's Bend go directly against the high hopes Jefferson entertained for a republic of independent farmers. The commodification, in *The Hamlet* and elsewhere, not only of the land, but of virtually everything, including the human body, the greed characteristic of nearly all of the male inhabitants of Yoknapatawpha, the lack of any sense of responsibility attached to the idea of ownership—all these leave little room for the stable, republican order Jefferson imagined. Such conditions pave the way for the rise of Flem Snopes, a figure Jefferson would no doubt have associated with the commercial world of Alexander Hamilton that he despised, not with that of a virtuous agrarian republic.

Flem Snopes, for more reasons than one, is among Faulkner's most controversial figures. It is interesting to note that in the context of the late 1930s, the years in which Faulkner worked on *The Hamlet*, Flem's decision to get "out of [farming] soon as [he] can" (750), hardly merits the censure the novel accords it. Despite—and partly because of—the efforts of the New Deal, the plight of tenant farmers, white or black, was terrible.[16] They were hardly any better off than they had been in the 1890s, the decade in which the events of the novel take place. The novel explicitly acknowledges their sorry lot in the descriptions of Mink Snopes's bitter toil. Why, then, does Flem receive so little sympathy in *The Ham-*

let? He is the only one who manages to free himself from an economic system that Faulkner certainly did not condone, that of tenant farming and sharecropping. As Ab Snopes says in "Barn Burning," it rests on the idea that the landlord owns his tenants "body and soul."[17] Should Flem have stayed on the land, then? Clearly not. But Faulkner is obviously reluctant to grant him a right to economic growth and expansion, even though the methods employed to achieve that growth are basically the same as the ones used by the Varners or, for that matter, V. K. Ratliff. The career he pursues is that of a ruthless capitalist. It is conceivable that in Flem's rise to power Faulkner reflects upon the "second revolution" in the South, in which the precapitalist, patriarchal system of tenant farming gave way to modern forms of capitalism, including those of wage labor. In this regard his career may express Faulkner's criticism of the economic changes that occured in the South between the 1890s and the late 1930s.[18] At the same time, it may reflect Faulkner's more general reservations about that "utopian dream of democracy" which he had ironically alluded to in "Father Abraham." The nagging question remains, however, regarding what else Flem Snopes should have done. If neither tenant farming nor modern day capitalism is the answer, where do we go?

Hovering in the background of *The Hamlet*, as in that of many other Faulkner novels, I believe, is a desire for a world as yet uncorrupted by commercialism and greed. It is a wish, almost against better knowledge, to believe in the beneficence of an agrarian order—witness the evocation of "the mooned or unmooned sleeping land" (857), of rich soil and fertile fields, which suggests that perhaps there are other options than those of the downtrodden farmers I have mentioned. Ab Snopes's life before he "soured" or "curdled," as Ratliff says, may have been pleasant enough; similarly, it is conceivable that the unnamed farmer in *The Hamlet*, had he been a less driven person, could have led a happier existence. Most strongly, the episode around the idiot Ike Snopes and the cow projects a longing to return to an earlier, pristine world in which man and nature exist in harmony with each other, without a need for speech, without, indeed, a need for toil or effort. But this is a dream, of course, a vision of a mythical past, and as such far removed from the actuality of rural life in the 1930s or at any other point in history. Yet some such wish to be close to the soil, at one with it and in tune with the seasonal cycles of growth and harvest, must have been at work in Faulkner himself, as his frequent posturing as a farmer indicates. That his was a real desire, at least occasionally, and more than the whim of an intellectual wanting to live in the country, is demonstrated by the seriousness he periodically exhibited about Greenfield Farm.

In a series of stories composed in the early 1940s Faulkner comes close to translating his vision of "a world elsewhere," and his dream of an alternative to the lives of either Mink or Flem Snopes, into concrete political terms. The stories are not among his best, and are at times unabashedly sermonizing, even jingoistic. In the present context, "The Tall Men" is the most interesting one of the group, as it echoes Jefferson's creed of the independent farmer more strongly than any other Faulkner text. At issue is the right of the Federal government not only to register men for the military service in times of peace, but to control the agricultural production on any given piece of land. It is the government's interference with the individual farmer's freedom to choose whichever crop he wants to grow—and, by implication, how he wants to run his and his family's life—that comes under Faulkner's strongest attack. The McCallum's, the country family he had many years earlier portrayed in warm terms in *Flags in the Dust,* resist such attempts and insist on their "freedom and liberty to make or break according to a man's fitness and will to work," on their right also to live by themselves in a remote corner of the county,

> with the rest of the world all full of pretty neon lights burning night and day both, and easy, quick money scattering itself around everywhere for any man to grab a little, and every man with a shiny new automobile already wore out and throwed away and the new one delivered before the first one was even paid for, and everywhere a fine loud grabble and snatch of AAA and WPA and a dozen other three-letter reasons for a man not to work. [19]

Here, a Jeffersonian kind of individualism is demonstratively held against the governmental measures of the New Deal, for which Faulkner obviously had little sympathy. Against governmental programs of any kind, but also against an easy life that relies on manufactured goods like neon lights and "shiny new automobiles" Faulkner posits the independence of the sturdy backwoods farmer. In the early 1940s, then, he clearly allied himself with a Jeffersonian tradition of thought, much more outspokenly so than was his wont.[20]

Finally, we should note that the sense of humor and the warmth with which Faulkner usually portrayed the rural world, and the attitude of bemused respect and understanding he shows towards its inhabitants and their foibles, are rarely present when he creates a sense of the city, especially of Chicago—here again he seems to side with Jefferson, who abhorred "the mobs of great cities" and found that they "add to the support of pure government, as sores do to the strength of the human body" (*Notes on the State of Virginia*, 165). Throughout *The Wild Palms*, Chicago is associated with death and corruption—"the defunctive days dying in neon upon the fur-framed petal faces of the wives and daughters of cattle and timber millionaires"; its people are seen as an anonymous mass—"the employees' chute . . . discharging presently the regimented black satin, the feet swollen with the long standing, the faces aching with the sustained long rigid grimacing."[21] The lot of Faulkner's country people is often grim and dismal, as Mrs. Armstid in *The Hamlet* demonstrates, yet with few exceptions they retain a measure of dignity which in descriptions like these Faulkner deliberately seems to withhold.

* * *

"Go back North. Marry: a man in your own race," Ike McCaslin tells the young black woman in "Delta Autumn" who has borne Roth Edmonds's child.[22] He cannot bear to think about the possibility of intermarriage between blacks and whites. Instead, he dreams of an earlier America, a racially "pure" land where "*Chinese and African and Aryan and Jew*" did not "*all breed and spawn together until no man has time to say which one is which nor cares,*" and where black men did not yet own plantations or live in "*millionaires' mansions on Lakeshore Drive*" (269) in Chicago. Faulkner, of course, is not to be identified with Ike McCaslin, yet there can be no doubt that the "sense of exhaustion" that is so pervasive in "Delta Autumn"—the term is Michael Grimwood's—is closely bound up with the issue of racial "mixing," particularly with the sexual transgression committed by Roth Edmonds, and with his subsequent failure to accept the consequences of his action, a failure in which Ike McCaslin is implicated and which mirrors the long and troubled history of the McCaslin family as a whole.

None of Faulkner's works more clearly echoes Thomas Jefferson's fears of the consequences of slavery than *Go Down, Moses*. "I trouble for my country when I reflect that God is just, that his justice cannot sleep forever," Jefferson had said in *Notes on the State of Virginia* (163). As if to demonstrate the truth of his contention that "the whole commerce between master and slave is a perpetual exercise of the most boisterous passions, the most unremitting despotism on the one part, and degrading submissions on the other" (162), Faulkner has Isaac McCaslin imagine the affair between Old Carothers McCaslin and the young slave Eunice, and, more devastatingly, the incest Carothers commits with his daughter Tomasina, the offspring of his union with Eunice. Jefferson argued that neither the whites nor the blacks would ever be able to forget the cruelties perpetrated under the system of slavery. On the side of the whites, they would leave "deep-rooted prejudices," on that of the blacks "ten thousand recollections . . . of the injuries they have sustained" (138). What if not the memory of "injuries sustained" leads Lucas Beauchamp to ask his haunting question, "How to God . . . can a black man ask a white man to please not lay down with his black wife? And even if he could ask it, how to God can the white man promise he wont?" (46) Similarly, when Roth Edmonds as a child suddenly turns away from his black friend Henry Beauchamp, we are reminded of Jefferson's warning that the children of the masters early on "learn to imitate" their behavior and "thus nursed, educated, and daily exercised in tyranny, cannot but be stamped . . . with odious peculiarities" (162). If in *The Unvanquished* Faulkner at times seems willing to gloss over the traumatic effects of slavery, in *Go Down, Moses* his verdict is unequivocal.

As it is in *Absalom, Absalom!* Thomas Sutpen may well serve as another example of "the unremitting despotism" Jefferson thought of as an inherent part of the system of slavery. As Richard Godden has argued, Faulkner in *Absalom, Absalom!* dramatized an aspect of the "peculiar institution" that among the ruling class of the planters was rarely openly acknowledged—the idea, namely, "that slavery is an undeclared state of war, in which black revolution is a permanent risk." It is because he recognizes this "permanent risk" that Sutpen fights his slaves, enacting "the preemptive counterrevolution crucial to the authority of his class."[23] If Godden's reading is correct (as I believe it is), we would find that Faulkner in *Absalom, Absalom!* discusses concerns which Jefferson *did* openly express. For Jefferson, "a revolution of the wheel of fortune, an exchange of situation," meaning an open conflict between blacks and whites, was a very real possibility, and he feared that "the Almighty has no attribute which can take side with us in such a contest" (163). In his views of the Almighty, Jefferson, it is interesting to note, was considerably less optimistic than Ike McCaslin, who after all believed that God was forever on the side of the South and even in the Civil War "turned once more to this land which He still intended to save because He had done so much for it" (211).

Jefferson today is most notorious for his ideas, however tentatively advanced, that the system of slavery in the South could in some way be justified because the blacks, in contrast to the Greek slaves in Roman times, were in certain ways doomed by nature, and inferior to the whites. "In general," Jefferson wrote in a famous passage in *Notes on the State of Virginia*, "their existence appears to participate more of sensation than reflection," and went on to claim not only that "their griefs are transient" and that "love seems with them to be more an eager desire, than a tender delicate mixture of sentiment and sensation," but that "in reason [they are] much inferior" (139). I am aware that in my imaginary dialogue between Faulkner and Jefferson I have reached a most delicate point that perhaps I should not dwell upon. That Faulkner strongly disagreed with some of Jefferson's pronouncements is obvious. A story like "Pantaloon in Black," to name only one example, reads as if it had been written with the explicit intention to refute one of Jefferson's more extraordinary claims. On the other hand, some of the passages in which Faulkner comments about the results of the Emancipation Act are not all that far removed from the reservations expressed by Jefferson—e.g., the case of the ex-slave Sickymo in "The Bear," now a "United States marshal in Jefferson who signed his official papers with a crude cross" (216), or the caricature of Percival Brownlee who disappears from the area, to turn up years later as the "well-to-do proprietor of a select New Orleans brothel" (217). Though not an ex-slave, but a Northerner, and the son of a slave, the anonymous husband of Ike's black cousin Fonsiba also belongs to this group. He is dealt with in the most derisive fashion, as a pretentious fool who proudly quotes the Founding Fathers and their promise of "freedom, liberty and equality for all" (206), but who cannot even provide sustenance for his wife. The perspective is Ike McCaslin's, but through Ike's anger and sense of frustration at the man holding "the lenseless spectacles . . . like a music master's wand in the . . . workless hand" (206) we can hear the irritation of the author himself.

Jefferson, as is well-known, was reluctant about emancipation. "Brought from their infancy without necessity for thought or forecast," the slaves are "by their habits rendered as incapable as children of taking care of themselves," and therefore depend on the help of the whites, he wrote.[24] More importantly, he always coupled his proposals about emancipation with the provision that the former slaves "should be colonized to such place as the circumstances of the time should render most proper" (*Notes on the State of Virginia*, 138), "such place" being separate territories on the American continent or, preferably, in Africa. What he feared most of all was the blacks' "amalgamation with the other color"—this would produce "a degradation to which no lover of his country, no lover of excellence in the human character can innocently consent."[25]

We will probably never know for certain to what extent Jefferson's fears of black and white "amalgamation" involved his own, personal situation. Of interest here is the prominence he gives to the moral and psychological apects of what was later to be called "miscegenation." Is there an echo of his fears of "degradation" in the presence of the last of Sutpen's black descendants in *Absalom, Absalom!*, the idiot Jim Bond who haunts the ruined house at the end of the book? As in Jefferson's writings, miscegenation in Faulkner is primarily conceived of as a psychological issue, an offense outweighing that of incest, as the sentence ascribed to Charles Bon, "*I'm the nigger that's going to sleep with your sister*," famously demonstrates.[26] The century and a half that separated Jefferson from Faulkner, it appears, did not assuage the dark fears he expressed.

In his stand on race Faulkner often has not fared much better in the hands of his critics than Jefferson. Yet who can doubt that in their struggle with the question of slavery and race Jefferson and Faulkner shared a genuine wish to do justice to the issue, a concern "to do right," and an acknowledgement at the same time that, if pressed, they could only go so far? Some of Faulkner's public statements in the 1950s are an indication of such an attitude, as is Jefferson's obvious reluctance in his later years to take action where perhaps he could have acted. Both men, in any case, came closer to facing the problem at hand than many of their contemporaries. They knew that they could not solve the "American dilemma," but they were willing at least to take on its burden.

* * *

More clearly than in the question of an "agrarian" economic order and more sharply than in the murky area of racial fears and reservations, the gulf that separates Faulkner from Jefferson manifests itself in Faulkner's view on what is usually referred to as America's civil religion, on the concept of individual freedom and man's ability to govern himself. It is here that the contrast between the two men is perhaps most visible. "Ambuscade," the first chapter of *The Unvanquished*, offers an instance of the grim turn Faulkner's thoughts on the idea of freedom could take. Young Bayard Sartoris has a dream which deserves to be quoted in full:

> I was dreaming, it was like I was looking at our place and suddenly the house and stable and cabins and trees and all were gone and I was looking at a place flat and empty as the sideboard and it was growing darker and darker and then all of a sudden I wasn't looking at it, I was there: a sort of frightened drove of little tiny figures moving on it, they were Father and Granny and Joby and Louvinia and Loosh and Philadelphy and Ringo and me and we were wandering around on it lost and it getting darker and darker and we forever more without any home to go to *because we were forever free.*[27]

The passage is one in a series of similar ones in the novel suggesting that freedom may be a mixed blessing. These passages usually refer to slaves, or former slaves, but here Bayard includes himself and his family in his bleak view of what freedom means—darkness, confusion, and a loss of home. Bayard's black friend Ringo sums up his experience of the newly won freedom in the sentence, "I done been abolished" (454), while the family servant Loosh, who early on proclaims that "the Race gonter all be free" (334), eventually returns to the household he has left, even though it is still run by John Sartoris, "the man that buried [him] in the black dark" of slavery (369). John Sartoris, on the other hand, is cheered by his troop of irregulars when, in his efforts to restore "order" in Jefferson, he shoots the two Burdens and, with no effort to conceal his intention, publicly rigs an election.[28]

Faulkner enters into a more extended discussion of the idea of freedom in *Go Down, Moses*. Here Ike McCaslin's dream of a "dimension free of both time and space" (261) which, for a while, he believes he has found in the wilderness, is contrasted with the freedom his cousin Fonsiba postulates for herself when she says, echoing Ike's words, "I'm free" (207). But her freedom, too, is compromised by the context into which Faulkner places its expression. I have already alluded to the contempt with which her husband's references to the Founding Fathers is met; Ike speaks of the man's "sonorous imbecility" and his "baseless and imbecile delusion." (206) The circumstances in which he finds the couple, "the muddy waste fenceless and even pathless, . . . the drafty, damp, heatless, negro-stale negro-rank sorry room—the empty fields without plow or seed to work them," indicate that the freedom Fonsiba declares is subject to the charge expressed in Ike's retort to her husband, "Freedom from what? From work?" (206).

As if to exonerate "those upon whom freedom and equality had been dumped overnight and without warning or preparation," Faulkner a few pages later has Ike proclaim that "human beings always misuse freedom," and that the wisdom *"necessary for a man to distinguish between liberty and license"* (214) is rarely attained by either blacks or whites. When he traces his own freedom to the son of an Indian chief and a black slave—"Sam Fathers set me free" (222)—Ike implicitly contrasts it to the freedom the Founding Fathers believed they had achieved for the country. As we have seen, Ike contemptuously rejects such a belief, much as he would like to accept the proposition that America represents "that whole hopeful continent dedicated as a refuge and sanctuary of liberty and freedom" (210). The only freedom exempted from any criticism or stricture is that of Old Ben, the bear, who is "ruthless with the fierce pride of liberty and freedom, jealous and proud enough of liberty and freedom to see it threatened not with fear nor even alarm but almost with joy, seeming deliberately to put it into jeopardy in order to savor it and keep his old strong bones and flesh supple and quick to defend and preserve it" (218–19). Such freedom, we are led to conclude, will never be available to mere men.

If in *The Unvanquished* and *Go Down, Moses* Faulkner addresses the Jeffersonian ideology of a free and sovereign people inversely—by negating it—, in *A Fable* he tackles Jefferson's political ideas head on. Although the novel is constructed as a parable around the second coming of Christ, who returns to earth to stop the ongoing World War I, parts of it, if not the whole, can also be read as a *political* parable, as a story about a powerful establishment that is challenged by the people. The mutiny of the French regiment, as Joseph Urgo has shown, is an act of rebellion;

its legitimacy and efficacy are discussed at length.[29] For the purposes of my argument, the runner is the more interesting figure than the corporal. Like Ike McCaslin, he claims that he is free; to become free, he has to divest himself of the rank of officer and join the common people. Only when he is no longer "barred and interdict from the right and freedom to the simple passions and hopes and fears" does he learn about the thirteen French soldiers.[30] After the mutinying regiment, the corporal, and his disciples have been arrested, the runner instigates the second and even more disastrous step of the rebellion against the military hierarchy. He persuades the troops—a whole battalion, it appears—to leave the trenches unarmed, and convinces even the British groom to join in the effort. In a way that Faulkner leaves unexplained, the German troops have been moved to take the same step, and after four years in "the mud in which they had lived like animals," they all rise to their feet together, standing "erect" for once, with the groom "not even realising that he had said 'we' and not 'I' for the first time in his life probably, certainly for the first time in four years" (963). Their rebellion is short-lived; it ends seconds after it has begun by a barrage ordered by the military establishments of both sides and directed at the soldiers who have left the trenches unarmed. The runner, however, has the last word. He survives, terribly maimed and crippled for life. " 'They cant kill us! They cant! Not dare not: they cant!' " (964), he shouts, words which he affirms on the very last page of the book, when he says: " 'Tremble. I'm not going to die. Never' " (1072).

The power structure thus challenged, the military establishment, is based on an international conspiracy; its only purpose is to remain in power. To achieve this, its leaders have to keep the war going. "It is man who is our enemy: the vast seething moiling spiritless mass of him," says the French corps commander (693); the view expressed by the old marshal would seem to support him: " '[The people] dont want to know. . . . They want only to suffer' " (884). Rather than "lose the world to man" (971) and let him have his will, i.e., allow the mutiny to spread, the marshal has decided to contact the enemy and "offer him too an alternate to chaos" (972). The incidents Faulkner invents to bring about the continuation of the fighting—the meeting between the generals—may strike us as a bit contrived and theatrical, but they make his intention clear. The military does not need an "agreement" to continue the war (952); they use their power so that it appears as if the mutiny has never happened. Not only do they order the barrage that kills their own troops, but they have General Gragnon, the officer who is willing to accept the blame for the mutiny—and who wants to have the mutinying soldiers shot—murdered in such a way that it will look as if he has died in the front lines. This is the "alternate to chaos" and the "order" the old general represents.[31]

Jefferson had argued more than once that "a little rebellion now and then is a good thing, & as necessary in the political world as storms in the physical."[32] "What country can preserve its liberties if their rulers are not warned from time to time that their people preserve the spirit of resistance," he asked, and praised the French revolution: "Let them take arms. . . . The tree of liberty must be refreshed from time to time with the blood of patriots & tyrants. It is its natural manure."[33] Above all, he put his trust in the people: "I am persuaded myself that the good sense of the people will always be found to be the best army. They may be led astray for a moment, but will soon correct themselves. The people are the only censors of their governors: and even their errors will tend to keep these to the true principles of their institution."[34] *A Fable* suggests that Faulkner shared Jefferson's distrust of those in power. The mutiny around which the novel revolves is an act of resistance which appears to be not only morally justified, but—for a while at least—successful at the same time. Yet it is also clear that Faulkner does not share Jefferson's enthusiasm for the people. In a curious way, *A Fable* withholds judgment on the events it so laboriously constructs. Although the runner succeeds in persuading the battalion, the crowds of civilians described in the novel are not on his side. They are depicted as mindless masses, tossed about and subject to sudden impulses, shifting directions and allegiances for no discernible reason. Far from supporting the mutiny, they curse the corporal as its "ringleader"; similarly, the runner at the end of the novel is almost lynched by the people of Paris when he dares to disturb the funeral of the marshal. The marshal, on the other hand, about whose ruthless exploitation of power the novel leaves no doubt, is portrayed as a gentle, wise old man, who is honored and revered by the world. If the runner appears as an idealist, the marshal is a realist, whose sense of order triumphs, challenged though it may be by the ideas the runner claims will never die.

Finally, then, the "Jeffersonian impulse" (Myra Jehlen)[35] we can sense in the principles the runner advocates is checked by a deeply disillusioned view of the people. Yet Faulkner never lets us forget that the system represented by the old marshal, a seemingly benign patriarch who addresses everyone around him as "my child," rests on no authority other than that of power. It is a hierarchy in which the will of a few determines the fate of the many. And it is morally corrupt. If *A Fable* is indeed "an American interpretation of existence," as Heinrich Straumann once called the novel, it is an exceedingly bitter one.[36]

* * *

Which of Jefferson's "principles of order within the human condition" did Faulkner subscribe to, where did he disagree with the Virginian? So far, I have deliberately excluded Faulkner's public statements from the dialogue between the two men that I have been constructing. In some of them Faulkner explicitly echoed the Founding Father whose name is so ubiquitous in his work, and no doubt a case could be made that *publicly* he was a staunch defender of Jeffersonian virtues. Thus he acknowledged "[n]ot just the right, but the duty of man to be responsible, the necessity of man to be responsible if he wishes to remain free. . . . [T]o be free, a man must assume and maintain and defend his right to be responsible for his freedom."[37] More than once he referred to the Declaration of Independence and its doctrine of individual happiness, which he interpreted as "not just pleasure, idleness, but peace, dignity, independence, and self-respect; that man's inalienable right was, the peace and freedom in which, by his own efforts and sweat, he could gain dignity and independence, owing nothing to any man."[38] In his essay "On Privacy," he expounded at length on "the American Dream" and, in deploring its demise, asserted its inherent value all the more strongly.[39] Moreover, one could argue that in his public pronouncements Faulkner, like Jefferson, was usually forward-looking, demanding that the changing times be met. He spoke of man's "temerity to revolt and the will to change what one does not like," and asserted that "I don't hold to the idea of a return. That once the advancement stops then it dies. It's got to go forward and we have got to take along with us all the rubbish of our mistakes and our errors. We must cure them."[40] Similarly, Jefferson had argued that "the earth belongs in usufruct to the living," and, calculating the time-span of one generation to be exactly nineteen years, proposed that in theory all laws and rules passed by one generation should after such a period of time be subjected to revision by the succeeding generation.[41] I have already mentioned Faulkner's repeated assertion that "life is motion"; Jefferson no doubt would have agreed.[42]

In his fiction, as we have seen, Faulkner was usually much more skeptical about "verities" like these than in his public statements. Nonetheless, his fiction, too, seems to suggest a certain affinity between the two men. It is an affinity that would link Faulkner with the "conservative" rather than with the "progressive" Jefferson. Thus Faulkner would probably have agreed with Jefferson's invectives against "the mobs of great cities" and "the moral corruption" they bring, as he would have sided with Jefferson in the latter's struggle against Alexander Hamilton's program of an expansive, market- and growth-oriented economy supported by "the moneyed interests." It is this conservative, agrarian Jefferson who was extolled by the Vanderbilt Agrarians and other opponents of unrestricted industrial and commercial growth. Faulkner often echoed their fears—witness his doubts about the rise of men like Flem Snopes, or the contempt expressed in *Go Down, Moses* for the people who populate "the little lost county seats as barbers and garage mechanics and deputy sheriffs and mill- and gin-hands and power-plant firemen" who make up "the lynching mobs" (215) against which there seems to be no help. The affinity I am speaking of seems to be based on an awareness that the great democratic experiment in America might have a dark underside, and that economic expansion would take its toll. Faulkner would probably have admitted his reservations about this experiment more readily than Jefferson—but then he lived at a much later age and had observed the course of the nation for a much longer period of time than the Virginian. The two men, finally, shared a sense of despair over the issue of race. They were both deeply conscious of the burden imposed on the country by the institution of slavery and its consequences, and neither Jefferson nor Faulkner was hopeful that the problem of race could be solved in the near future.

Faulkner's skepticism regarding a Jeffersonian kind of democracy is most pronounced in *A Fable*, a novel which I read as a direct attempt to come to terms with Jefferson's position on the liberty of the people and the power of an entrenched establishment bent on defending its privileges. While agreeing with Jefferson's insistence that power always needs to be subjected to control, the novel leaves little hope that such control can ever be achieved. The people, by whom the author of the Declaration of Independence set such great store, are found to be sadly wanting—they are inarticulate, easily swayed, and have no idea who controls them.[43] Is it a mere coincidence, then, that Faulkner first started thinking about *A Fable* in the very year in which the nation once again celebrated the statesman from Virginia? On April 13, 1943, on Jefferson's birthday, President Roosevelt unveiled the Jefferson Memorial in Washington. In his short address he praised Jefferson as the "apostle of freedom" to whom the nation was "paying a debt long overdue." "He believed, as we believe," Roosevelt said, "that men are capable of their own government, and that no king, no tyrant, no dictator can govern for them as well as they can govern for themselves. . . . He, as we, saw those principles and freedoms challenged. He fought for them, as we fight for them."[44] If in his public statements Faulkner may have supported America's "civil religion" as it is here announced, in *A Fable* he obviously thought of it as no more than the "utopian dream" to which he had referred in the fragment "Father Abraham." The extent to which he struggled with its basic ideas is perhaps suggested by the immense effort that went into the composition of the novel—to refute Jefferson, or the image he presented to the nation at large, clearly was no easy task.

NOTES

1. William Faulkner, *Requiem for a Nun*, in *Faulkner: Novels 1942–1954*, ed. Noel Polk and Joseph Blotner (New York: Library of America, 1994), 492. Subsequent references to this text are made parenthetically.

2. As Noel Polk has shown, the story about the naming of the town of Jefferson is not to be dismissed lightly. It can be read as a serious parable about questions of citizenship and government, individual freedom and communal responsibility, and as such has its place in a novel which, much like *A Fable*, revolves around questions of civic order and organization. Noel Polk, *Faulkner's "Requiem for a Nun": A Critical Study* (Bloomington: Indiana University Press, 1981), 22–53.

3. William Faulkner, *Father Abraham*, ed. James B. Meriwether (New York: Random House, 1983), 13.

4. Merrill Peterson, *The Jefferson Image in the American Mind* (New York: Oxford University Press, 1960 [1962]), 350.

5. Ibid.

6. Claude G. Bowers, *Jefferson and Hamilton: The Struggle for Democracy* (Boston: Houghton Mifflin, 1925), 97.

7. *Faulkner in the University: Class Conferences at the University of Virginia, 1957–1958*, ed. Frederick L. Gwynn and Joseph L. Blotner (New York: Vintage, 1959), 266, italics added.

8. Ibid., 212.

9. Myra Jehlen, *Class and Character in Faulkner's South* (New York: Columbia University Press, 1976), 23; Cleanth Brooks, "Faulkner and the American Dream," in *On the Prejudices, Predilections, and Firm Beliefs of William Faulkner* (Baton Rouge: Louisiana State University Press, 1987), 136–47; esp. 142.

10. Jehlen, 23; on Jefferson's "fundamental ambiguity" see Peterson, 394.

11. For a summary of the discussion, see Garrett Ward Sheldon, *The Political Philosophy of Thomas Jefferson* (Baltimore: Johns Hopkins University Press, 1991).

12. William Faulkner, *The Hamlet*, in *Faulkner: Novels 1936–1940*, ed. Noel Polk and Joseph Blotner (New York: Library of America, 1990), 750. Subsequent references to this text are made parenthetically.

13. *I'll Take My Stand: The South and the Agrarian Tradition*, by Twelve Southerners, ed. Louis D. Rubin, Jr. (Baton Rouge: Louisiana State University Press, 1977), 205.

14. Thomas Jefferson, *Notes on the State of Virginia*, ed. William Peden (New York: Norton, 1972), 164f. Subsequent references to this text are made parenthetically.

15. On Faulkner's use of the term "peasants" see Michael Millgate, "Faulkner and the South: Some Reflections," in *The South and Faulkner's Yoknapatawpha: The Actual and the Apocryphal*, ed. Evans Harrington and Ann J. Abadie (Jackson: University Press of Mississippi, 1977), 195–210, esp. 200ff. On the question of Faulkner's "agrarian" sentiments in *The Hamlet* see Lothar Hönnighausen, *William Faulkner: Masks and Metaphor* (Jackson: University Press of Mississippi, 1997), 223–61.

16. Cf., among others, Jack Temple Kirby, *Rural Worlds Lost: The American South, 1920–1960* (Baton Rouge: Louisiana State University Press, 1987), esp. 142–44; Van L. Perkins, *Crisis in Agriculture: The Agricultural Adjustment Administration and the New Deal, 1933–1938* (Berkeley: University of California Press, 1969), esp. 1–35; Richard Godden, *Fictions of Labor: William Faulkner and the South's Long Revolution* (Cambridge: Cambridge University Press, 1997), 56–58.

17. *Collected Stories of William Faulkner* (New York: Random House, 1950), 9.

18. See Richard Godden, *Fictions of Labor*, esp. 115–22. On Flem and Mink Snopes as examples of a "rebellious spirit" see Joseph R. Urgo, *Faulkner's Apocrypha: "A Fable,"*

Snopes, and the Spirit of Human Rebellion (Jackson: University Press of Mississippi, 1989), 151ff.

19. *Collected Stories*, 56, 58.

20. I should note that one of the many ironies in the story of the changing image of Jefferson in American politics is the fact that both the advocates of the New Deal and those who strongly opposed the measures the Roosevelt Administration tried to push through claimed Jefferson as their guiding figure. See Peterson, *The Jefferson Image in the American Mind*, 355–76. On Faulkner's aversion to the New Deal, see Joel Williamson, *William Faulkner and Southern History* (New York: Oxford University Press, 1993), 265.

21. William Faulkner, *If I Forget Thee, Jerusalem*, in *Faulkner: Novels 1936–1940*, 576, 579.

22. William Faulkner, *Go Down, Moses*, in *Faulkner: Novels 1942–1954*, 268. Subsequent references to this text are made parenthetically.

23. Richard Godden, *Fictions of Labor*, 51, 53.

24. Thomas Jefferson to Edward Coles, August 25, 1814, in Thomas Jefferson, *Writings*, ed. Merrill Peterson (New York: Library of America, 1984), 1345.

25. Ibid.

26. William Faulkner, *Absalom, Absalom!*, in *Faulkner: Novels 1936–1940*, 294.

27. William Faulkner, *The Unvanquished*, in *Faulkner: Novels 1936–1940*, 335, italics added.

28. I have elaborated on this in my article " 'Because we were forever free': Slavery and Emancipation in *The Unvanquished*," *Faulkner Journal* 10:81–91.

29. *Faulkner's Apocrypha*, 94–125. Urgo calls *A Fable* "a meditation on rebellion" and Faulkner's "most blatantly anti-authoritarian and anti-establishment novel" (105).

30. William Faulkner, *A Fable* in *Faulkner: Novels 1942–1954*, 726. Subsequent references to this text are made parenthetically.

31. As Urgo observes, "in the Old General, Faulkner has created a prototype not of the modern demagogue but of the modern politico, who is in office to maintain not some principle or in the name of some constituency, but to maintain the authority necessary to remain in office." *Faulkner's Apocrypha*, 113.

32. Letter to James Madison, January 30, 1787, in *Writings*, 882.

33. Letter to William S. Smith, November 13, 1787, in *Writings*, 911.

34. Letter to Edward Carrington, January 16, 1887, in *Writings*, 880.

35. Jehlen, 143.

36. Heinrich Straumann, "An American Interpretation of Existence: Faulkner's *A Fable*," in *William Faulkner: Three Decades of Criticism*, ed. Frederick J. Hoffman and Olga W. Vickery (East Lansing: Michigan State University Press, 1960), 349–72. See also Noel Polk, "Faulkner and World War II," in Neil R. MacMillen, ed., *Remaking Dixie: The Impact of World War II on the American South* (Jackson: University Press of Mississippi, 1997), 131–45: "The bleakest final point is power's absolute bind: unillusioned itself, it must feed the illusion of the masses, not merely to conserve itself in power, but simply to invest the masses with direction, to keep them from trampling each other to death. It is indeed a bleak fictional portrait of the very humanity that Faulkner, from his Nobel Prize pulpit, had expressed such faith in" (143). But Faulkner, it is important to note, never really gives the masses a chance to articulate themselves. Would they "trample each other to death" if left to their own devices? Urgo's reading of the masses is more optimistic; he sees in them "the embodiment of the spirit's potential" for both good and evil, with Marthe illustrating the positive side. See *Faulkner's Apocrypha*, 119, 121f.

37. William Faulkner, *Essays, Speeches, and Public Letters*, ed. James B. Meriwether (New York: Random House, 1965), 129, 131.

38. Ibid., 127–28.

39. Ibid., 62–75.

40. *Lion in the Garden: Interviews with William Faulkner, 1926–1962*, ed. James B. Meriwether and Michael Millgate (New York: Random House, 1968), 131. Joseph Urgo believes that the attitude expressed here in a public statement is reflected also in Faulkner's fiction. Urgo speaks of *Go Down, Moses* in almost Jeffersonian terms: the novel, he says,

"affirms the power and the right of the living generation to assert its will on the world"; "if there is a dirty word in *Go Down, Moses*, that word is heritage." *Faulkner's Apocrypha*, 215, 219.

41. Letter to James Madison, September 6, 1789, in *Writings*, 959ff.

42. Cf. *Lion in the Garden*, 253.

43. As the crowd scenes in *Light in August, Absalom, Absalom!*, or *The Hamlet* demonstrate, this pessimistic view is not limited to the late Faulkner. He never trusted man's "ability to move *en masse*" (*A Fable*, 839).

44. *The Public Papers and Addresses of Franklin D. Roosevelt*, compiled with special material and explanatory notes by Samuel I. Rosenman, 1943 volume: *The Tide Turns* (New York: Harper & Brothers, 1950), 162ff.

Writing *A Fable* for America

CATHERINE GUNTHER KODAT

> O righteous God: Thou hast directed
> how everything must befall.
> Then to whom is the reward presented:
> him who wants or cannot want things else?
> —ARNOLD SCHOENBERG, *Moses und Aron*

In recent years the world of Faulkner scholarship has seen several compelling reevaluations of what might be termed the author's "second drawer" works, but the 1954 novel *A Fable* has not been included, for the most part, in the new dispensation of sympathy for Yoknapatawpha after *Go Down, Moses*.[1] While there has been a minority effort to upwardly revise critical opinion of the work,[2] most current assessments of *A Fable* largely repeat the commentary that greeted the novel when it was first released. Initial critical reaction ran a rather narrow gamut: sympathetic readers called the book "a heroically ambitious failure," while those with less patience termed it "a calamity" (for his part, Ernest Hemingway said it was "not pure shit but 'impure diluted shit' ").[3] More recently, scholars have described *A Fable* as "troublesome," a "failed political novel," "a book of badness simply astonishing for Faulkner." Thirteen years ago André Bleikasten grouped *A Fable* with a cluster of misbegotten literary productions from Faulkner's later years, all of them offspring of the post-Nobel conjugation of Faulkner "the writer" with Faulkner "denizen of the world." "For a long time a watchful angel kept" these two Faulkners apart, Bleikasten wrote. "I wish they had never met."[4]

It is tempting to conclude that this last characterization of *A Fable* as Faulkner's "hideous progeny"[5] actually indicates a hopeful future for the work: like *Frankenstein*, perhaps all *A Fable* needs to do is stick around long enough to catch the paradigm shift that will finally provide the key to a fuller appreciation of the work. Faulkner himself predicted that it would take "maybe 50 years before the world can stop to read" *A Fable*.[6] But Bleikastan's sly description of the novel as the product of two aspects of a single "Faulkner" forces us to consider that, as monsters go, *A Fable* is more like Dolly the sheep than Victor Frankenstein's creature—who, after all, emerged through a recycling of sundry ill-fitting parts into a new, if seemingly ungainly, whole. The difficulty with *A Fable* is not that it is too various but that it is too much the same: from its status as allegory (which forces the text to negotiate its meaning via the same story as Christ's) to its textual aspects (as Bleikasten notes, the narrative voice itself "all too often sounds like a mocking echo . . . Faulknerian to the point of self-travesty"[7]), *A Fable* sets its readers on edge largely through its insistence on going over (and over) narrative ground covered thoroughly, and better, before. For readers who know and love the work of the 1930s, Faulkner's insistent self-referentiality in *A Fable*—a self-referencing that seems to signal a certain imaginative exhaustion and that approaches a rather gruesome self-consumption—is among the text's most painful qualities.

My favorite contemporary description of *A Fable* appears in the "Chronology of William Faulkner's Life and Works" at the beginning of *The Cambridge Companion to William Faulkner*. There, Philip M. Weinstein describes *A Fable* as Faulkner's "most premeditated novel," and that single word, "premeditated"—implying, as it does, that the book represents the scene of some monstrous crime, and that the perpetrator knew exactly what he was doing—provides the starting point for my discussion of the novel.[8] For the most part, I share the misgivings of *A Fable*'s detractors, misgivings that arise primarily from what it feels like to read the book. One might not expect the experience to be pleasurable, but neither is it invigorating or productively challenging. The novel makes all of the demands of a Faulknerian text (multiple intersecting plots, abstruse allusions to literary and social history, a scrambled chronology, periodic sentences running a page or more in length) but offers none of the usual compensations (a moment in which those seemingly unrelated plots crystallize into a complex pattern of meaningful interdependence; a unexpected yet stunningly apt intervention in the *uses* of literature and history; the emergence of a hidden chronological pattern; breathtakingly beautiful language). *A Fable* takes all of the achievements of the Faulknerian vision and hollows them out. Now, as scholars and critics, we can (and have) argued that this hollowness is precisely the point of the book,[9] but that interpretive sleight of hand does little to make up for feeling, after finishing *A Fable*, that one has been toyed with rather cold-bloodedly. In fact, it was precisely in an effort to mute that impression that Saxe Commins decided to withhold Faulkner's pre-publication statement about *A Fable*, which begins with the assertion that the novel "is not a pacifist book" and goes on to insist that it has no "aim or moral."[10]

Having confessed that I, too, have trouble with *A Fable*, let me hasten to add that, though I may find it hard to praise the text, my aim here certainly is not to bury it. Rather, I want to take that experience of reading *A Fable*—the sense of having been dallied with, of having overinvested oneself in a text that finally never moves beyond the *promise* of fulfillment—as an important indicator of the novel's method and meaning, both of which, I believe, arise from Faulkner's engagement with the manipulations of American mass cultural entertainment—what Theodor Adorno and Max Horkheimer have termed the "culture industry"—when the phenomenon of U.S. "cultural imperialism" first clearly emerged as a historical possibility.[11] Faulkner called *A Fable* his "big book" not merely because of its length—437 pages—or the amount of time he dedicated to writing it—ten years—but because he believed it would be his "crossover hit," the text that would bring modernism to the masses by rigging out a well-known "uplifting" story with the abstruse tackle of modernist literary technique. In the course of accomplishing this, *A Fable* lays bare the interconnections and interdependencies of "high" modernism and commodified, consumerist mass culture, and it is this persistent double-voicedness, this sentimental modernism, that accounts for much of what is repellent in the text.[12] In a famous letter to Walter Benjamin, Theodor Adorno writes that both the works of elitist modernism and mass cultural productions "bear the stigmata of capitalism. . . . Both are torn halves of an integral freedom, to which however they do not add up"; I want to suggest that one way to think of *A Fable*'s textual shortcomings is to see them as demonstrating the ways in which these "torn halves" of modern life fail to "add up."[13] Like Arnold Schoenberg's twelve-tone compositions, *A Fable* articulates the lures and structures of modern commodification even as it seeks to transcend them: not suprisingly, reading Faulkner's novel turns out to be about as easily enjoyable as listening to *Moses und Aron*.[14] Unlike Schoenberg, however, Faulkner could not content himself with the abstract integrity of modernist negation; unlike *Moses und Aron*, *A Fable* truly seeks to please—and to sell.

I want to propose that—appearances to the contrary[15]—the frustrating and ungainly aspects of *A Fable* are best accounted for when we read the novel as a book about America, as a text that offers Faulkner's most sustained meditation on American philosophies and American aesthetics at the moment of the United States' postwar ascension to global power via the twin forces of military victory and mass cultural expansion. In its exploration of the rhetoric of freedom and equality via ideologies of brotherhood (through the resistance of the corporal and his twelve followers, through the secret fellowship of Masonry, and through the global fraternity of officers and generals); in its recognition of the importance of a sentimental Christianity both as a method of U.S. national identity formation and, in the postwar era, as a means of shoring up domestic support for diplomatic adventuring in the fight against "godless" Communism; in its anticipation of the ways in which the modernist negation of "unfreedom" (to use an Adornian term) would be increasingly and indiscriminately linked, in service to the U.S. pursuit of a capitalist global hegemony, with mass cultural phenomenon like Hollywood films and major league sports (even Eisenhower's golf stroke was fuel for the propaganda work of the United States Information Agency), *A Fable* registers the peculiarly American-inflected triumph of consumerist mass culture and the concomitant "decline of modernism" in the aftermath of the second World War.[16] Framed in this way, *A Fable* emerges as an importantly problematic text of the new "American century": it is not, as Faulkner predicted, his "War and Peace close enough to home, our times, language, for Americans to really buy it," but it is, perhaps, his *Uncle Tom's Cabin*.[17]

Stowe's text provides a useful point of comparison here, for, like *A Fable*, it employs aspects of the Christian myth as crucial narrative scaffolding. And, also like *A Fable*, it is not a text that goes down easily, though its importance to American literary history is impossible to deny. A proper accounting of the ongoing debate over the merits of literary sentimentalism occasioned by the recanonization of *Uncle Tom's Cabin* requires more space than I have here, but I would like to briefly revisit some aspects of that debate in order to more clearly fix my claim that the technique of *A Fable* is perhaps best understood as a sentimental modernism. A good starting point would be Shirley Samuels's comment that sentimentality in the U.S. is "a national project: in particular, a project imagining the nation's bodies and the national body."[18] In other words, as a political and social project as well as an artistic one, sentimentalism deploys an expressive register that was not limited to, or invented by, women writers. In fact, Elizabeth Barnes has traced the tradition of the American sentimental back to the founding of the republic and concludes that representing structures of sympathetic relations became an important way for our earliest citizens to imagine themselves as interconnected members of a single social enterprise: "a sentimental vision of union . . . eventually becomes the ideal for both men *and* women."[19] In Barnes's reading, the Declaration of Independence emerges as "a definitive example of American sentimental politics," deriving its power from "a suprising conflation of the personal and the political body—a vision of 'the people' as a single and independent entity, asserting its liberal privilege in a body at once collective and individual" (ix). As Barnes explains, the Declaration's assertion that all men are created equal "epitomizes the power of sentimental representation—a power to reinvent others in one's own image" (2).

Barnes's view of sentimental fiction represents a new direction in the ongoing dispute over whether (to put it in its baldest terms) sentimental literature is "good" literature. I'd like to suggest that it has been the persistent gendering of sentimentalism that has fuelled this dispute; Barnes reminds us that, while the sentimental mode certainly reached a peak in the United States through the work of nineteenth-century women writers, there is nothing in the style to render it "essentially" feminine.[20] It is more usefully defined as a discourse of identification: "sentimental fiction essentially puts self-interest to affective work, reconciling the seemingly irreconcilable division between internal and external authority, between individual rights and the needs of the community to which the individual belongs" (Barnes 18). According to Barnes, sentimental fiction accomplishes its affective work in several ways; for the purposes of discussing *A Fable*, it is necessary to note only two: the invocation of familial structures and the celebration of vicarious feeling.

Sentimental narratives "stage political issues as personal dramas" largely through an appeal to familial structures, in which "sameness, rather than difference, offers the key to democratic equality and, hence, to national identity" (Barnes 16). In sentimental narratives, families are as families do: acting *as if* someone is your brother is enough to make him so; feeling comes to stand for being. Similarly, "vicarious relations, like the sentimental construction of sympathetic identification, blur the boundary between action and emotion to suggest that sympathetic feeling itself is an act that holds society together" (Barnes 116). The hallmark of the sentimental text is the substitution of feeling for being and acting, through an appeal to a recognition of sameness. Barnes is careful to explore how the sentimental reconciliation of differences has difficulties as well as virtues: the transformation of self-interest into an engine of social cohesion can as easily become a model of appropriation and consumption as of universal brotherhood. Though I cannot do justice to the subtleties of her work here, Barnes's analysis refines and clarifies a point made many years ago by Ann Douglas in her impressive (though deeply problematic) study of sentimentality in American culture, a point that, despite its draconian terms, is useful to keep in mind when thinking about *A Fable*: "There is an enormous and vital distinction between an interested, respectful acceptance of the full human condition and a glorification of the death of the critical instinct—between acknowledging human limitations and celebrating them. . . . The first is a religious impulse, the second is finally a commercial one, and eventually involves the preparation of the individual for the role of consumer."[21] While Douglas sees religious and commercial impulses occupying separate poles that are rightly kept far apart, Barnes suggests that religion and commerce are best imagined as *recto* and *verso* of a single American document.

Part of the usefulness of *Uncle Tom's Cabin* to my analysis of *A Fable* is that it makes explicit the importance of Christianity to the sentimental discourse of "fellow feeling." The mystical body of Christ emerges as the place that equates feeling and action: through Christ, we become members of one family; Christ's suffering for our sins presents a model of the virtue of vicarious action. Barnes's discussion of Thatcher Thayer's *The Vicarious Element in Nature and Its Relation to Christ*, a religious tract published thirty-six years after Stowe's novel, makes clear the importance of the Christ myth to American efforts to form a more perfect union:

> The ruling tenets of republicanism and liberalism, seen by most twentieth-century critics as competing ideologies of the postrevolutionary and antebellum eras, respectively, are brought together in Thayer's vision of vicarious relations. Thayer simultaneously depicts the individual body—and the senses attached to it—as the epistemological center of a national universe and yet dissolves the individual body into a larger body, a body constituted 'more for others' than for oneself. . . . It is the individual body writ large, producing, as if of one accord, a 'national sentiment.' Thayer's rhetorical transition from the political to the spiritual, from the vicarious element in nature to its supernatural incarnation in Christ, marks the crowning achievement of sympathy's sociopolitical work. For Christ becomes the representative whose ability to identify completely with all humanity signifies the unifying power of sympathy. In Christ we get not only a theological but a *political* model for the unification of diverse individuals into one corporate body—Christ's own. (188–219)

Barnes's linking of the Christian body with the corporate body brings us back to *A Fable*, where, as many scholars have noted, the Christ-figure Stefan Brzonyi is known throughout the text primarily (and symbolically) as "the corporal," a naming clearly meant to draw the reader's attention to the importance of Christ to the task of creating corporations. The corporation of which Stefan is the chief representative body is the twelve; they, in turn, represent the entire regiment that refuses an order to go over the top in the spring of the last year of World War I. The furious and humiliated division commander Charles Gragnon wishes to execute the entire regiment for this mutiny, but proper attention to Christian allegory dictates that the execution of the corporal will stand vicariously for the punishment of all. This sentimental appeal to the vicarious is complemented in the narrative by the familial structure the corporal is able to impose upon the twelve: they are as brothers, and it is out of loyalty to his brothers ("There are still ten" the corporal replies to the marshal's claim that "the brotherhood of your faith and hope" has been shattered by the betrayals of Pierre and Polchek[22]) that the corporal goes to his death.

Readers of *A Fable* have already seen fraternity in action well before the old marshal explicitly names the corporal's band a "brotherhood." The section Faulkner sought to sell to *Partisan Review* as "Notes on a Horsethief" relies heavily on the unifying power of American Freemasonry in order to make convincing its tale of common-man resistance to the commercialization of "the best, the brave" (*Fable* 816). In Steven C. Bullock's study of Freemasonry in the United States, the fraternity emerges as an important instancing of the general American sentimental discourse. In the creation of "the American social order," Freemasonry "played an important role in shaping the momentous changes that first introduced and then transformed the eighteenth-century Enlightenment in America, helping to create the nineteenth-century culture of democracy, individualism, and sentimentalism."[23] Bullock's interest is in the golden years of Masonry, when the fraternity was called upon to solemnize the dedication of the Capitol and when George Washington made it a point to stand for a portrait wearing his Masonic regalia, and he convincingly demonstrates the importance of Masonic ideals (which, among other things, promised a future in which all the world would "rejoice together as brethren of one common family"[24]) to the founding of the republic—even as (or especially as) he acknowledges the ways in which Masonry limited itself (only freeborn men could join, and the dues structure made membership nearly impossible for the lower classes). By the time Faulkner was writing "Notes on a Horsethief," however, the glory years of Masonry were long over; the organization was nearly destroyed in the national Anti-Masonic movement that emerged in the wake of the 1826 disappearance of a member who had threatened to publish a pamphlet revealing Masonic secrets. When Masonry reappeared in the 1850s, it was largely as a social order devoted to "moral uplift and self-improvement, inculcating the traditional virtues of sobriety, thrift, temperance, piety, industry, self-restraint, and moral obligation"; Masons imagined their lodges as second homes promising peaceful asylum from the outside world.[25] In other words, Freemasonry was a masculine organization that managed to translate successfully its public mission into a private one by claiming to inculcate many of the same values prized by the promoters of the similarly sentimental, though feminized, cult of domesticity.

One final digression about Freemasonry before returning to the problem of brotherhood in *A Fable*: the ostensible concern of fraternalism is with the promotion of universal amity, but it is crucial to remember—as Mary Ann Clawson points out in a study tracing the history of the fraternal ideal from the guilds of medieval Europe to the trade unions of nineteenth-century America[26]—that fraternalism has important economic as well as political and religious registers, and it is in this economic register that the "corporate" aspects of the "corporal" move to the fore. As Clawson explains, "a corporate concept of society assumes that groups, not individuals, are the basic units of society, and that people act, not primarily as individuals, but as members of collectivities. It assumes, moreover, that social institutions are governed not only collectively, but hierarchically. Corporatism is the social metaphor that most forcefully asserts that unity of interest is compatible with hierarchy and inequality" (39). In fact, as Clawson notes, modern Freemasonry emerged in eighteenth-century England largely through the desire of members of the British elite to take on the symbolic trappings of craftsmen, thus expressing "their commitment to the emerging market economy and to the social value of craft labor and material productivity" while retaining their own privileged position in that new economy (16). By a process of vicarious identification with the craftsman, members of the gentry sought to paper over the class conflicts of the new industrial order while simultaneously maintaining their high status within that order. Another important function of modern American fraternalism thus can be described as an effort to simultaneously articulate and contain the contradictions of democratic capitalism: "fraternal forms of association have reached across boundaries, tending to unite men from a relatively wide social, economic, or religious spectrum. At the same time, fraternalism bases itself on a principle of exclusion, from which it derives much of its power" (Clawson 11). Or, to put it another way: through Masonry, a sentimental appeal to "fellow feeling" provides the cover story that enables exploitative economic relations to operate unchecked.

Faulkner's Masons in the story of the racehorse manifest all of the complications and contradictions I've just described; indeed, this section of *A Fable* uses the Masons in order both to endorse sentimentally and to critique abstractly our largely unexamined notions of the benignity of brotherhood. How much Faulkner knew of the history of U.S. Masonry remains a very open question, but it is not likely that he missed noting the one Masonic cultural retention still recognized by all Americans: the eye above the pyramid on the Great Seal of the United States adorning the back of the dollar bill. The brotherly impulses of the Masons in "Notes on a Horsethief" are motivated not by sympathy for the efforts of Tobe Sutterfield and the sentry to honor the heroic desire of the racehorse simply to run, but by a corporate desire to guarantee "that everybody . . . had a share in what it won" (843). Tobe Sutterfield insists that, in racing the horse, he, his grandson, and the sentry had no interest in wealth: "There wasn't no money . . . There never was none, except just what we needed, had to have. . . . We never had time to bother with winning a heap of money to have to take care of. We had the horse" (849). The crippled racehorse thus emerges as a kind of ideal of modernist negation, "the mark of a free man . . . to say *no* for no other reason except *no*" (825–26; original emphases). But it is, of course, largely through the corporate protection—indeed, one might nearly say the sponsorship—of the Masonic brotherhood that the sentry, the reverend, and his grandson are able to pursue their commodity-free dream of "the best, the brave."

After the death of the horse, a Tennessee "lodge room" serves as shelter for the sentry (Mister Harry, or "Mistairy" [mystery] in his cockney accent [804]), the place where he takes "his last degree in Masonry" before leaving for the war in Europe (847, 849). It is in warfare that the practice of brotherhood is quite explicitly linked to the proliferation of capital: the sentry's loansharking succeeds largely because he transform his debtors into brothers (through his "Association" [798]), successfully mystifying the nature of their relationship (even though, as an exchange between the runner and another soldier makes clear, *the money* is "the Association" [798]). In the absence of the racehorse, the blandishments of corporate brotherhood are thus reconfigured as compensation for the collapse of the heroic vision "[T]o save that horse that never wanted nothing and never knowed nothing but just to run out in front of all the other horses in a race" (849).

In *After the Great Divide*, Andreas Huyssen makes clear the interdependence of high modernism and popular mass culture; the mass productions of the culture industry are in truth "the repressed other of modernism, the family ghost rumbling in the cellar," while modernism itself emerges as "the strawman desperately needed by the system to provide an aura of popular legitimation for the blessings" of mass culture (Huyssen 16–17). John T. Matthews has used Huyssen's work to examine Faulkner's early critical participation in the Hollywood film industry, focusing in particular on the screenplays and short stories of the early 1930s, written when Faulkner was new to Hollywood, his contempt for commercial culture was at its sharpest, and his willingness to express that contempt was least checked.[27] Matthews's analysis is convincing; certainly, the Faulkner of the 1930s was well aware of, and well equipped to take on, the contradictions of both modernism and the culture industry. In emphasizing the Faulkner of the 1930s, however, we leave unexplored the possibility that the Faulkner of the 1940s (and later) could represent perhaps more than a simple object lesson on the dangers of alcohol, marital misery, and fiscal fecklessness. I submit that Faulkner's increasingly parlous negotiations of the artistic demands of those later years (and his letters provide an eloquent testimony to the painfulness of those negotiations) need to be read as resulting from more than personal difficulties: they testify to the collapse of the exquisitely sustained, and mutually sustaining, tensions between art and commerce that marked not only Faulkner's finest work but much of the American variety of the "high modernist" mode itself. Or to put the issue another way: while close attention to the popular productions that Faulkner wrote in the 1930s reveals his insistent, if covert, efforts to make those productions accommodate some self-critique (and *Sanctuary* is exhibit A here), attention to the serious work of the later period forces us to reckon with the ways in which "modernism itself is held hostage by the culture industry" (Huyssen 42). *A Fable* is an escaped hostage, come back with the news that "in the vortex of commodification there was never an outside" (Huyssen 42).

I take Faulkner's complaints, in his letters to Harold Ober and Robert Haas, that "movie scription" had damaged his writing less as evidence of real authorial failure than as a sign that the previously covert (and thereby powerful) relationship between commerce and art had begun to move forcefully into the open, where its power began to dissipate.[28] *A Fable*, after all, was not a product of Faulknerian inspiration; as he repeatedly reminded his correspondents, "the idea belongs to a director in Hollywood."[29] Henry Hathaway, the director (and World War I veteran) who came up with the idea of making a movie about the enigma of the Unknown Soldier, was "the consummate Hollywood professional"; the producer William Bacher was "a nonstop talker and a hypnotic salesman."[30] Joseph Blotner suggests that, when the two of them approached Faulkner in 1943 with the idea that "the three of them would make the picture together and share alike in the profits," Faulkner agreed to the project largely because he believed it would ensure that he "might never have to return to Hollywood" again.[31]

Like Poe's purloined letter, *A Fable* hides its mass cultural origins out in the open in its highly unusual acknowledgment page, which fixes the provenance of the text in the American film industry ("To William Bacher and Henry Hathaway of Beverly Hills, California, who had the basic idea from which this book grew into its present form") and daily newspaper journalism ("to James Street in whose volume, *Look Away*, I read the story of the hanged man and the bird" [*Fable* 667][32]). The acknowledgment also registers, however obliquely, Faulkner's attempt to reshape this popular material into something approaching a high modernist production (as well as his conviction that such work was going unappreciated) by memorializing his unsuccessful effort, via *Partisan Review*, to reproduce James Joyce's 1927–29 publication of sections of *Finnegans*

Wake, under the title "Work in Progress," in *transition* ("and to Hodding Carter and Ben Wasson of the Levee Press, who published in a limited edition the original version of the story of the stolen racehorse" [667]). Faulkner's letters amplify this sense that his efforts to continue the modernist project by popularizing it were largely thankless: the rejection by *Partisan Review* prompted a remarkable note to Harold Ober in which Faulkner expressed both his serious doubts about the project ("I have never had an opinion from you . . . about it. . . . What is your opinion of this section in question? Dull? Too prolix? Diffuse?") and his conviction that current times were too "beat and battered" (and, as his simile clearly implies, too industrial and commercial) to appreciate his work: "that magazine does not exist now which would have printed sections from Ulysses [*sic*] as in the 1920s. And that man crouching in a Mississippi hole trying to shape into some form of art his summation and conception of the human heart and spirit in terms of the cerebral, the simple imagination, is as out of place and in the way as a man trying to make an Egyptian water wheel in the middle of the Bessemer foundry."[33]

This paper began with a quotation from Schoenberg's *Moses und Aron*, and I would like to return to that work briefly as a way of framing my conclusions about Faulkner's fable for Americans. Schoenberg conceived *Moses und Aron* in 1930, at the opening of the decade that should have seen the fulfillment of his career. The work arose in the midst of Schoenberg's "Jewish identity crisis"; by 1933 he had abjured his conversion to Protestantism, returned to the faith of his fathers, and fled Germany for the United States, where he settled in Southern California and taught at UCLA amid growing personal poverty and professional underappreciation.[34] Schoenberg intended *Moses und Aron* both as an important endorsement of his Jewish faith and as a testament to his unshaking belief in heroic modernist abstraction; this latter theme emerges in the opera through the mutually constitutive relationship of Moses and his brother Aaron. The powerful yet inarticulate Moses, who seems to speak for Schoenberg himself, insists that God is invisible and unrepresentable, while the glib popularizer Aaron advises his brother that it is best to "be understood by all the people in their own accustomed way."

Moses und Aron remained unfinished, "a magnificent torso,"[35] partly because Schoenberg found no time to complete it: what had been a promising career in Germany collapsed in the United States, where he was forced to support himself largely through his teaching. Like Faulkner, Schoenberg too found himself "sharecropping in the Golden Land"[36]; his letters repeatedly deplore the frittering away of his creativity in pedagogical duties.[37] Unlike Faulkner, however, Schoenberg would not let Aaron speak for Moses; though his atonal style was quickly picked up and parodied in horror movie soundtracks, Schoenberg himself declined to work for films and maintained a steadfast aversion to popular art.[38] Six years after his 1945 Guggenheim application was rejected, Schoenberg was dead, and the two works he saw as his greatest contributions to modern music, *Moses und Aron* and the oratorio *Die Jakobsleiter*, remained in fragments.

As Moses speaks for Schoenberg, so the runner in *A Fable* speaks for Faulkner: not only because he articulates the antinomies that so characterize the Faulknerian imagination,[39] but because his project echoes, and so explains, Faulkner's project in writing *A Fable*. The runner recognizes the hidden connection between heroic individualism (modernism) and modern corporate life (mass culture); he believes, further, that willfully making this connection overt represents humanity's best chance to honestly fulfill the seemingly opposed promises of individual autonomy and human fellowship. In acting on this belief, however—in forcing the sentry to mobilize the members of the Association to say no to the war (*Fable* 959–64)—the runner becomes "a mobile and upright scar," divided exactly down the middle so that "one entire side of his hatless head was one hairless eyeless and earless sear" (*Fable* 1070); he becomes the living sign of the catastrophic effort to combine the two halves of a torn freedom. In rendering the runner monstrously mutilated as a result of his attempted reconciliation, Faulkner registers the mutilated status of *A Fable* itself. I have already described the reactions of the literary community to the novel; I should perhaps add that Hollywood, too, found the book baffling and repellent. William Bacher wanted nothing to do with it as a possible film project; after Henry Hathaway read *A Fable* he remarked, "I couldn't find my story. I didn't recognize anything."[40]

Joseph Blotner notes quite accurately that, while Faulkner "had no alternative" to working as a screenwriter, "it had been only himself who had driven him to complete the struggle to finish *A Fable*."[41] The book was clearly important to Faulkner, and I've tried here to outline why that was so: Faulkner believed *A Fable* would be his "big book" because it would bring him his largest readership yet. Americans would "really buy it,"[42] but the novel would also win him new intellectual respect, and it would do this by giving a mass readership both what it already wanted and what it did not yet understand. Here resides the didactic aspect of Faulkner's fable: Americans would see that what they did not understand was actually what they really needed to know, while what they thought they knew and wanted was actually a distraction designed to maintain an exploitative status quo. *A Fable* has pleased no one, however, and it seems to have remained in print largely because it is a book by William Faulkner, and for that reason alone important. Yet *A Fable* is also important for what it tells us about the collapse of the high modernist project, its transformation into what Peter Bürger has called "modernist conformism."[43] To a significant degree, the United States was both witness to and collaborator in this collapse. Cold War propaganda needed something to set in opposition to Soviet Realism, leading the architects of U.S. cultural diplomacy to appropriate modernism as uniquely expressive of American freedom and autonomy. As a result, modernist art, and modernist artists, became cultural footsoldiers in the Cold War. Faulkner's willing (even eager) participation in this co-opting of modernist negation is well-documented; what my reading of *A Fable* suggests is that Faulkner embraced this collapse partly because it confirmed the losses registered so vividly in the novel. It may be that the modernist impulse to say no to things as they are is "not going to die. Never" (this is, of course, the runner's promise at the end of *A Fable*), yet it is also the case that *A Fable* shows us how that impulse comes to grief (the last words of the novel are, "What you see are tears" [*Fable* 1072]). And faced with grief and nothing, we all know the choice Faulkner would recommend.

NOTES

1. For an example of recent scholarship that argues for a positive reevaluation of works previously deplored (or ignored), see Richard C. Moreland's *Faulkner and Modernism: Rereading and Rewriting* (Madison: University of Wisconsin Press, 1990), which argues strongly for positive rereadings of *The Reivers* and *Requiem for a Nun*. Regarding the latter work, Moreland was preceded in the project of scholarly reclamation by Noel Polk's important *Faulkner's "Requiem for a Nun": A Critical Study* (Bloomington: Indiana University Press, 1981). John T. Matthews recently has uncovered complex strategies of cultural analysis in some of Faulkner's more neglected short stories and in his work for Hollywood; see "Faulkner and the Culture Industry" in *The Cambridge Companion to William Faulkner*, ed. Philip M. Weinstein (Cambridge: Cambridge University Press, 1995), 51–74. Cheryl Lester's analysis of Faulkner's "Appendix: Compson: 1699–1945," in "To Market, to Market: *The Portable Faulkner*," *Criticism: A Quarterly for Literature and the Arts* 29 (1987): 371–89, similarly argues that what has long been considered a "problematic" text is actually an important scene of Faulknerian critique.

Joseph Urgo's study *Faulkner's Apocrypha: "A Fable," Snopes, and the Spirit of Human Rebellion* (Jackson: University Press of Mississippi, 1989) argues not only for a sympathetic rereading of Faulkner's later works, but places *A Fable* squarely in the center of that project. While Urgo and I have similar views about Faulkner's resistance to what one might call the "Cowley-fication" of his work—and while I agree with Urgo's assessment that *A Fable* "is impossible to read with the political blindspot of New Criticism [yet] equally impossible to read in the context of social realism or of naturalism" (100)—we finally interpret the corporal's resistance, and Faulkner's representation of that resistance, rather differently.

2. In the (small) world of partisans of *A Fable*, Noel Polk easily prevails as the work's most consistent and persistent champion: see "Woman and the Feminine in *A Fable*," in his study *Children of the Dark House: Text and Context in Faulkner* (Jackson: University Press of Mississippi, 1996), 196–218; " 'Polysyllabic and Verbless Patriotic Nonsense': Faulkner at Midcentury—His and Ours," in *Faulkner and Ideology: Faulkner and Yoknapatawpha, 1992*, ed. Donald M. Kartiganer and Ann J. Abadie (Jackson: University Press of

Mississippi, 1995), 297–328; "Enduring *A Fable* and Prevailing," in *Faulkner: After the Nobel Prize*, ed. Michel Gresset and Kanzaburo Ohashi (Kyoto: Yamaguchi Publishing House, 1987), 110–26; and "Roland Barthes Reads *A Fable*," in *Faulkner's Discourse: An International Symposium*, ed. Lothar Hönnighausen (Tübingen: Max Niemeyer Verlag, 1989), 109–16. The last essay, along with Urgo's study, has been especially useful to my thinking about the novel.

For other sympathetic readings of *A Fable*, see Warwick Wadlington, "Doing What Comes Culturally: Collective Action and the Discourse of Belief in Faulkner and Nathanael West," in *Faulkner, His Contemporaries, and His Posterity*, ed. Waldemar Zacharasiewicz (Tübingen: A. Francke Verlag, 1993), 245–52; and the following essays in the collection *Faulkner: After the Nobel Prize*: "The Imagery in Faulkner's *A Fable*," by Lothar Hönnighausen, 147–71; "The Indestructible Voice of the British Battalion Runner in *A Fable*," by Ikuko Fujihara, 127–46; "The Critical Difference: Faulkner's Case in *A Fable*," by Fumiyo Hayashi, 91–109; "William Faulkner's Late Career: Repetition, Variation, Renewal," by Hans H. Skei, 247–59.

3. Joseph Blotner, *Faulkner: A Biography*, 2 vols. (New York: Random House, 1974), 2:1502. Charles Rolo, writing in the *Atlantic*, provided the first quotation; Brendan Gill, of the *New Yorker*, the second. Hemingway's remark appears in Blotner, 2:1644.

4. John E. Basset, "*A Fable*: Faulkner's Revision of Filial Conflict," *Renascence* 40 (1987): 15; Richard H. King, "*A Fable*: Faulkner's Political Novel?" *Southern Literary Journal* 17:2 (1985): 10; Harold Bloom, "Introduction" to *Modern Critical Interpretations: William Faulkner's "Absalom, Absalom!,"* ed. Harold Bloom (New York: Chelsea House Publishers, 1987): 3; André Bleikasten, "A Private Man's Public Voice," in *Faulkner: After the Nobel Prize*, 59. Bleikasten made these remarks in 1985, though they were not published until 1987.

5. Mary Shelley, "Introduction to *Frankenstein*, Third Edition (1831)" in *Frankenstein*, ed. J. Paul Hunter (New York: W.W. Norton & Company, 1996), 173.

6. Joseph Blotner, ed., *Selected Letters of William Faulkner* (New York: Random House, 1977), 262.

7. Bleikasten, 53.

8. Philip M. Weinstein, xix.

9. Both Polk, in "Roland Barthes reads *A Fable*," and Nicholas Moseley, in "Faulkner's Fables," *Review of Contemporary Fiction* 2:2 (1982): 79–86, claim, in different ways, that "*A Fable* is a fable about people's use of fables" (Moseley 80).

10. James B. Meriwether published the rejected preface as "A Note on *A Fable*," *Mississippi Quarterly* 26 (1973): 416–17, noting that "Faulkner wrote this statement concerning *A Fable* in response to a request" from Commins, who "disagreed with what Faulkner said in the statement, and had decided not to use it" (416).

11. Max Horkheimer and Theodor W. Adorno, *Dialectic of Enlightenment*, trans. John Cumming (New York: Continuum Publishing Company, 1989); see the chapter "The Culture Industry: Enlightenment as Mass Deception." John Tomlinson, *Cultural Imperialism* (Baltimore: Johns Hopkins University Press, 1991).

12. I should indicate my debt to the well-established vein of Faulkner scholarship that examines the polarities of the author's imagination. For two examples of this work, see Michael Millgate's essay "William Faulkner: The Two Voices," in *Southern Literature in Transition: Heritage and Promise*, ed. Philip Castille and William Osborne (Memphis: Memphis State University Press, 1983), 73–85, and Michael Grimwood's *Heart in Conflict: Faulkner's Struggles with Vocation* (Athens: University of Georgia Press, 1987). Both authors employ a largely psychological approach in explaining Faulkner's "heart in conflict with itself"; Grimwood adds that Faulkner's simultaneous embrace and rejection of literature as a vocation arose from "his attunement to the liabilities of pastoralism" (11). I have no disagreement with Grimwood and Millgate's assertions; in considering *A Fable*, however, I want to explore cultural and historical explanations as well as psychological ones.

13. *Aesthetics and Politics: Theodor Adorno, Walter Benjamin, Ernst Block, Bertolt Brecht, Georg Lukács*; Ronald Taylor, translation editor; afterword by Frederic Jameson (New York: Verso 1995), 123.

14. I here repeat and slightly modify a point made by Andreas Huyssen in *After the Great Divide: Modernism, Mass Culture, Postmodernism* (Bloomington: Indiana University Press, 1986), 34. Subsequent quotations from this work will be cited parenthetically within the text.

15. Most of *A Fable* is set in Europe; virtually all of the main characters are British or European.

16. Walter L. Hixson's discussion of the USIA's "feature packets" describes the State Department's wide-bore consumption, reproduction, and dissemination of images of American virtue and prosperity during the "People's Capitalism" propaganda campaign of the mid-1950s. Feature packets with titles such as "The Hollywood Story" and "Hollywood and the Church" (!) were circulated cheek-by-jowl with packets entitled "The Operas of Gian-Carlo Menotti" and "The Eisenhower Golf Stroke." See Hixson, *Parting the Curtain: Propaganda, Culture, and the Cold War, 1945–1961* (New York: St. Martin's Press, 1997), 134–37. I take the phrase "decline of modernism" from Peter Bürger's essay of the same title, in *The Decline of Modernism*, trans. Nicholas Walker (University Park: Pennsylvania State University Press, 1992), 32–47.

17. *Letters*, 238.

18. Shirley Samuels, introduction to *The Culture of Sentiment: Race, Gender, and Sentimentality in Nineteenth-Century America*, ed. Shirley Samuels (New York: Oxford University Press, 1992), 3.

19. Elizabeth Barnes, *States of Sympathy: Seduction and Democracy in the American Novel* (New York: Columbia University Press, 1997), 13. Subsequent quotations will be cited parenthetically within the text.

20. Janet Todd's study *Sensibility: An Introduction* (New York: Methuen, 1986) performs a similarly corrective function, reminding readers that "the sentimental impulse is recurrent in literature" and noting that, because "sentimental techniques and their appreciation" can be "associated with a variety of social and cultural phenomena" among which "there is no hard association or simple cause and effect," the question of the virtues of sentimental literature "is, then, a matter of emphasis and number, not of complete identification and opposition" (10).

Suzanne Clark's *Sentimental Modernism: Women Writers and the Revolution of the Word* (Bloomington: Indiana University Press, 1991) attends, as I do, to the interdependencies of sentimental and modernist discourses. For various reasons, however, Clark is interested in continuing the discussion of sentimentality as a gendered phenomenon, and she does not connect sentimentalism with a commodified mass culture, as I do here, following Huyssen.

21. Ann Douglas, *The Feminization of American Culture* (New York: Doubleday, 1988 [1977]), 189.

22. *A Fable*, in *Faulkner: Novels 1942–1954* (New York: Library of America, 1994), 986–87. All subsequent quotations from the novel will be cited parenthetically in the text.

23. Steven C. Bullock, *Revolutionary Brotherhood: Freemasonry and the Transformation of the American Social Order, 1730–1840* (Chapel Hill: University of North Carolina Press, 1996), vii.

24. Ibid., 1.

25. Lynn Dumenil, *Freemasonry and American Culture, 1880–1930* (Princeton: Princeton University Press, 1984), xii.

26. Mary Ann Clawson, *Constructing Brotherhood: Class, Gender, and Fraternalism* (Princeton: Princeton University Press, 1989). Subsequent quotations will be cited parenthetically within the text.

27. See the essay "Faulkner and the Culture Industry."

28. *Letters*, 248–49.

29. Ibid., 178.

30. Ephraim Katz, *The Film Encyclopedia*, 2nd edition (New York: HarperCollins Publishers, 1994), 599; Blotner, 2:1149.

31. Blotner, 2:1149.

32. Robert W. Hamblin has pointed out that the story of the condemned man and the bird appears nowhere in *Look Away!* ("James Street's *Look Away!*: Source (and Non-

Source) for William Faulkner," *American Notes & Queries* 21:9–10 (May–June 1983): 141–43]). I am less interested here in fixing the source of the bird anecdote than in noting Faulkner's sense that the story had come from a commercial source. Street worked as a reporter for a variety of newspapers in the South; *Look Away!* is presented as a compendium of some of his more memorable assignments: "Most of my adventures were experienced only because I am a reporter and not because I am a native Southerner." See *Look Away! A Dixie Notebook*, by James H. Street (New York: Viking Press, 1936), v.

33. *Letters*, 261.

34. "In 1945, Arnold Schoenberg's application for a grant was turned down by the Guggenheim Foundation. The hostility of the music committee . . . was undisguised. The seventy-year-old composer had hoped for support in order to finish two of his largest music compositions, the opera *Moses und Aron* and the oratorio *Die Jakobsleiter* (*Jacob's Ladder*), as well as several theoretical works. Schoenberg had just retired from the University of California at Los Angeles; since he had been there only eight years, he had a pension of thirty-eight dollars a month with which to support a wife and three children aged thirteen, eight, and four." Charles Rosen, *Arnold Schoenberg* (Chicago: University of Chicago Press, 1996), 1.

35. Donald Jay Grout, *A History of Western Music*, rev. edition (New York: W. W. Norton & Company, 1973), 708.

36. Bruce Kawin, "Sharecropping in the Golden Land," in *Faulkner and Popular Culture: Faulkner and Yoknapatawpha, 1988*, ed. Doreen Fowler and Ann J. Abadie (Jackson: University Press of Mississippi, 1990), 196–206.

37. "Now just think: I am surely the only composer of my standing there has been for at least a hundred years who could not live on what he made from his creative work without having to eke out his income by teaching." *Arnold Schoenberg: Letters*, selected and edited by Erwin Stein; translated from the original German by Eithne Wilkins and Ernst Kaiser (Berkeley: University of California Press, 1987), 163.

38. See, for example, his 1945 response to a Guggenheim committee query about the merit of an applicant's work: "I have no reason to change my opinion of Mr. Anis Fuleihan's talent. . . . It seems to me I can recommend the awarding of a Guggenheim Fellowship as warmly as I did the first time. And I am not surprised that he needs this support again. No serious composer in this country is capable of living from his *art*. Only popular composers earn enough to support oneself and one's family, and then it is *not art*." Ibid., 233; original emphases.

39. " 'You want to go back to ranks,' the company commander said. 'You love man so well you must sleep in the same mud he sleeps in.'

" 'That's it,' the other said. 'It's just backward. I hate man so' " (*Fable* 721).

40. Blotner, 2:1503.

41. Ibid.

42. *Letters*, 238.

43. Bürger, 38.

Where Was that Bird? Thinking *America* through Faulkner

JOSEPH R. URGO

Yoknapatawpha County and thereabouts is Faulkner's performance of America. It is purely textual, envisioned and mapped by its founder, from textual fiction ("We the People of the United States") to nation, from Yoknapatawpha to twentieth-century United States literature. Do I confuse the nation's founding with the textual foundations of a Yoknapatawpha-based fictional cosmos? I think I do. Perhaps it is because much of what we consider to be distinctive in Faulkner's fiction reflects the performative nature of the founding of the United States of America. The preface to the Constitution begins, "We the People of the United States," and ends by referring to "this Constitution for the United States of America." At the time, there was (or were) no "United States of America" as a nation-state, but simply a collection of independent states, seeking to be united in commerce and in defense, but lacking the formal processes necessary to carry out any purposeful action. Because we know so much about the history of the founding of the United States, we can better articulate the imaginative roots of all nation-states, the way nation-states emerge over time like fictional projects.[1] Today I ask you to consider Faulkner's Yoknapatawpha as national intellectual space, and allow me to map a sense of Faulkner's America as an aesthetic vision. The unwieldy texts, some nearly off the chart of literary patience and others indispensable, today, to any discussion of the novel, reflect, on balance, the equally unwieldy project of the United States nation, some of which also makes sense, and some of which does not.

What nation? Nowhere in the founding documents of the United States will you find discussion or suggestion of its name. "[N]either the Declaration of Independence nor the Constitution provides a name for the country. At a later time, Thomas Jefferson proposed to make ten states out of the land between the Ohio River and the Mississippi and to give them such names as Dolypotamia, Metropotamia, and Assenisippia. In the Declaration of Independence, however, Jefferson shows no intention of naming the country. . . . The burden of the Declaration is to convert a group of united colonies into a group of united states—just as that of the Constitution is 'to form a more perfect Union' among 'the United States of America.' "[2] Thus, if we trace the source of the nation's name, if we want to find out where the name came from, we find that in fact it has no consensual, descriptive name. What it bears instead is a prescriptive name, a performative name. "We the people of the United States" is more accurately understood as "we who will be the people of what will become the United States" and so forth. Apparently, there was no strong motivation to call the nation anything other than what it was doing, which was uniting states. The action (or inaction) was no doubt politically expedient, and fortunes would amass as a result of political unification. At the same time, *uniting states* established that a clear sense of *doing* was more vital and profitable than a thorough consensus regarding *being*. After all, who we are has changed tremendously in two centuries, while the stage directions for our performances—governmental and commercial—have changed only slightly.

I want to explore the ways in which Faulkner writes in and perpetuates this performative cast of mind. *Requiem for a Nun* describes the naming of Jefferson as an act accomplished not to found a town (because the town existed already as a trading post) but to "cope with a situation which otherwise was going to cost somebody money."[3] When the name of the town is spoken, the experience is described as a transcendent performance, somewhat like a musical sounding:

> at last one spoke for all and then it was all right since it had taken one conjoined breath to shape that sound, the speaker speaking not loud, diffidently, tentatively, as you insert the first light tentative push of wind into the mouthpiece of a strange untried foxhorn: "By God. Jefferson."
>
> "Jefferson, Mississippi," a second added.
>
> "Jefferson, Yoknapatawpha County, Mississippi," a third corrected. . . . (494–95)

Jefferson is not only the name of the town but the name of Thomas Jefferson Pettigrew, the mail rider whose cooperation is needed to avoid the situation which otherwise was going to cost somebody money. If we trace the name of Faulkner's town, thinking we will find some form of foundational homage to the author of the Declaration of Independence, we don't arrive there. Quite explicitly, in *Requiem for a Nun*, the town is *not* named for its famous namesake, but is spoken into being, as a way of coping with a situation unrelated to its obvious, but not immediately relevant, reference. That Jefferson, Mississippi, is not named for Thomas Jefferson is critical; Faulkner's imaginary town does not represent or refer to the historical Thomas Jefferson, but to yet another fiction. Pettigrew's mother did name her son for Thomas Jefferson, so he would have some of Jefferson's "luck," a word, her son explains, that she did not mean. "She didn't know the word she wanted to say" (490).

The American practice I am locating in Faulkner might be understood as a flight from the representational in favor of the performative. What is observed here for Jefferson may also be applied to Yoknapatawpha, to Faulkner's Mississippi, and ultimately, to Faulkner's America. It is not so much a representation of America that we find in Faulkner—although of course we do find images and characters and places and events that bring social and historical matters to mind. Of much greater importance, we find in Faulkner a way to *think* America, a cognitive practice rooted in an American cultural ecology. Faulkner's America is performative, where the national experience is one that records the human capacity for incidental establishment, reflected by a literary project that suggests the futility of tracing representation to meaningful source materials. Accomplishment rarely occurs for its own sake; a source is not always used for its intended purpose. I do not consider these Faulknerian tendencies insignificant, or idiosyncratic.

In between the dedication page and the first page of *A Fable*, there is an acknowledgments page that reads:[4]

> To William Bacher and Henry Hathaway of Beverly Hills, California, who had the basic idea from which this book grew into its present form; to James Street in whose volume, *Look Away*, I read the story of the hanged man and the bird; and to Hodding Carter and Ben Wasson of the Levee Press, who published a limited edition of the original version of the story of the stolen racehorse, I wish to make grateful acknowledgment. W. F.

Those who know Faulkner well know that we'd better be on our guard when he's written introductory materials to a novel. One needs to read the preface to the Modern Library edition of *Sanctuary* very carefully to get from the description of that novel as "a cheap idea" to the incredibly understated assessment of it as "a fair job."[5] Similarly, close scrutiny of the prefatory note to *The Mansion* warns against getting distracted by "contradictions and discrepancies" within the *Snopes* trilogy as a whole,[6] asserting very cryptically—probably too cryptically—a theory of destabilized textuality that still challenges readers and critics. Very simply put, a Faulkner preface is never a throwaway, never something to be taken lightly or read simply as authorial indulgence.

In the prefatory note to *A Fable*, Faulkner thanks Bacher and Hathaway, colleagues in Hollywood in the 1940s, for the basic idea in the novel. Joseph Blotner, however, reports that "When Henry Hathaway finally read [*A Fable*], he said, 'I couldn't find my story. I didn't recognize anything.' "[7] Well, that's interesting, and raises questions about the nature of the debt Faulkner felt toward these men. Alone, the reference may not be such a problem, and neither is the standard acknowledgment for the advance publication of "Notes on a Horsethief." The problem is with this clause: "to James Street in whose volume, *Look Away*, I read the story of the hanged man and the bird." I have read Street's book and there is no story in it of a hanged man and a bird. Nancy Butterworth and Keen Butterworth, authors of the annotations to *A Fable*, corroborate the fact that "the story . . . does not appear in Street's book."[8] Robert Hamblin preceded the Butterworths, calling *Look Away* a "non-source" for *A Fable*.[9] Why would Faulkner make a *specific* citation to a source for a novel that is, in fact, overflowing with textual allusions (as the Butterworths' annotations make clear) and, even if he wanted to make the acknowledgment, why would he get it wrong? We know *A Fable* was not written quickly; on the contrary, Faulkner devoted ten years to it, revising it, rewriting sections numerous times, adding materials to it when it was in production, and composing an interpretive introduction. Like the allusion to the cheap idea of *Sanctuary* and the discrepancies in *Snopes*, one must suspect there is much more than meets the eye in this reference to James Street. The cue provided us by Faulkner's "grateful acknowledgment" is, I will suggest, of signal importance to our understanding of Faulknerian representation, and especially to any consideration of Faulkner in America. I'm not done with Street, but first, an exploration into why Faulkner nods to him in *A Fable*.

Mississippi (and through it, America) erupts twice in *A Fable*, first in the long three-legged racehorse tale, to which I shall return, and then in a brief anecdote told by the Old General to his son, the mutinous corporal. The Supreme Commander wishes to spare the life of his rebellious son and so tells him that nothing is more valuable than living, "merely knowing that you are alive—Listen to this. It happened in America, at a remote place called by an Indian name I think: Mississippi" (990). He then tells a story of a hanged man and the bird, which in *A Fable* concerns a condemned murderer who insists upon his innocence, despite the court judgment against him. A priest manages to convince the murderer to confess, "and so making his peace with God," he was prepared to die. However, on the gallows, just before his execution, the man sees a bird alight on a tree and begin to sing. In the Old General's words: "whereupon he who less than a second before had his very foot lifted to step from earth's grief and anguish into eternal peace, cast away heaven, salvation, immortal soul and all, struggling to free his bound hands in order to snatch away the noose, crying, 'Innocent! Innocent! I didn't do it!' even as the trap earth, world and all, fell from under him—all because of one bird, one weightless and ephemeral creature which hawk might stoop at or snare or lime or random pellet of some idle boy destroy before the sun set—except that tomorrow, next year, there would be another bird, another spring" (991–92). The tale from Mississippi is employed by the Old General to warn the Corporal away from consenting to die for a cause, when a simple utterance (whether "Innocent!" or "Guilty!"), even if false, can bring into being his future and save his life. In the end, as we know, this Faulknerian son accepts the need to end his life, if for no other reason than to deny his father's power to save it. Throughout *A Fable* the larks sing overhead, signaling, to those humans below who can hear them, that there is more to this life than that which is grounded on earth. The Supreme Commander interprets the Mississippi anecdote; he extracts applicable meaning from the bird's song to the condemned murderer and offers it to his son: "Then take that bird. Recant, confess, say you were wrong; that what you led was—led? you led nothing: you simply participated—an attack which failed to advance. Take life from me; ask mercy and accept it. I can give it, even for a military failure" (992). The Old General knows that facts, like birds, are weightless and ephemeral, and can (and are often) manipulated to achieve human desires. In a performative world, facts are secondary to their usefulness.

Now, there *is* a hanged man in *Look Away: A Dixie Notebook*, by James H. Street, published in 1936.[10] Will Purvis appears in a kind of tag-incident at the end of chapter 17, "The Story of Richburg," and he is also a man who has been convicted of murder. His public hanging is described by Street as the occasion for a town holiday, complete with a picnic, horseshoe throwing, and political speeches. I'll read you the hanging part:

> Will's hangman never before had executed a man and didn't know the tricks of the trade. A good hangman will grease his rope and stretch it between two mule-drawn singletrees. The trouble with most hangings is that they use new ropes which spring and give.
>
> Will was led to the scaffold and told to speak his last words. He looked at the multitude, smiled rather weakly, and said clearly:
>
> "I didn't do it, my friends."
>
> The rope was adjusted and the trap was sprung. Will dropped through the hole and the rope slipped over his head. He was uninjured but dazed. The rope scorched a cut on his neck, but he walked unaided through the opening at the base of the scaffold. Women fainted as he walked into view.
>
> "It's the will of God," someone shouted and started a hymn. Soon the whole gathering was swaying and "stomping" to the hectic melody of the chant. The sheriff was dumbfounded.

> "Free him," the crowd roared. "God has saved him."
>
> The spectators who came to see the death believed they had seen a miracle and became hysterical. They became so emotional that the public hanging was converted into a revival meeting. Some of the sinners climbed trees and barked. They called it the "holy bark." Others gibbered in "unknown tongues" and shrieked. They said they were holding a person-to-person conversation with God. Women flung themselves into the dust and lay there, quivering and panting. Others went into trances. (121–22)

The sheriff was inclined to hang Will over again, but the governor, "either convinced that God had manifested Himself or a bit fearful of the hysterical voters" (122) commuted the sentence to life imprisonment. Fifteen years later, another man confessed to the murder for which Will had been sentenced, and as a result the condemned man is freed and given a five thousand dollar compensation for wrongful imprisonment.

What was Faulkner acknowledging? What did he do when he borrowed the phrase, "I didn't do it!"? The connection between Will Purvis's declaration of innocence, his bungled hanging and subsequent liberation, and the Old General's story about the condemned murderer who declares his innocence as he is executed, "all because of one bird"—the story referred to by Faulkner as "the story of the hanged man and the bird" which he read in Street's book—is tenuous to say the least. It seems hardly worth a formal acknowledgment, unless, of course, the nod to Street has less to do with Street's book and more to do with locating weightless and ephemeral matters generally. In the acknowledgments to *A Fable*, Faulkner places us on an impossible source hunt, one that calls into question the very idea of referentiality—, as does *A Fable*, we should recall.

The relation between Street's story and Faulkner's is not at the level of representation—you may look for a bird in *Look Away!* but you won't find it. The bird is not what Faulkner got from Street. What he got from Street was a way to think about the relation between human declaration, the will to live, human justice, and the ability (and tendency) to ascribe to heaven or to God the workings (and failings) of human beings. It's as if Faulkner, in the acknowledgments to *A Fable*, points out that literary representation can neither be traced to origins (Hathaway does not recognize his "idea") nor to sources. The single literary source acknowledged in any published prefatory statement by Faulkner is Street's "story of the hanged man and the bird." In Faulkner's novel, the man really was guilty, but proclaimed his innocence because he heard a bird's morning call of life, and wanted to live even more than he wanted to go to heaven properly confessed and forgiven according to the strictures of his faith. The story is used in *A Fable* to convince another guilty man to confess, and to choose life. But in the source story the condemned man is not guilty, and he proclaims his innocence not because of a bird but because he is, in fact, guilty of no murder, and when his hanging fails it is not because of God but because the hangman bungled the job—though the people see it as divine intervention, a view later corroborated by the man's eventual vindication. To the Old General, "take that bird" means to "recant, confess" and say whatever you need to say in order to do what it is you want to do. To declare, even if to lie, is to perform one's desire and to live out the results of one's speech.

And so, here we are, in Mississippi, at the source, where we should be able to hear that bird, track it down. By specifically acknowledging Street's text, *Look Away*, as the source of the story of the hanged man and the bird, I think Faulkner issues public warning against interpreting his texts as *representations* of their subject matter. The specific acknowledgment in *A Fable* is to *Look Away*—maybe the pun is intentional. Faulkner's America is not necessarily to be found in the mimetic qualities of Faulkner's Yoknapatawpha novels, any more than France or World War One can be found in *A Fable*, as many readers have noted in desperation. So, to the title of my essay, Where exactly was that bird?

As the twentieth century closes it will be identified, in literary history, as Faulkner's century. In that century, scholars attended to what Faulkner represents in his fiction—the Southern qualities and the depictions of matters important to us, such as race, sex, gender, and class issues. Such critical efforts have responded to Faulkner as a kind of macroprocessor, if you will, a storehouse of information about the South and the United States on which to test the critical concerns of the academy. One unintended consequence of this scholarship, as useful and necessary as it has been, is that we still do not possess, one hundred and one years after the birth of Faulkner and thirty-six years after his death, an adequate understanding of his mind. Faulkner the intellectual remains enigmatic. To this day we have images proffered that Faulkner was a simple, uneducated man; that he barely understood his own genius; and more recently, that he suffered midlife brain disorders.[11] I decline to accept that, as it were. If we leave aside the images through which Faulkner represented America—his mimesis—and work toward the way Faulkner *thought* America, the cognitive processes of his aesthetic vision, we may come to a better understanding of the reasons why the twentieth has emerged as Faulkner's century. This is not a bird-hunting expedition, in other words.[12]

I prefer this premise: A fictional text is only incidentally about its representational qualities. By such a statement I mean that what is represented in the text—the South, some War, a bird, a Bear—are simply the tools, as Faulkner would say, employed to give shape to the imaginative activity of the mind that produced the text. I take my lead on this matter from Faulkner's responses to nine questions about his art at the University of Virginia:[13]

1. When asked whether "this fictitious county you've made" should be understood as a "pageant," Faulkner responded: "No, it was not my intention to write a pageant of a county, I simply was using the quickest tool to hand. I was using what I knew best, which was the locale where I was born and had lived most of my life. That was just like the carpenter building the fence—he uses the nearest hammer" (3).
2. When asked about inconsistent characterizations from one book to the next: "There again I am using the most available tool to tell what I am trying to tell"(9).
3. What about the your use of sensationalism? "Sensationalism is in a way an incidental tool, that he might use sensationalism as the carpenter picks up another hammer to drive a nail" (49–50).
4. Regarding the Easter dates in *The Sound and the Fury*: "Now there's a matter of hunting around in the carpenter's shop to find a tool that will make a better chicken-house. And probably—I'm sure it was quite instinctive that I picked out Easter, and that I wasn't writing any symbolism of the Passion Week and all. I just—that was a tool that was good for the particular corner I was going to turn in my chicken-house and so I used it" (68).
5. Regarding his long sentence structure: "That is a matter of the carpenter trying to find the hammer or the axe that he thinks will do the best job" (84).
6. Regarding what's better, using autobiographical materials or making up stuff: "I would say that the writer has three sources, imagination, observation, and experience. . . . That he is writing about people, and he uses his material from the three sources as the carpenter reaches into his lumber room and finds a board that fits the particular corner he's building" (103).
7. Was the Joe Christmas–Christ symbolism in *Light in August* intentional? "No, that's a matter of reaching into the lumber room to get out something which seems to the writer the most effective way to tell what he is trying to tell" (117).
8. How about social justice themes, are they intentional? "The fiction writer . . . will use the injustice of society, the inhumanity of people, as a—as any other tool in telling a story, which is about people, not about the injustice or inhumanity of people" (177).
9. What's more important, the story or the theme? "If I understand you right, in that case the message would be one of the craftsman's tools, that—well, that's perfectly valid. A message is one of his tools, just like the rhetoric, just like the punctuation" (239).

Faulkner scholars are more likely than not to dismiss these statements as evidence of a biographical mask, where Faulkner plays the simple farmer or carpenter instead of owning up to the fact that he is an artist, an intellectual, who was doing considerably more than building chicken-houses with axes and hammers. Alternatively, the comments have been seen as evidence that Faulkner was himself mystified by his literary genius, and was no better at explaining it than the students in the classrooms at Virginia. The carpenter metaphor stresses performance (using the nearest hammer; finding a board that fits) over essence, and is striking for its consistency throughout the Virginia interviews.

The artist possesses an imagination like any of us, but the artist possesses one thing we do not possess: the capacity to give shape to that imagination so that it can be captured and conveyed. In Faulkner's words, he possessed agility with the tools and the materials necessary to give recognizable, communicable shape to his imagination. The tools were the local materials, the narratives, the plots and structures of the texts we know. The materials were mostly Mississippi, but also New Orleans, Georgia, Virginia, Boston, and France. The narrative tools varied widely, and we may imagine that Faulkner had one of those great big red Sears Craftsman toolboxes marked "narrative structure" and a smaller box marked "materials and setting." But to Faulkner, these tools were somehow separate from the way he considered the finished product, the thing that was built "to tell what he is trying to tell."

We have spent much time on the tools and the materials Faulkner employed, and less time on the imagination itself, the cognitive modes that called the materials into form and necessitated the use of the tools. There have been exceptions, of course, such as Donald Kartiganer's study of cohesive fragmentation in the novels.[14] In the absence of sustained attention to Faulkner's intellect, we perpetuate certain skewed perspectives on Faulkner. His use of local, northern Mississippi materials is astounding. Even after sixty years, the tools with which he employed Sutpen, Compson, Bundren, Christmas, Drake, and McCaslin continue to arrest motion, thought, and critical acumen. But because these tools and materials are so astounding, we cannot seem to assimilate the cognitive content of Corporal and General, Mink and I. O., Lucius and Ned. Instead, we want to see these as bungled tools.

My thesis, again: Faulkner provides us a way of thinking America and a pun on the conference title: *Faulknerin' America*. The novels, as a whole, perform an intellectual drama not especially valuable for simply thinking *about* America—not a way to learn what it's like to live in the South (and why anybody would want to, as Shreve says)—but a peculiar, specific, and nationally revealing cognitive process. Faulknerin' America, then, signals less a series of representations and more a mode of cognition. In *Absalom Absalom!*, we know that comprehension does not hinge on the events themselves so much as on the capacity of Quentin and Shreve (and Rosa and Mr. Compson) to envision, interrogate, and then declare the meanings of the events they confront. Various images—pebbles in the water, narrow umbilicals, marriages of speaking and hearing—evoked by Faulkner lay stress to intellectual processes and performances. Faulkner leads us to consider "America" as a way of thinking, one that is among the world's most vital and still contested resources for imaginative activity. Yoknapatawpha is less a place, real or mythical, as it is an American performance whose genealogy may be traced to the performative founding of the nation itself.

Martin Kreiswirth explored the performative nature of Faulkner's aesthetics in a paper delivered here in 1993. Referring to "irresolvable base-level contradictions" throughout Faulkner's fiction, contradictions that "are not ambiguities, not interpretive irregularities, but textual instabilities," Kreiswirth demonstrates that in Faulkner "something always will be suppressed, disavowed, hidden away,"—like that hanged man's bird, we might say. Kreiswirth quotes the narrator's assertion in *Absalom, Absalom!* that "there might be paradox and inconsistency but nothing fault or false" in the tale created by Quentin and Shreve. "For Yoknapatawphan intertextuality, the false and fault are not errors or discrepancies but performatives. And what they perform is transgression—textual, semiotic, and generic—which calls upon the reader to engage in a certain kind of transgressive interpretive activity,"[15] or yet another set of performatives. And this performative quality, I will now say, is particularly American. At the very core of the national experience, from the journeymen's and colonists' declarations that those people were *Indians*, to the naming of the very landmass *America*, the link between utterance and act has been forged cable-strong in United States history.

Note the sheer performative nature of the following statement: "We the People of the United States, in Order to form a more perfect Union, establish Justice, insure domestic Tranquillity, provide for the common defense, promote the general Welfare, and secure the Blessings of Liberty to ourselves and our Posterity, do ordain and establish this CONSTITUTION for the United States of America." "This CONSTITUTION" was a handy tool for the founding carpenters, whose real purpose was to form (or, perhaps, *perform*) a more perfect union where justice, tranquillity, commerce, and liberty could endure. The decision to ordain and establish the national constitution was the quickest tool at hand, as it were, for the maintenance of certain conditions, most particularly, the more perfect Union—the tightest chicken-house. What is established in the *Constitution* is not a Union (since that is acknowledged to exist already, however imperfect and fragmented), but a text. What is performed in the document is a nation. Only through the application of that document, in the performance of its legislative and electoral processes, for example, do the people, in their various states of union, become "the United States of America." The states already exist as entities; it is the performative text that unites the states into a single Union, or Nation. A logic whereby text follows experience and at the same time *legalizes* it, declares it, authorizes it—simultaneously evoking and invoking a reality, is the "united state" between Faulkner and America.

Addie Bundren may be correct in her assertion "that words are no good; that words don't ever fit even what they are trying to say at,"[16] which fits well with Faulkner's own distrust for weightless and ephemeral facts and, as we know, sources. But as performance, words are *real good*. Anse's word to Addie assures her burial in Jefferson. Faulkner's words, "sole owner and proprietor," are emblematic of the entire performance of Yoknapatawpha, the veneer of Faulkner laid over the landscape of America.

Once we begin to contemplate Yoknapatawpha as the material performance of Faulkner's thinking, linked cognitively to a more perfect Union or a well-tempered chicken-house, we might turn our attention away from the planks and boards and the kinds of hammers and nails used (or the structures of government and the balance of powers), and toward the kind of thinking evoked by the novels—or why they were written at all. Read cognitively, fiction is understood not to represent the world, but to participate in it and to perpetuate it. America is, above all, the product of thought and performance, of textual invocations and declarations. Recall the less-scrutinized clause in the famous beginning of the Declaration of Independence, where the signers proclaim their belief that "a decent respect to the opinions of mankind requires that they should declare the causes which impel them to the separation." Here is the complete, initial statement: "When in the Course of human events, it becomes necessary for one people to dissolve the political bands which have connected them with another, and to assume among the Powers of the earth, the separate and equal station to which the Laws of Nature and of Nature's God entitle them, a decent respect to the opinions of mankind requires that they should declare the causes which impel them to the separation."

The Declaration of Independence is an ingenious performance, a performance that has become the hallmark of American political discourse (and repeated ritualistically on the Fourth of July in many places). Performative speech lies at the heart of the nation's establishment, and therein lies one key to its endurance. The new nation, to be called simply by its component or structural parts, "The United States of America," is rooted in texts. Before nationhood it existed as a colony of Great Britain, and it emerged as an independent country by way of formal, written declaration, and a war fought not for nationhood but for the right of declaration. "And for the support of this declaration," the document concludes, "with a firm reliance on the protection of divine providence, we mutually pledge to each other our lives, our fortunes, and our sacred honor."

The first paragraph of the Declaration of Independence reasons that it is not enough to *become* a separate nation, but that independence must be accompanied, or followed, by a performative text. The Continental Congress had already voted and passed a formal Resolution of political independence on July 2, 1776, two days before finalizing the language of the public declaration. July 2 is thus the historically accurate, technically precise date of American independence. But it seems not to matter, nationally. The declaration is necessary, according to the text, because "a decent respect to the opinions of mankind requires" it. However, it is not clear exactly how it is that the opinions of mankind demand such declaration, or how these opinions have been gathered to warrant such a conclusion. A political issue between England and several of its remote colonies was unlikely to interest the majority of mankind in the late 18th century. Furthermore, few nations in existence in 1776 had come into being in the same manner, and so it is difficult also to know what these opinions, once located, would be based upon. Ultimately, the requirement of published declaration is a peculiarly American one. The casting of national goals as a text, the attempt to locate unity or disunity, consensus or dissensus, in the guise of language, is the way in which America is performed. In the United States, the existence of the nation is rooted not so much in the material existence of land or in traceable lines of ethnicity but in documents, in language.

A recent, historical study of language and literary form in colonial America refers to the "improbable claim that the United States was actually 'spoken into being,' " referring thus to "the American sense of national fabrication as an intentional act of linguistic creation, the belief that the nation was made out of words."[17] Moreover, we should recall that "the Declaration was written to be read aloud. . . . On July 4 the Continental Congress ordered not only that 'the declaration be authenticated and printed,' but that 'copies of the declaration be sent to the several assemblies, conventions, and committees, or councils of safety, and to the several commanding officers [so] that it be proclaimed in each of the United States.' "[18] The colonies were free and independent—what was lacking was the narrative, the publication of the cognitive link between experience and textuality. In Faulknerian terms, it could not be "is" until it "was." And so the document asks Americans to fight not so much for independence (because they are said to already possessed that quality), but for the right to declare their status. "Lives . . . Fortunes, and . . . sacred Honor" are pledged, not to self-evident truths specifically but to one another, "for the support of this Declaration."

The opening words of the Constitution, "we the people" make United States citizens both subjects and objects of the nation, the component results as well as the agents of that result. The people make the union, and the union results in "the people." America might thus be understood a verb, as in "we america" or "the people america," so the "the United States of America" is like saying, the united states of being, of doing, or of performing America. Faulkner's performance, *Faulknerin' America*, is rooted in powerful cognitive experiences. Throughout Faulkner, events are secondary to their narrative performance, to their mode of declaration. Early critics, so taken by Faulkner's technique, often echoed Sartre's sense that in Faulkner "the present does not exist, it becomes; everything *was*."[19] However, this and similar formalist observations need to be linked to an American cultural ecology. For example, we have a sense of the "frozen moment" in isolation, apart from its function in American historical forms, where frozen moments—signing the Declaration, seceding from the union, a motorcade in Dallas—punctuate American consciousness. The performance imperative in Faulkner and in America demands that narrative be employed to discover what happened, and by so declaring, bring into being what *was* as a means of shaping what is, and what will be.

Faulkner often invoked the idea of the "unfinished" nation, an important American concept. "We the people" exist to *make* "a more perfect union," we should note, not to continue to *be* a perfect union. "What's wrong with this world is, it's not finished yet," Faulkner said in 1953. "It is not completed to that point where man can put his final signature on it and say, 'It is finished. We made it, and it works.' "[20] The incomplete nature of the world calls for more texts, more performance, more thought regarding its nature and its construction. Abraham Lincoln's words at Gettysburg, "The world will little note, nor long remember what we say here, but it can never forget what they did here," achieve American irony. The world has indeed remembered what Lincoln said on that battlefield, at least as well, if not more vividly, than what the soldiers did there. Acts that Lincoln suggested were impossible to accomplish with words (*we can not dedicate—we can not consecrate—we can not hallow—this ground*) were in fact possible only by declaration. Lincoln concluded that "It is for us the living, rather, to be dedicated here to the unfinished work which they who have fought here have thus far so nobly advanced."[21] The sense of work left undone, and of performances scheduled to play, is a deep source of national cohesion in the United States.

Perhaps the strongest and clearest statement of the performative basis of United States public philosophy is articulated in "The American Scholar," by Ralph Waldo Emerson. "Each age, it is found, must write its own books; or rather, each generation for the next succeeding. The books of an older period will not fit this." Emerson links this eternal necessity for revision not to generational antipathy or to change for its own sake, but to the same philosophical principle that underlies the idea of a pursuit of happiness and a more perfect union—to the faith (and it is article of faith) that the cosmos, the world, and the nation are *unfinished* entities. "It is a mischievous notion that we are come late into nature; that the world was finished a long time ago." It is the task of human beings to work toward completion by effecting their world through their own pursuits, and by affecting the worlds—moral, political, and personal—of others. "Not he is great who can alter matter," Emerson declares, "but he who can alter my state of mind."[22] Alteration, not continuation, is Emerson's ideal act, as it must be to one whose faith holds that the world is unfinished. Lincoln, in the Gettysburg Address, invoked the same faith. The dead contribute not so much to a battleground as to a continuation of a project of perfection. In his Nobel Prize Acceptance Speech, Faulkner defined the duty of writers and poets as being "one of the props" to remind human beings of their transcendent capacities.

The cognitive demands made by Faulkner have profound implications for public life in America. In *A Fable*, the narrator defines *thinking* in such a way as to reverberate back through all the novels.[23] "To think: not that dreamy hoping and wishing and believing (but mainly just waiting) that we would think is thinking, but some fierce and rigid concentration that at any time—tomorrow, today, next moment, this one—will change the shape of the earth" (933). It is *thinking* that Faulkner's novels are mainly about, once we accept the idea that representation was of secondary importance to this novelist. Hence, the centrality of *A Fable* to the idea of Faulkner in America. In *A Fable*, "America," the performative, is cast, representationally, as one rather tremendous, illegal, perhaps immoral, mutinous, thieving, and impossibly successful achievement—one tremendous bird's song, sourceless and untraceable, encapsulated by the "song" of the hanged murderer but given fuller treatment by the tall-tale of the three-legged racehorse. The placement of American materials in this novel set, as it were, in France, provides an indispensable way to think about the placement of Yoknapatawpha in American culture.

While no Americans are involved in the mutiny of Gragnon's division, Faulkner sets the mutiny at the moment when the American troops are first arriving in France. Similarly, at the very moment when the runner is about to engage in action, he hears the tale of the sentry and the racehorse. The sentry is the prototypical American, the performative individual, who is transformed by his dual-migration, to and from the United States, as a prototypical bird of passage. "[S]o that when late in 1914 he returned to England to enlist, it was as though somewhere behind the Mississippi Valley hinterland where within the first three months he had vanished, a new man had been born, without past, without griefs, without recollections" (805). This new man's metamorphosis occurs as a result of his experience in America with the three-legged horse, whose story (the story of the horse) emerges in *A Fable* as "the affirmation of a creed, a belief, the declaration of an undying faith, the postulation of an invincible way of life: the loud strong voice of America itself out of the westward roar of the tremendous and battered yet indomitably virgin continent" (820–21).

The story is impossible; it is inconceivable that a stolen three-legged horse could run, let alone run fast, let alone win races. Such inconceivability and impossibility are clearly linked to the similar attributes of the novel's main focus, the incarnation of Christ as a French corporal and the mutiny of thousands of troops in 1917. The voice that tells the horse-tale is that of an African American, a preacher who preaches a kind of secular humanism. The casting of this preacher as the novel's singular American voice is neither impossible nor inconceivable, but not insignificant, either. The Reverend Sutterfield's genealogy is phenomenal, as is his appearance in France during the war, as an agent of humane orders. The sheer impossibility of so much of *A Fable* is linked to the equivalent, historical impossibilities at the core of the existence of the United States, of Faulkner's America. The physical facts, the sources, the representational references are not traceable, and not as important to knowing the nation as are the performance. The horse thieves in *A Fable* steal the racehorse not to save its life, "not just to keep it alive," we are told. "The reason was so that it could run, keep on running, keep on losing races at least, finish races at least even if it did have to run them on three legs because it was a giant and didn't need even three legs to run them on but only one with a hoof at the end to qualify as a horse" (816). Not the horse itself—you'll find a three-legged race horse in the same place where you'll find the story of the hanged man in the bird, which is no-place—but the performance of it, is what constitutes Faulkner's America: the "we the people" part of American existence.

Acts of declaration and the repository of the spoken word in texts have created and maintained United States national existence. Ours is a textual nation, where national celebrations turn to founding documents and acts of declaration for validation. Long after whatever they did there is forgotten, what they said there (*I regret I have but one life to give for my country; Remember the Alamo; The only thing we have to fear is fear itself*) remains as part of the national consciousness. The compulsion to declare, to make known one's intentions, to turn deeds into words not simply for the historical record but for public dissemination, to be heard and read by others as a ritualistic acts of community—this compulsion defines American nationalism as profoundly as any resulting public policy or political institution. The brilliance of Lincoln's Address at Gettysburg is that it simultaneously invoked the tradition of declaration while proffering its denial, which would mean the end of the nation. At the beginning of the speech, Lincoln invoked the Declaration at the nation's founding by referring to the bringing forth "on this continent, a new nation . . . dedicated to the proposition that all men are created equal." He then denied the power of human declaration, evoking the horror that the world will not remember what we say here—and thus by implication, that the founding Declaration be forgotten. For if the world forgets what we say, and if American declarations fall on deaf ears, the idea of the United States of America would become, literally, a historical impossibility, a three-legged horse incapable of running anywhere. American declarations must be heard, and read, and read and heard again. The idea of the nation is rooted in the significance of human declarations, and sustained by the various performances of what Faulkner called "the poet's voice" that articulates "not merely the record" of national fact, but provides "one of the props"[24] necessary for the construction of the future, the predicament of human beings who must endure incompletion. While searching for the bird's origins we must keep our eyes on its eternally receding flight, always anticipating morning, when another weightless and ephemeral creature will change the shape of the earth, toward our more perfect union.

NOTES

1. The most influential explication of the nation as an imaginative entity is Benedict Anderson, *Imagined Communities: Reflections on the Origin and Spread of Nationalism* (New York: Verso, 1993).

2. Terence Martin, *Parables of Possibility: The American Need for Beginnings* (New York: Columbia University Press, 1995), 29.

3. William Faulkner, *Requiem for a Nun* (1951), in *Faulkner: Novels 1942–1954* (New York: The Library of America, 1994), 475. All subsequent references are to this text.

4. William Faulkner, *A Fable* (1954), in *Faulkner: Novels 1942–1954* (New York: Library of America, 1994), 667. All subsequent references are to this text.

5. William Faulkner, *Sanctuary*, with a new introduction by the author (New York: Modern Library, 1932), v, vii.

6. William Faulkner, *The Mansion* (New York: Random House, 1959), no page number.

7. Joseph Blotner, *Faulkner: A Biography*, 2 vols. (New York: Random House, 1974), 2:1502.

8. Nancy Butterworth and Keen Butterworth, *William Faulkner: Annotations to the Novels: A Fable*, ed. James B. Meriwether (New York: Garland, 1989), 2.

9. Robert W. Hamblin, "James Street's *Look Away!*: Source (and non-source) for William Faulkner," *American Notes & Queries* 21:9–10 (1983), 141–43.

10. New York: Viking Press. Subsequent references are to this edition.

11. On Faulkner's self-conscious use of masks and public personae, see Lothar Hönnighausen, *Faulkner: Masks and Metaphors* (Jackson: University Press of Mississippi, 1997); for the speculation that he suffered brain damage, see Daniel J. Singal, *William Faulkner: The Making of a Modernist* (Chapel Hill: University of North Carolina Press, 1997).

12. It could be. At the beginning of *A Fable*, the Sergeant-Major's shout is described as "a thin forlorn cry hanging for a fading instant in the air like one of the faint, sourceless, musical cries of the high invisible larks now filling the sky above the city" (671). When General Gragnon is ordered back to headquarters, he disobeys and drives to the line. Then—

> So at first he did not realise what had startled, shocked him. He said sharply: "Stop." and sat in the halted car in the ringing silence which he hadn't even heard yet because he had never heard anything here before but guns . . . [and remembering, or becoming a child again,] listening now to the same cicada chirring and buzzing in a tangle of cordite-blasted weeds. . . . Then he heard that lark too, high and invisible, almost liquid but not quite . . . until he said, loud and harsh: "Drive on!"—moving on again; and sure enough, there was the lark again, incredible and serene, and then again the unbearable golden silence, so that he wanted to clap his hands to his ears, bury his head, until at last the lark once more relieved it. (699–700)

Gragnon, the man who wants to execute his entire division, hears the song of life when larks supplant artillery.

The runner (who will make a futile attempt to emulate the corporal) watches the crew load the blank shells "and at midnight was in another wood—or what had been a wood, since all that remained now was a nightingale somewhere behind him—, not walking now but standing against the blasted corpse of a tree, hearing still above the bird's idiot reiteration the lorries creeping secretly and steadily through the darkness" (741). The crowd in Paris moves below "the lark-loud sky" (787) and turns and moves "all at one instant as birds do" (788). Finally, at the moment of the corporal's execution, the orders are read by the declarant, "his voice sounding clear and thin and curiously forlorn in the sunny lark-filled emptiness among the dead redundant forensic verbiage talking in pompous and airy delusion of an end of man" (1022).

A quality reverberates throughout Faulkner in these evocative birdcalls. There is the bird that sang while Popeye and Horace stared at each other across the spring for two hours, and Temple Drake's haunting image of the cries of marsh-fowl in *Sanctuary*. While Quentin fights Dalton Ames in *The Sound and the Fury*, he hears "a bird singing somewhere beyond the sun"; and then there are the jaybirds that menace those who are awake on Easter morning: they "came up from nowhere . . . screaming into the wind" (William Faulkner, *The Sound and the Fury* [1929; New York: Vintage, 1990], 266). In *A Fable* the sound of birds signals spiritual life—not spirituality romanticized, but simply the will to live, as in the ambitions of the child-Gragnon, the anxiety of the Paris crowd, and the protest of the guilty man—not qualitatively different, to Faulkner, than the protest of an innocent man. But I promised that this would not become a bird-hunting expedition, and I will keep that promise. These birds have flown to endnotes.

13. *Faulkner in the University: Class Conferences at the University of Virginia, 1957–1958*, ed. Frederick L. Gwynn and Joseph L. Blotner (New York: Vintage, 1959).

14. Donald Kartiganer, *The Fragile Thread: The Meaning of Form in Faulkner's Novels* (Amherst: University of Massachusetts Press, 1979).

15. Martin Kreiswirth, "'Paradoxical and Outrageous Discrepancy': Transgression, Auto-Intertextuality, and Faulkner's Yoknapatawpha," *Faulkner and the Artist: Faulkner and Yoknapatawpha, 1993*, ed. Donald J. Kartiganer and Ann J. Abadie (Jackson: University Press of Mississippi, 1996), 161–80.

16. William Faulkner, *As I Lay Dying*, in *Faulkner: Novels 1930–1935* (New York: Library of America, 1985), 115.

17. Christopher Looby, *Voicing America: Language, Literary Form, and the Origins of the United States* (Chicago: University of Chicago, 1996), 4. The following discussion of the idea of incompletion in American history is given fuller treatment in Joseph R. Urgo, *In the Age of Distraction* (Jackson: University Press of Mississippi, 2000).

18. Jay Fliegelman, *Declaring Independence: Jefferson, Natural Language, and the Culture of Performance* (Stanford: Stanford University Press, 1993), 25.

19. Jean Paul Sartre, "Time in Faulkner: *The Sound and the Fury*," in *William Faulkner: Three Decades of Criticism*, ed. Frederick J. Hoffman and Olga W. Vickery (New York: Harcourt, Brace, and World, Inc., 1963), 228.

20. "Address to the Graduating Class, Pine Manor Junior College," *Essays, Speeches, and Public Letters*, ed. James B. Meriwether (New York: Random House, 1965), 135.

21. Abraham Lincoln, "The Gettysburg Address," in *An American Primer*, ed. Daniel J. Boorstin (New York: Penguin, 1966), 436–37.

22. Ralph Waldo Emerson, "The American Scholar," in *The Portable Emerson*, ed. Carl Bode (New York: Penguin, 1981), 53, 65.

23. I do not hold to the view that Faulkner in the 1950s, the "public" Faulkner, was a very different author from the brooding and private man of the 1930s and 1940s, whose fiction is often assumed to be unconcerned with public affairs and nation-building. The failure has been one of perception. For example, there is Benjamin Compson in *The Sound the Fury*, "trying to say" and persecuted for it. There is one brother, Jason, seeking a public voice in the capitalist marketplace; another brother, Quentin, trying to explain himself in a public court of law. There is the move by Anse Bundren, in *As I Lay Dying*, from intensely private inarticulateness to a boldly public declaration, "Meet Mrs Bundren." In *Light in August*, the private anguish of Joe Christmas becomes the public issue of Gavin Stevens, and in *Sanctuary* Temple Drake transforms her subjective experience into a public performance of the roots of civil responsibility. The public address system in *Pylon* offers continuous declarations, turning the peculiar vocation and private motivations of pilots into public metaphors for courage and daring. Quentin and Shreve seize as public property the private, family drama of the Sutpen clan, making national myth of it. A retreat from public engagement marks Ike McCaslin's failure in *Go Down, Moses*. It is certainly true that it the later 1940s and throughout the1950s, Faulkner emphasized the public dimension of his thinking. *Intruder in the Dust* and *Requiem for a Nun* are intensely public, the former for its engagement in contemporary racial politics, and the latter for its application of a local, fictional evocation to national history. Nonetheless, to see the public concerns of Faulkner in the 1950s as aberrations would be a mistake.

24. The quoted phrases are from the Nobel Prize Acceptance Speech.

"A-laying there, right up to my door": As American *As I Lay Dying*

CHARLES A. PEEK

Dedicated to William Shaver, longtime participant and supporter of Yoknapatawpaha.

Critics have often noted that Faulkner seems to have wide sympathies, a deep understanding, even affection for his characters, noting interviews where he refused to label as villains some of the characters who seem villainous to many.[1] However, in the midst of such praise, we often find readings of his work possible only by dividing the sheep from the goats. To me, to read Faulkner is to strive for that perspective which allows me, too, to suspend judgment, to share in Faulkner's affections for all his characters, less daunted by their failures than awe-struck by their efforts, always aware of the difficult, even impossible situations within which they must live, be, and do. Melville suggests to us that sooner or later an author always reveals his face in his work; my suspicion is that the closest glimpse we ever get of Faulkner's face is in the brief dialog between Gavin Stevens and V. K. Ratliff, admittedly neither Faulkner's *voice*, in *The Mansion*, the penultimate story in the Yoknapatawpha cycle:

> Stevens: "People just do the best they can."
> Ratliff: "The pore sons of bitches."

How precarious are our judgments, with what wisdom we would suspend them in a kind of love, is driven home in the final images Darl invokes on his way to Jackson, in a scene that asks us to ponder what shall be the relation between our economic realities and our spiritual ideals. "A nickel has a woman on one side and a buffalo on the other; two faces and no back. I dont know what that is. Darl had a little spy-glass he got in France at the war. In it it had a woman and a pig with two backs and no face. I know what that is. 'Is that why you are laughing, Darl?' "[2] On the one hand, in Darl's spyglass, we see the arrangements of our still frontier-driven system of values and judgments: the woman and the pig, two backs with no faces, confrontational, the bestiality of seeing nature as only to be consumed, the human only as consumer, an obscene relation between the human and the natural. On the other hand, on the nickel, arrangements appear as we might profess them to be: two faces and no backs, nature and the human as two faces of the same coin, nature and humanity in back-to-back solidarity creating one value, the common coin of the land. Exploitive confrontation, productive solidarity: Faulkner seems to me always to be exposing the former and encouraging the latter.

Faulkner's public discourse suggests that he believed in a state where the free choice of solidarity—"confederation" he called it—was encouraged, where the state empowered rather than coerced, represented our ideals rather than capitulated to our baser arrangements, contributed to our willingness to risk for our aspirations rather than contribute to our dependence by pandering incestuously to our panic for security. As Darl says, "When something is new and hard and bright, there ought to be something a little better for it than just being safe" (117).

As Patrick O'Donnell argues, the state's role is properly the control of movement, of who and what goes where and on what; the state controls nomadism or, in a word, builds and controls traffic on roads. Our wagons should ride on the state.[3] But Faulkner did not believe that our lives or our spirits should do the same. Much of what we mean by the words *individual* and *family* refer to what we do inside the house, constitutionally separate from the state. O'Donnell rightly claims that *As I Lay Dying* is not merely the Freudian Family Romance, but this should not suggest that no kind of Family Romance plays any part in the novel. *As I Lay Dying* examines rural conditions influenced by the passing of the Frontier, a frontier yet today marked by its roads, trails, routes, and destinations. But the novel also focuses, within those conditions, on a kind of metafamily, its secrets and its sharing, its aspirations, falsifications, and frustration, its illusions and disillusioning.

In *As I Lay Dying*, Faulkner shapes portraits of Family and Frontier by evoking as their context the philosophical concepts which underpin the rise of an American people, ideas we know most commonly as "a state of nature" and a "social contract," the concepts at the heart of the debates rendered by Hobbes, Locke, and Rousseau. We hear these concepts echoed in Cora's language of "natural affection" (19) and "human nature" (22), in Dewey Dell's discussions of how much neighbors do for the Bundren family, in the family's desire not to be beholding, in the contrasting of men and machines, in Darl's ideas about what men naturally prefer (119), in Cash groaning like "a natural man" (140), and in Cash's and Tull's reflections on the mutability of the human condition. It would not be amiss, then, to read the novel as vectoring the assumptions behind Jeffersonian democracy—pun of course intended.

To examine our foundations as a national people, to ameliorate our judgments, to works out its concern for authority and autonomy, for state and individual, Faulkner gives extensive development to two metaphors, a metaphor of the road, with obvious connections to the idea of the Frontier, and a metaphor of the house, with connecting links to the idea of the Family.[4] Both ideas surface repeatedly in American life and thought. Two passages that exemplify Faulkner's method and subject. First, midway through *As I Lay Dying*, Cash and Darl, riding in the wagon where they are described as crouching, "flagrant and unabashed in all the old terror and the old foreboding, alert and secret and without shame" (128), set to discussing Vernon Tull. Their conversation goes like this:

> [Darl]: "I reckon we're still in the road, all right."
> [Cash]: "Tull taken and cut them two big whiteoaks. I heard tell how at high water in the old days they used to line up the ford by them trees."
> [Darl]: "I reckon he did that two years ago when he was logging down here. I reckon he never thought that anybody would ever use this ford again."
> [Cash]: "I reckon not. Yes, it must have been then. He cut a sight of timber outen here then. Payed off that mortgage with it, I hear tell."
> [Darl]: "Yes. Yes, I reckon so. I reckon Vernon could have done that."
> [Cash]: "That's a fact. Most folks that logs in this here country, they need a durn good farm to support the sawmill. Or maybe a store. But I reckon Vernon could."
> [Darl]: "I reckon so. He's a sight."
> [Cash]: "Ay. Vernon is. Yes, it must still be here. He never would have got that timber out of here if he hadn't cleaned out that old road." (128)

Faulkner compresses logging, sawmill economics, Tull's status among the locals, the prevalence of stories told about one another, and bits of Scot dialect, in this brief space between two framing comments about the road and its history. Shortly later, passing now from the frontier and its roads to the house and its family, Addie reflects: "My father said that the reason for living is getting ready to stay dead. I knew at last what he meant and that he could not have known what he meant himself, because a man cannot know anything about cleaning up the house afterward. And so I have cleaned my house. With Jewel—I lay by the lamp, holding up my own head, watching him cap and suture it before he breathed—the wild blood boiled away and the sound of it ceased. Then there was only the milk, warm and calm, and I lying calm in the slow silence, getting ready to clean my house" (162).

These two passages, then, are not simply descriptive reports; rather, they evoke the two poles which give the novel its dynamic and arrest our tendency to prejudge, to label. The change in idiom—cleaning out the road but cleaning *up* the house—is only a token of their vastly different import. Faulkner guides our reflection by alternating his focus between these two metaphors for life, the metaphor of the road, the journey, and the metaphor of the house, the family; around the former he evokes the socioeconomic conditions of their material culture and around the latter he gathers their religious beliefs, doubts, and heritage. To ask which came first, the house or the road, is to ask about priorities, contexts, values.[5]

These two poles also create the methodology of the novel: by how he treats each focus, and especially by their continuous alteration, Faulkner compels a suspension of judgment, casting into doubt our prejudices, giving us a kind of love for the Bundrens and their neighbors so that we see them as neither heroes nor villains but as people facing all types of circumstances, types less remote from us than we might believe. If we acquaint ourselves with both the people and their circumstances, we will find how readily we can identify with them, how suspect (and ultimately snobbish and condescending) are both idealizations and criticisms of them.[6]

1. The Road and Its Progenitors

As I Lay Dying is replete with references to the motif of road and journey. Faulkner mentions roads twenty-four times, bridges thirty-three times, and fords (as in river crossings) ten times. All these references surround the thematic statement Faulkner places at the beginning of Anse's first monologue, "Durn that road," allowing Anse to explain his antipathy: "Putting it where every bad luck prowling can find it and come straight to my door, charging me taxes on top of it. . . . trying to shorthand me with the law. Making me pay for it" (31, 32). Anse lays to its charge Cash's taking the notion to be a carpenter, which led to his fall from a church roof; blames it for "Talking me out of" Darl, "threaten[ing] me out of him"; and believes it created the situation in which Addie is dying. Anse complains, "She was well and hale ere a woman ever were, except for that road" (32). These objections, both immediate and visceral, have in their turn led Anse to his notorious speculation about people and roads, a speculation within which Anse, too, echoes Faulkner's two metaphors. He says,

A-laying there, right up to my door, where every bad luck that comes and goes is bound to find it. I told Addie it want any luck living on a road when it come by here, and she said, for the world like a woman, "Get up and move, then." But I told her it want no luck in it, because the Lord put roads for traveling: why He laid them down flat on the earth. When He aims for something to be always a-moving, He makes it long ways, like a road or a horse or a wagon, but when He aims for something to stay put, He makes it up-and-down ways, like a tree or a man. And so He never aimed for folks to live on a road, because which gets there first, I says, the road or the house? Did you ever know Him to set a road down by a house? I says. No you never, I says, because it's always men cant rest till they gets the house set where everybody that passes in a wagon can spit in the doorway, keeping the folks restless and wanting to get up and go somewheres else when He aimed for them to stay put like a tree or a stand of corn. Because if He'd a aimed for man to be always a-moving and going somewheres else, wouldn't He a put him longways on his belly, like a snake? It stands to reason he would. (31–32)

According to Allen Tate, Faulkner said the seed for the whole novel was Anse Bundren's bitterness toward the road which he felt had ruined his livelihood and his luck, both true as we shall see.[7] Anse's statements of this theme are reinforced at the emotional heart of the novel, the disastrous attempt to cross the flooded river. In this scene, coming and going, impassable roads, bridges down, and fords lost all come together, and here Faulkner takes the opportunity to draw out the economics that link road and livelihood.

The only remarks about roads that precede Anse's are Tull's assurances that, "with the roads like they are now, it wont take you no time to get her to town" (17) and "the roads is good now" (25). These comments, apparently only relatively true at best, suggest a time when the roads were not good, introducing the subject of roads by suggesting an important history attaches to them. Some of that history, the replacement of fords with bridges, is told by Uncle Billy: "I dont know ere a man that's touched hammer to it in twenty-five years. . . . It was built . . . in the year 1888" (78), a history which evokes this reflection,

> "Lots of folks has crossed it that wont cross no more bridges," Houston says.
> "It's a fact," Littlejohn says. "It's so."
> "One more aint, no ways," Armstid says. (79)

These reflections serve to connect the bridge with death and dying, among the outer limits of the life span which no individual can write for herself so that even our own stories are not solely our own. And, in its turn, our mortality connects us to our lot, our actual situation, how it limits us, what it demands of us.

Roads, then, form a major thematic statement and emotional center for the action of *As I Lay Dying*, one of the two poles that create its dynamic. What then do we, children of the Interstate Highway system, know about roads circa the last quarter of the nineteenth century and the first quarter of twentieth? Howard Lawrence Preston, in *Dirt Roads to Dixie*, examines the good roads movement, particularly as it affected the South.[8] The original impetus to the movement was directed toward populist farmers and intellectuals and aimed at improving the country's worst road system so that farmers could better get their produce to market. Expediting transportation of farm products would allow increased access to markets and price advantage once at market. It would also break the dependence of the farmer on the railroad whose escalating freight costs, escalating to satisfy Eastern financial interests, were an anathema to the populist movement. Its promoters claimed that good roads "prolonged animals' lives . . . increased farmland values, and facilitated the substitution of more profitable crops" (15).

The goals of the good roads movement required first justifying and then activating federal involvement in supporting local roads. Southerners in particular had held that such federal involvement "usurped the rights of the states and violated the Constitution" but federal involvement became justified in "1896 when Congress inaugurated Rural Free Delivery (RFD) and began building a series of post roads to facilitate mail delivery" (Preston 19). This iniative was followed up "between December 1911 and July 1912 [when] some sixty good roads bills were introduced in Congress" (36). Advocates of the shift argued that, "since farmers were 'the producers of the food products and many of the raw materials upon which the world lives and grows fat in body and finance,' it was the moral duty of Congress to shift the burden of paying for road improvements off the backs of farmers" (33).

This phase of the good roads movement, however, failed to garner support for a curious reason. Southern states had a system of tax exemptions for road upkeep whereby a farmer would contribute to maintenance and improvement of roads by working on them himself a certain number of days. Mississippi's statute read, "All male persons over eighteen and under fifty, unless exempt by law, shall be required annually to perform not to exceed ten days of work on the public roads" (quoted in Preston 20). A good deal for tax-hating populists, a deal enhanced by taking full advantage of both the exemption and the provision that work not exceed ten days! Preston recounts from an 1889 article in *Scribner's Magazine* "a typical day working on the roads":

Arriving on the ground long after the usual time of beginning work, the road-makers proceeded to discuss the general questions of road-making and other matters of public concern, until slow-acting conscience convinces them that they should be about their task. They then with much deliberation take the mud out of the road-side ditches, if, indeed, the way is ditched at all, and plaster the same on the center of the road. A plough is brought into requisition, which destroys the best part of the road, that which is partly grassed and bushgrown, and the soft mass is heaped up to the central parts of the way. . . . An hour or two is consumed at noon-day lunch and further discussion of public and private matters. A little work is done in the afternoon, and at the end of the day the road making is abandoned until next year. (quoted 21–22)

Preston's account gives credibility to Uncle Billy's claim that he doesn't know "ere a man who has touched hammer to [the bridge]," a situation that has persisted for twenty-five years. Preston's account gives credibility to Uncle Billy's memory. When Anse complains about paying taxes for the road by his house, he may be regretting the loss of a previous exemption and echoing the sentiments expressed by a Moore County, North Carolina, farmer: "The road over which I travel is good enough for me. . . . Why should I vote to tax myself to help others?" (Preston 24–25).

Preston notes that a second phase of the good roads movement was more effective, though in this phase emphasis had shifted from rural roads for the benefit of farmers to tourist routes for the benefit of towns. The second phase attracted as its apostles "middle class executives, politicians, and land developers, chamber of commerce members, bank presidents, sales representatives, real estate agents, and trade board members" (41). The railroad participated, advocating roads as an extension of the rails. These advocates redefined progress in terms of "wealth and commercial and industrial achievements and not the accessibility of farmers to markets" (5). It is no wonder then that farmers, who "did not like having their needs made subordinate to those of urban merchants" now "felt abandoned by the good roads movement and its new leadership" (64). And this sense of betrayal was occasioned not only by the shift from rural road improvement to building tourist highways but by the consequent shift from wagons to cars. Preston notes, "Unlike midwesterners, farmers in the South . . . disliked and distrusted the noisy, citified automobiles that frightened their livestock, tore up their dirt roads, and sometimes damaged their property" (48).

The awareness that market advantage for farmers had yielded to tourist advantage for commercial interests, that wagon had yielded to car, accounts for the emphasis in Darl's account of the Bundrens' arrival in Jefferson, "passing the signs for sometime now: the drug stores, the clothing stores, the patent medicine and the garages and cafés" (209) on streets "where cars go back and forth" (214). The identification of billboards and automobiles with Jefferson links the farmers' distrust in roads to the deeper sense of the difference between townsfolk and country folk, contributing to the system of class distinctions which belittle the Bundrens and limit their prospects.

The principal embodiment of the farmers' disillusionment is seen in the conditions of roads, bridges, and fords described in the novel. Sometime between 1888 and 1905, improvements came to the roads around the Bundrens accompanied by the expense of taxation for their improvement. The promised benefits had never been realized, a failure for which farmers were not to blame but in which they had been complicit. As for their own mobility, bridges, once new but later in disrepair, succeeded in diminishing the once usable fords, so that during rainy seasons when the bridges were down, crossing the river was possible only on horseback and then as an act of courage. Road taxes, assessed to already marginal farmers, had only served to advantage the commercial interests of the towns, further distancing the farmer by placing him, as country person, in an even more inferior position to townsfolk.

In the novel, the road, therefore, stands for the material culture which disadvantages the farmers and constitutes a national betrayal of the final pioneers, those of the farming frontier. Appropriately, it is the impassability of the roads, the impossibility of finding and using the fords, and the decrepit conditions of the bridges which continually thwart the Bundren's journey. The road motif and the nine days of false starts and delays in the Bundren journey stand for all those forces which exploit and degrade people, just as surely as do all the events which delay Odysseus' journey and extend it to nine years. Both show how sorely we are tested—whether by a sea lane as in *The Odyssey* or by a country path as in *As I Lay Dying*—when the road becomes inimical to the journey, both actually and metaphorically. And in *As I Lay Dying*, as in *The Odyssey*, the thwarted journey becomes an emblem of all that keeps us from finding home, keeps us coming and going, and prevents us from turning space into place. Knowing something about roads as features of material culture makes it more possible for us to feel Pa's "ultimate outrage" (68) and say with him, "Durn that road." And we might recognize with him, however intuitively, that the conditions of life, symbolized in the journey, cannot be escaped in the epic of life where the way forward is never around but only through.

2. The House and Its Progeny

Faulkner's road metaphor invites us into an inspection of the brutal conditions of life for the marginal farmer, an inspection which contextualizes the Bundrens in America's history; it is this dimension of the novel which allows John Matthews to call *As I Lay Dying*, in an adaptation of Vardaman's phrase, "a book that continues to hurt the heart" (94). But a second cluster of images invites us to see what transcends those circumstances, what makes it possible for the Bundrens to go through their obstacles, sustain their journey, even if they are unsuccessful or only partly successful in capturing its spirit or achieving its ends. It is in this second cluster of images that the novel will, in T. W. Adorno's terms, "slough off a repressive, external-empirical mode of experiencing the world" (6).[9]

Here the material is so rich and the commentary so plentiful our discussion can focus on two elements of the extended metaphor, beginning first with possibly the most obvious and memorable feature of the novel, Vardaman's line/chapter, "My mother is a fish" (74). Faulkner places this line for dramatic irony between Cash's notorious version of "thirteen ways of looking at a blackbird," his explanation of why he is building the coffin as he is, and Tull's "mutability canto," his account of Addie's funeral. After this, the line is repeated or recast four more times (89, 137, 180, 182). In his important study, Joseph Urgo proposes that "one's role in the drama of meaning is largely determined by one's mastery of the use of the figurative. . . . True understanding, the kind of understanding that teaches and communicates, is achieved through figuration." On this basis, he extols "the triumph of Vardaman's emblematic 'My mother is a fish.'" Granting that, like all young boys, Vardaman can be obtuse, he nevertheless rescues Vardaman from his usual oblivion by pointing out that "Vardaman . . . emerges as the author-figure in the novel."[10]

The depth of Vardaman's wisdom can be seen in what is the likely source for Faulkner's construction of his phrase. Vardaman, concerned for what a technical jargon might term "the range of signification" of the concept of "mother," echoes a significant moment, recorded in all three synoptic gospels, where Jesus first questions, "Who is my mother? and who are my brethern?" and then, pointing to his followers, asserts that "whosoever shall do the will of my Father . . . the same is my brother, and sister, and mother."[11] Shocking as this must be to today's fundamentalists who claim that a Christian America teaches their narrow set of family values, it must have been even more shocking to Jesus' mother and brother and sister! Jesus is here portrayed as reformulating home and family, separating them from biology, kinship, and home economics and reconstituting them on a spiritual basis. It is not necessary to give Vardaman's phrase the same meaning in order to see that it performs a similar function, as is born out further by the novel's parallel extension of the question of who my mother is into its necessary corollary, who is my brother?, which Vardaman answers often, naming a member of the family as his brother, as in "Cash is my brother" (181 but see also 89). By extension, though again not presented as figures, each scene with neighbors Tull, Samson, or Armstid raises another question to which Jesus responds in a similar fashion, the question "who is my neighbor" (Luke 10:29). And parallel to these is the similar assertion about Jewel, "Jewel's mother is a horse" (84, 89, 181, 182, 195), which, although in my opinion untrue, nevertheless adds to the figurative exploration and creation of meaning that surrounds Addie's death and intertextualizes with the gospels. To these we would need to add Darl's assertions that he has no mother (89) and that "*Are* is too many for one woman to foal" (90).

Urgo is limiting his focus on the figurative to metaphors for the core experience of the novel when he claims Vardaman "is the only Bundren who has made the link between comprehension and the production of meaning" (21).[12] It is true, only Vardaman deals figuratively with Addie's actual being and death; but related issues, such as kinship, paternity, identity, and even God's incarnations in earthly forms, all receive figurative treatment, some in similes so extended as to become virtually metaphoric. The extended community of farmers is itself sustained by the figurative so that, while Vardaman may be the exemplar, he sees more because, as Eliot reminds us, he stands on others' shoulders.

These extensions of figuration which Vardaman brings to the forefront suggest, too, that we are amiss to deal only with one term of Vardaman's metaphor. Having looked at a source for the term *Mother* and the subject of kinship, we need to look as well at how Vardaman figures these as a fish. Christian connotations surrounding the fish further help connect this metaphor to its scriptural source. There is Christ's promise that he will make his followers fishers of men (Matthew 5:19) and the legend that the letters making up the Greek word "fish" also form an anagram for a simple creed. The presence of fish in the scriptural feeding stories which underlie the Eucharist (e.g., Matthew 14:17) are echoed in the story by Vardaman's sense of the fish that "tomorrow . . . will be cooked and et and she will be him and pa and Cash and Dewey Dell" (60), echoing the words of the Book of Common Prayer: "that we may evermore dwell in him, and he in us."[13]

Once again, however, Vardaman's fish is only the most noticeable instance of a larger animal motif whose figures penetrate *As I Lay Dying*. Beyond the horse, identified as we know with Jewel, Faulkner permeates his character portraits with animal imagery. Peabody describes husbands as "some trifling animal" and wives as being treated no better than "packhorses" (41); Pa's silhouette has an "owl-like quality" (45); and he looks to Dewey Dell "like right after the maul hits the steer and it no longer alive and dont yet know that it is dead" (55) and to Addie like "a tall bird hunched in the cold weather" (156). Vardaman looks to Tull "just like a drownded puppy" (63); Addie's children are referred to as foals (90); Cash's head turns "like an owl's" (95); Dewey Dell's breasts are generalized as "mammalian" (150); Pa rides up "hang-dog" (175); Addie's coffin seems to Darl like "a cubistic bug" (201); Cash looks to Darl like "one of these bull dogs" (218); and the new Mrs. Bundren is "duckshaped" (241). In addition, there are the cows in both the Bundren and the Gillespie barns as well as the one that clops into the square as Vardaman awaits Dewey Dell, sundry mules, and varying numbers of buzzards. The list is rounded out with Cora's eggs, which become fertilized in Darl's description of the sun as "a bloody egg" (35), and by Cash's inclusion of animal magnetism in his coffin check list.

While certain animals may have their own specific connotations, for instance the Freudian and Thoreauvian associations with Jewel's horse or the mythic sources for the cow in the square, for the most part significance here comes not from any particularity but from the accumulated power of the images, suggesting that somehow, some way the animal world offers a source for evaluating the human world.[14] In a novel with so many scriptural sources as well as religious concerns (these we will look at shortly), it would seem likely that this imagery overall and the purpose to which it is put would have a Biblical analog as well. Faulkner's likely source was Job 12:7, in keeping with other of the novel's allusions to Job.[15] Indeed the whole context surrounding Job 12:7 proves interesting to themes and motifs in *As I Lay Dying*. Verse 3, "But I have understanding as well as you; I am not inferior to you: yea, who knoweth not such things as these?," echoes in the feelings the Bundrens have toward townsfolk, as in Dewey Dell's "We are country people, not as good as town people" (54). How the neighbors talk about Anse as a laughing stock (here in a passage that frames the later depiction of Christ in his passion) is prompted by verse 4: "I am as one mocked of his neighbor, who calleth upon God, and he answereth him: the just upright *man is* laughed to scorn." Cash building the coffin by lantern light, scoffed at for doing so, and on his way to falling a second time, comes from verse 5: "He that is ready to slip with *his* feet *is as* a lamp despised in the thought of him that is at ease." Verse 6, "The tabernacles of robbers prosper, and they that provoke God are secure; into whose hand God bringeth *abundantly*," suggests how the road enhanced the prosperity of the town, where every Bundren is robbed of something. Verses 7 and 8, "But ask now the beasts, and they shall teach thee; and the fowls of the air, and they shall tell thee," are the source of the animal imagery, extended even here to land and fish. And Addie's testing of words and Anse's new teeth are both suggested in verse 11: "Doth not the ear try words? And the mouth taste his meat?" (Job 12:3–8, 11, italics in the original). The Job passage is too suggestive for readers to ignore the possible connection, but what might the complex images from Job mean? Verses 9 and 10 capture their import in the original: "Who knoweth not in all these that the hand of the Lord hath wrought this?" and "In whose hand *is* the soul of every living thing, and the breath of all mankind."

Thus we can see that a cluster of Biblical illusions undergirds the "mother and brethren" metaphor and its extension into animal images, with the suggestion that animals—mammal, fish, and bird—might constitute a kind of wisdom, a wisdom that transcends the Bundren's painful awareness of their situation, their inability to find an exit ramp off the road they're on. Moreover, taken in their accumulated power, the illusions invoke the sense these country folk continually express: that their lives are a work of the Lord, that his breath is the life of mankind, the soul of every living thing.[16]

3. Because "if there is a God what the hell is He for"? (14)

Many critics seem to assume that, except possibly for Addie's, any religious sentiments in *As I Lay Dying* are hypocritical, so it interesting that Faulkner didn't regard even Whitfield as hypocritical, saying instead that he was a victim of a convention by which he was forced to live (Gwynn 114). The novel does, of course, deal with hypocrisy. Indeed, from 1900 onward, in the intellectuals' revolt against the village, there was a growing sentiment against what was seen as, and often was, hypocrisy in American religious life, a hypocrisy the intellectuals attacked under the names of Puritanism, Victorian Morality, or Calvinism. The climate created by the attack was partially what brought about the movement of the New Woman and the sexual revolutions of the Gay Nineties and Roaring Twenties. In the attack on religious hypocrisy, those moments which American religion had seemingly sanctified—especially the gendered moments of Marriage, Birth, Motherhood—came to be considered shams.

Faulkner makes use of all this in his portrait of Addie, her experiences of marriage and childbearing, and her comments about her own marriage, children, and adultery. Her recognition that she "had been tricked by words older than Anse or love" (159) expresses an awareness of the sham of idealizing these moments; and her assertion that she "hid nothing . . . tried to deceive no one . . . would not have cared" (161) expresses her own refusal to be a hypocrite. She is an embodiment of the new sexual freedom and anti-Puritan feeling which were the grass roots version of the intellectuals' sentiments.[17] Yet it is important to recall that, however aware Faulkner may have been of the intellectual sentiments of his day, he often asserted himself as a writer by denying being an intellectual, a denial which almost certainly was meant to indicate that his roots were in the rural, parochial life of his South, a background which, as his own life and career became increasingly complicated, he seems to have grasped with renewed fervor.[18]

Faulkner's dual sympathies, both for the intellectuals' revolt and for the area they found revolting, influenced how hypocrisy, far from being ubiquitous, is sharply focused in the novel, first on the self-serving Cora, her lack of self-awareness and her ironic pontifications, and second, in what are often counted as the mixed-motives for the funeral journey. Vernon Tull's begrudging respect for Cora, however, might temper even our judgment of her and suggest that she is less hypocritical than inconsistent. And while there will be more said about the motives and spirit of the journey, the other religious sentiments expressed in the novel seem curiously free from hypocrisy.

The religious sentiments of Faulkner's characters do, however, present a piety plagued by doubt. Their mixed feelings are caused by the radical distance between life on the road and life in the house, between external economic demands on people barely better off than sharecroppers and internal religious beliefs and spiritual aspirations which have sustained them, somehow, between their suffering and their sins. The mixed feelings expressed in their religious views draw not so much from the widespread attack on hypocrisy as from another feature of the intellectuals' discontent. In what was perhaps the most influential work of its time, *America's Coming of Age*, Van Wyck Brooks wrote, "So it is that from the beginning we find two main currents in the American mind running side by side but rarely mingling—a current of overtones and a current of undertones—and both equally unsocial: on the one hand, the transcendental current originating in the piety of the Puritans, becoming a philosophy in Jonathan Edwards, passing through Emerson, producing the fastidious refinement and aloofness of the chief American writers, and resulting in the final unreality of most contemporary American culture; and on the other hand the current of catchpenny opportunism originating in the practical shifts of Puritan life, becoming a philosophy in Franklin, passing through the American humorists, and resulting in the atmosphere of our contemporary business community."[19] Brooks adds, and this sentence is telling for *As I Lay Dying*'s portraits of Darl and Jewel, that, "It is just here, at the moment of choice, that . . . there is nothing . . . but to lurch violently to the one extreme or the other . . . according as intellect or the sense of action preponderates" (13–14).

The era found a common trope for Brooks's dilemma in the hypothetical young men which populate its essays and fiction, young men sensitive but so divided as to want ballast, being blown to one expression or another of despair. Brooks, Randolph Bourne, and Joseph Wood Krutch were among those who created such portraits; and surely Darl and Jewel are Faulkner's embodiments of the type so prevalent in his day.[20] However, in others' accounts, this rarefied atmosphere of sensitive youth was characteristic only of young men. Faulkner extends the trope to the experience of women—Addie—and the collective experience of the country folk themselves, some of whom, in the Revolt of the Rednecks, became politicians the Faulkner family supported. And among them and in their religious utterances, Faulkner found a people whose ideals and realities, while horribly distanced from one another, were nevertheless tenaciously held together. Indeed, what characterizes their piety is this balancing act, the balance for which Cash continuously pleads.

A few representative passages show what is typical of the myriad of expressions of religious sentiments found in the novel. Leaving aside the obviously confused sentiments of Cora, these expressions are launched, as the title of this section indicates, by the reflections of Jewel which culminate in his exclamation, "if there is a God what the hell is He for"? (14). The question concludes a scene where Jewel puts himself in the place of God when Pa and Cash are injured. In God's place, Jewel would have let the two die, Pa so there would be no journey and Cash so there would not be "that goddamn adze going One lick less. One lick less and we could be quiet." Had Jewel been God, "It would just be me and her on a high hill" (14). This is the typical form taken by religious utterances in the novel: characters express varying degrees of acceptance of God coupled with questions about his wisdom or goodness in dealing with their situation, their problems, their suffering, but refusing withal to let go of God.

Following this pattern, Anse, in his turn, tells us, "Old Marster will care for me as for ere a sparrow that falls. But it seems hard that a man in his need could be so flouted by a road" (34). He echoes the sentiment when he says, "Eight miles of the sweat of his body washed up out outen the Lord's earth, where the Lord himself told him to put it" (97). Peabody tells us, "Too bad the Lord made the mistake of giving trees roots and giving the Anse Bundrens He makes feet and legs. If He'd just swapped them, there wouldn't ever be a worry about this country being deforested someday" (38). We hear the same pattern in Vardaman's "God made me. I did not said to God to made me in the country" (59). Tull puts his "trust in my God and my reward" but questions the holes bored into Addie's face: "If it's a judgment, it aint right. Because the Lord's got more to do than that. He's bound to have." Even more poignantly, Tull challenges,

"It aint right. I be durn if it is. Because He said Suffer little children to come unto Me dont make it right, neither" (66). The same pattern is voiced poetically in Dewey Dell's self-assurances, "I believe in God, God. God, I believe in God" (108).

In addition, there is that remarkable passage which for me still defies precise attribution, in which we hear what is apparently a "Carcassonne"-like dialog:

> *It's a fact. Washed clean outen the ground it will be. Seems like something is always happening to it.*
>
> *Course it does. That's why it's worth anything. If nothing didn't happen and everybody made a big crop, do you reckon it would be worth the raising?*
>
> *Well, I be durn if I like to see my work washed outen the ground, work I sweat over. It's a fact. A fellow wouldn't mind seeing it washed up if he could just turn on the rain himself. Who is that man can do that? Where is the color of his eyes?*
>
> *Ay. The Lord made it to grow. It's Hisn to wash up if He sees it fitten so.* (80–81)[21]

Even Cora qualifies her belief that "in my husband and children I have been more blessed than most" with the caveat, "trials though they have been." And it is Cora who, though she believes Heaven to be her great reward, calls it "the Great Unknown" (20).

The ordained Whitfield may believe that he "wrestled with Satan" (164), but these lay folk all see themselves as wrestling with God. In light of this struggle, when Anse truncates Job's phrase to its opening statement, "The Lord giveth" (26 for an instance), he is not trying to acknowledge God's giving while escaping his taking away. Rather, it would seem what Anse and others must assure themselves continually is that the Lord gives; all the evidence of their lives proves to them that he most assuredly takes away. Yet, assure themselves again and again they all do, balancing their experience of material decrease with spiritual increase, their losses with their rewards. Perhaps they could use a new god, one who encouraged them to take collective responsibility for the enhancement of their material lives. But what should they do in the meantime, while everything in their material environment conspires against that enhancement even as they are "doing the best we can" (189)?[22] Over against the way Van Wyck Brooks describes a division between values and practicalities in the American personality, these poor, mostly uneducated, certainly betrayed country folk have managed to keep the two balanced so that their personalities are defined by both. The material culture evoked by the road motif and the spiritual culture invoked by the motif of home and kinship, road and fish, frontier and family are held together through the piety of local speech. This is neither blind faith nor literalist belief; it becomes that only in one such as Cora, who unlike her neighbors is alienated from her own experience.[23] Indeed, Cora's insensitivity and Darl's and Jewel's oversensitivity are the extremes that frame the piety of the rest of this rural community, a piety that refuses to lose track either of its suffering or its salvation.

4. In the Balance

Such balance as their piety achieves is maintained in one other place, the funeral journey itself. Much has been written about the family's ulterior motives for this journey: Anse wants teeth, Dewey Dell an abortifacient (not so uncommon an expectation as Moseley would make us believe), Vardaman his red train. Of course these are, in fact, their desires; but the insistent force of these desires comes only from the reality which relentlessly presses in on them. We come upon them in sight of being reduced to sharecroppers: injured from falling off a roof (Cash), from being caught under a load of lumber (Anse), or from wearing, as a boy, bad shoes in wet conditions (Anse again); pregnant and unable to tell anyone about it (Dewey Dell); their cultivator and seeder given as chattel mortgage (176); taxed for road improvements that never materialize; feeding themselves on turnip greens; unable to achieve the American dream whether through frontiersmanship (Jewel), a work ethic (Cash), patriotic service (Darl), or education (Addie); all of them betrayed by both emotions and conventions, bereft of wife and mother; and (noting the title's diffuse application) all in some way dead—Darl killed by Dewey Dell, Anse by Addie, though she says, "He did not know he was dead" (160), Jewel as wooden as the coffin, Vardaman found sleeping like a dead steer, and Addie in her coffin. Pardon the pun, but none of this augurs well!

In the midst of hardship, such a showing of genuine concern for each other! Vardaman shows his love for Darl as he cries after burning the barn, Dewey Dell for Cash as he is dragged from the river and Jewel as he plunges into it, Darl for Vardaman as he tries to sort out his mother's dying, Pa, trying to smooth the quilt around his dying wife, Jewel recovering Cash's tools. These are, in Peabody's words, "what they mean by the love that passeth understanding" (41–42). Discounting the veterinarian, Billy Varner, the Bundrens' nearest source of medical care is Jefferson, also their nearest source for anything above subsistence, where commodities (from abortifacients to bananas, themselves only coming to be more common in the rural South of those times) beckon them. Yet to this same Jefferson they can only repair on rare occasion—their poverty makes it too costly, their roads make it too arduous. Perhaps they can be forgiven for thinking of teeth and trains, especially by those of us with ready access both to painless dentistry and to countless toys for all the girls and boys heaping up for endless garage sales. Most significantly, it is this journey which refuses to ignore either their obligation to Addie or their own physical and emotional needs, refuses to ignore the pressure exerted on them either by their poverty or by their promise. These are not heroes; neither are they villains. Rather, they express what Albert Murray calls the bedrock feeling of democracy, believing as they do, even against all evidence to the contrary, that they are as good as anyone.[24] The Bundren *world* is without hope; from it, there seems to be no exit, none of the formulas for escape in American jingoism promises escape from their births. But rich or poor, upwardly mobile or trapped, educated or ignorant, none of us can escape our births. That durn road and all that associates with it may well even represent Faulkner's own growing awareness, whether about race, class, or gender, that he could not escape that against which he struggled. But it also represents Faulkner's growing understanding that the struggle itself was enough, that where people persist in struggling, with both the basic realities of life and the basic concepts of American democracy, there, even if their world may be without hope, their *lives* are not.

The signboard for New Hope marks a cemetery. Going twice past that sign, the Bundrens and we learn it is not in escaping our circumstances, even the circumstance of our mortality, that we find hope; rather it is in the midst of death and all the lesser deaths and all their death-dealing conditions that hope can be found. As Faulkner balances real roads and figurative fish, the long-ways stretch of the journey and the up-and-down ways life of man, we are exposed repeatedly to a singular truth the Bundrens exhibit: there is more to life than the world. And sometimes it, too, is a-laying there right up to [our] door.

NOTES

1. Frederick L. Gwynn and Joseph L. Blotner, *Faulkner in the University: Class Conferences at the University of Virginia, 1957–1958* (New York: Vintage, 1965), 112. Subsequent references to this text are made parenthetically.

2. William Faulkner, *As I Lay Dying* (New York: Vintage, 1987), 235. Subsequent references to this text are made parenthetically.

3. Patrick O'Donnell, "Between the Family and the State: Nomadism and Authority in *As I Lay Dying*," *Faulkner Journal* 7:1/2 (Fall 1991–Spring 1992): 83–94.

4. Donald M. Kartiganer uses slightly different terms for his brilliant study of the narratology ("the game of narrative process" 293) of the novel: on the one hand the farm, the

vertical, the world of Being; on the other the journey, the horizontal, the world of Becoming. Through an examination of metaphor and metonymy, particularly as the shift from one to the other affects the set of mundane images (e.g., coffin, teeth, fish), he connects these two dimensions of the novel to a series of "theoretical dualisms that have come to dominate the way we think about modern and postmodern writing." He rightly notes of all the dualisms, especially of the "two complementary arenas of existence" in the novel, that "Each side of each set is an emphasis, not an isolated quality, an emphasis that seeps unmistakably into the other side, providing not only tension but resonance" (299). See "The Farm and the Journey: Ways of Mourning and Meaning in *As I Lay Dying*," *Mississippi Quarterly* 63,3 (Summer 1990): 281–303.

5. Tull evokes a physical image: shovels or perhaps a piece of farm equipment at work on what passes for a road. Addie evokes a spiritual activity in an emotional space. And quite pointedly, cleaning out, as in the road, is identified with a female, Addie Bundren. Vernon's kind of cleaning can be reported by two other men who have heard tell of it; Addie must tell us herself about an act, a choice, which no one else knows or even could know. Tull's act is part of a public world of stories which help form the minimal links connecting people; Addie's intent is part of a world of secrets which shape each character's aloneness and isolation. These differences raise questions of value whose answers are partially determined by whether our perspective is Tull's or Addie's. Both perspectives plunge us into paradox. In the world of economic forces whose dominance is constantly evoked in the novel, it would seem that houses (and for that matter, barns) come first; then a road is build connecting house to house. But the timber to build houses couldn't get out without a road in the first place. In the world of spiritual forces whose reality is also constantly evoked (even while its wisdom is constantly questioned) journeys and therefore roads have been the primary literary metaphor. But, if you will, they are metaphors for a metonymy, ways of talking about where we live, our "house" and all the scriptural parables where houses are metonyms for lives. Anse (yes, Anse!) is very clear that houses come first, that things of the house, spiritual beliefs, shape and move physical, economic, and social realities. However, his priority is called into question continually by a pervasive dissatisfaction with the human lot created by such realities. Thus, his questioning of God, his doubting of His wisdom, suggests that perhaps these poor, rural Mississippians might be better off if they toppled the old gods and made room for new ones, gods who would not so much expect them to suffer their lot as to shape their own economics destinies.

6. Some critics, such as Cleanth Brooks, have found the Bundrens heroic; others, like Diana York Blaine, have found in at least one or another, and even in Faulkner, a villainy as heinous as it is vivid. Cleanth Brooks, *William Faulkner: The Yoknapatawpha Country* (New Haven: Yale, 1963); Diana York Blaine, "The Abjection of Addie and Other Myths of the Maternal in *As I Lay Dying*," *Mississippi Quarterly* 47:3 (Summer 1994): 419–39.

7. Michael Millgate, *The Achievement of William Faulkner* (1966; Lincoln: University of Nebraska Press, 1978), 111.

8. Howard Lawrence Preston, *Dirt Roads to Dixie: Accessibility and Modernization in the South, 1885–1935* (Knoxville: University of Tennessee Press, 1991). Subsequent references are made parenthetically. Preston makes one other connection relevant to the novel when he cites John W. Abercrombie's contention that "Good roads and good schools are all but inseparable" (17). Significantly both Cora and Addie were teachers. The theme of modernization has been treated in John Matthews, "*As I Lay Dying* in the Machine Age," *boundary 2* 19:1 (Spring 1992): 69–94.

9. T. W. Adorno, *Aesthetic Theory*, trans. C. Lenhart (London: Routledge & Kegan Paul, 1972), 6. John Matthews uses Adorno extensively.

10. See Joseph R. Urgo, "William Faulkner and the Drama of Meaning: The Discovery of the Figurative in *As I Lay Dying*," *South Atlantic Review* 53:2 (May, 1988):14, 21, 12; this article later became part of his book, *Faulkner's Apocrypha* (University Press of Mississippi, 1989). Of the comparison of Vardaman and Faulkner, Urgo claims Vardaman "will insist, as Faulkner would insist from *As I Lay Dying* onward, that his figuration is real—as real an alternative as any to the literal, or to what often passes in fiction as realistic" (12).

11. Matthew's version reads this way:

While yet he talked to the people, behold, his mother and his brethren stood without, desiring to speak with him.

Then one said unto him, Behold, thy mother and thy brethren stand without, desiring to speak with thee.

But he answered and said unto him that told him, Who is my mother? and who are my brethern?

And he stretched forth his hand toward his disciples, and said, Behold, my mother and my brethren!

For whosoever shall do the will of my Father which is in heaven, the same is my brother, and sister, and mother. (12:46–50; see also Mark 3:31, Luke 8:19)

If Luke is considered the Ur-text, then possibly Vardaman's echoing phrase will be the Urgo-text. Darl's assertion that Jewel's mother is a horse, accepted by most critics, seems wrong to me. The horse is a male symbol. Jewel's maternity is not in question, nor is his relationship to his mother, which makes it unlikely that the horse was ever an Addie-substitute. It is his paternity that is problematic, and his purchase of the horse is portrayed more like a Freudian case of killing the father. Moreover, although this paper is not the place to deal with it, each of the Bundren youngsters mirrors facets of Faulkner himself, again bearing out Melville's contention that authors always reveal themselves in their narratives.

12. Though characters may be more or less adept at the figurative, it is pervasive in the novel, and need not apply only to verbal metaphors but to visual ones as well, e.g., Addie buried in her wedding dress. To whatever degree it is present in a given character, it performs the same sustaining and liberating function. For those who are students, let me suggest an area yet to receive adequate attention: the similes for eyes in *As I Lay Dying*, whose rich variety promises a useful study.

13. Book of Common Prayer (1928), 82. This would have been the book Faulkner used to worship with.

14. Doreen Fowler, "The Ravished Daughter: Eleusinian Mysteries in *The Sound and the Fury*," in Doreen Fowler and Ann J. Abadie, *Faulkner and Religion* (Jackson: University Press of Mississippi, 1991).

15. For instance Job 1:21 which both Peabody's reflections on the meaing of death (39, 42) and several of the responseries which begin, "The Lord giveth . . ." allude to.

16. Faulkner once said that in *The Old Man and the Sea* Hemingway had, "discovered . . . God": "God made the big fish that had to be caught, God made the old man that ad to catch the big fish, God made the shark that had to eat the fish, and God loved all of them" (Gwynn 147). Here, there was the river, there was the family and its journey, there was the log that *"surged up out of the water and stood for an instant upright upon that surging and heaving desolation like Christ"* (134)—and God loved them all; they were all, in the words of a Lindy Hearne song, precious in the eyes of Jesus.

17. The readiest sources regarding the intellectual revolt are Henry May, ed., "The Discontent of the Intellectuals: A Problem of the Twenties," *The Berkeley Series in American History* (Chicago: Rand McNally & Company, 1963); Harold Stearns, ed., *Civilization in the United States* (New York: Harcourt, Brace and Co., 1922); Frederick Lewis Allen, *Only Yesterday: An Informal History of the Nineteen-Twenties* (New York: Harper & Row, 1931); Warren I. Susman, "The Useless Past: American Intellectuals and the Frontier Thesis: 1910–1930," *Bucknell Review* 11 (March 1963): 1–19. Faulkner always pretended to be unaware of the work of the intellectual community, but recent investigation of his reading during the period leading up to *As I Lay Dying* suggests he had regular access to the journals in which they published. See Thomas L. McHaney's paper, "What Faulkner Read at the P.O." in *Faulkner at 100: Retrospect and Prospect* (Jackson: University Press of Mississippi, 2000), 180–87.

18. See Frederick R. Karl, *William Faulkner: American Writer* (New York: Wiedenfeld and Nicolson, 1989), 382–84.

19. Van Wyck Brooks, *America's Coming-of-Age* (Garden City, N.Y.: Doubleday and

Company, 1958). The title essay, however, was originally published in 1915; though there is not evidence Faulkner read it, we do know he had ready other of Brooks's works.

20. Brooks's account is referenced above; Bourne's appears in May, referenced above. Joseph Wood Krutch, *The Modern Temper* (New York: Harcourt, Brace and Company, 1929), 4–7.

21. For a careful study of some of these passages, especially of the Old Marster metastory, see Warwick Wadlington, *"As I Lay Dying": Stories Out of Stories* (New York: Twayne, 1991), especially chapter 7 where he discusses both "Old Marster" and the political leadership the Faulkners supported. Since the next to last utterance in the dialog echoes God in Job (see Job 38–41, especially 38: 26,34), it is possible that this is the medieval-like debate somewhat in the vein of "Carcassonne," here between a Cash- or Tull-like character on the one side and God on the other. It should be clear my concern here is not to evaluate the truth of falsity of their faith; after all, Tull's objection is based in part on misunderstanding how the word *suffer* is used in "Suffer the little children." I want only to demonstrate that these are people of faith and realism, that they hold in balance their impoverished and threatening material culture and their religious culture with its hopes and ideals.

22. I mean this question to reflect the similar issue Solzhenitsyn confronts in his chapter "Each Has His Own Interests" in *Cancer Ward*, which culminates in this dialog:

"What she suffers from is an underdevelopment of science," said Vadim. He had found himself a strong argument. "When science advances, all chickenhouses will be clean and decent."

"But until science advances you'll go on cracking three eggs into your frying pan every morning, will you?" said Shalubin. . . . "Wouldn't you like to work in a chickenhouse for a bit, while science advances?"

"He's not interested in that!" came the gruff voice of Kostoglotov. (383)

23. Note how Cora's interpretation of the log as "the hand of God" comes only at the expense of ignoring the log altogether: "Log, fiddlesticks" says Cora (literally ignoring the log in her own eye) and has in it none of the anguish in Darl's perception of the log as like Christ. Just as easily, she consoles herself for the loss of her eggs, "it's not like they cost me anything except the baking" (139, 134, 8). Anyone who "couldn't afford to use the eggs" herself (5), and yet counts her sweat, her baking for so little, lacks a serious grip on her own reality. Indeed, Cora's insensitivity and Darl's and Jewel's oversensitivity are the extremes which frame the piety of the rest of this rural community, a piety that refuses to lose track either of its suffering or its salvation.

24. Remarks to some of those assembled at Don and Lyn Kartiganer's, Oxford, Mississippi, after Murray addressed the 1997 Faulkner and Yoknapatawpha Conference.

Go Down, Moses: Faulkner's Interrogation of the American Dream

LINDA WAGNER-MARTIN

Faulkner had it too; it wasn't exclusively the province of the earnest Fitzgerald in *The Great Gatsby*, the detail-loving Lewis in *Babbitt*, or the ironic Hemingway in *The Sun Also Rises,* nor was it the sometimes sentimentalized icon of the American writers who have remained at the margins—Anzia Yezierska, Langston Hughes, Gertrude Stein, Ring Lardner, Nella Larsen and Zora Neale Hurston, Henry Roth. Early in the twentieth century, the American Dream was as real as Wall Street and Harlem, probably more real than William Carlos Williams's red wheelbarrow—an image which by 1940 was itself already nostalgic.

By 1940, too, the location of the American Dream was shifting and shifty; it was no longer to be found exclusively on Main Street or at the 42nd Parallel. The economic debacle of the Great Depression (always referred to during the 1930s as a "recession") had left more writers than Faulkner stunned, disbelieving, and ready to accept some lesser version of an earlier definition of both "dream" and economic "success." Diminished as it might have been amid the rubble of the depression and the storm clouds of the encroaching world war, the American Dream did maintain the integral component of possessorship to which Philip Weinstein refers when he describes the "collapse of the American dream of identity-as-property" in a Lockean sense.[1] Weinstein's focus then was on Faulkner's *The Sound and the Fury*, and his example was that neither Benjy nor Quentin Compson would ever be defined by their state of holding property; their stories were rather those of "interior dispossession."

Go Down, Moses gives us the same set of themes, of course. The most apparent fulcrum of the novel is Ike McCaslin's relinquishment of his property, a relinquishment that has prompted as much spilled ink as any other voluntary act in Faulkner's fiction.[2] I suggest that the reason Ike McCaslin has become such a conundrum, a character so prickly to readers' imaginations that he and his chosen dilemma could be said to dominate criticism of Faulkner's later work, is precisely because he acts to oppose the conventionally understood American Dream. For, in short, the American Dream is that of acquiring, of getting riches, and land, and social position, and a family that may lead to an eventual dynasty, to commmunity leadership, and to pride in self: kinds of possessions all.

This conventional American Dream is also inscribed with class- and race-marked values. Thinking of dynasties suggests more wealth—a greater level of acquisition—than most lower class or even middle class readers could imagine; it goes without saying that Lucas Beauchamp's $1000 bequest from Lucius Quintus McCaslin represents an enormity of riches, and that once seduced by the (white) McCaslin American Dream, Lucas finds himself an anomaly among blacks as well as most whites. Similarly, for a Native American reader, for example, the pride of individual possessionship germane to the American Dream of success might be unappealing. The Dream as we have usually accessed it also depends on heterosexuality: how else to procreate, how else to benefit from the legal code of primogeniture, the law that governed the conveyance of property?

In many respects, Ike McCaslin is an enigma because he has consciously shunned any fulfillment of the American Dream. Were Ike to have performed his expected role in acquiring the land that had been left to him, he—married, sexually able, intellectually competent—would have watched his life assume the shape of that of the well-off, white, landed Mississippian. By refusing his inheritance, Ike became both an oddity and a pariah. As Faulkner makes clear in the cameo scene of Ike's wife refusing him any further sex unless he takes his inheritance,[3] Ike's decision costs him all elements of his expected place, as well as, perhaps, his potency. Faulkner's creation of Ike's high-minded refusal made a shambles of the traditional plot for a success narrative.

It is, in part, this shambles of narrative form that has bothered many Faulkner readers. We know the story of Faulkner's own "mild" shock when he saw the jacket cover, *Go Down, Moses and Other Stories*—even though he had labored earnestly and well to form the early separate stories into a whole.[4] But in both Faulkner's first conception of the book, and in his later implementation of his plan, the central story is not the Ike McCaslin material, and only some of that relating to Lucas Beauchamp;[5] it is rather "Pantaloon in Black," the narrative of the great loss that strikes Rider and leaves him dumbfounded, able to conceptualize only death.

"Pantaloon in Black"

The enormity of this character's loss after he had seemed to *win* the American dream is so devastating that he creates the means of his own death as a result. I have been—most of us have been—intrigued with the positioning, and the power, of "Pantaloon in Black." Although it appeared not to fit, and critics quibbled—and continue to quibble[6]—about how or whether Rider was connected to the McCaslin lineage (the point being that he can be an admirable, perhaps more admirable, human being with*out* McCaslin blood), his story clearly was and is the most moving section of the novel.

Written early in 1940, almost immediately after the death of Caroline Barr (and the author's visible participation in her funeral, complete with eulogy—no matter how appropriate or inappropriate it may seem these fifty years later),[7] "Pantaloon in Black" moves back in time to the *commedia* figure of Faulkner's early poem sequence, and to a reprise of Harry Wilbourne's more restrained—but no less longing—grieving for Charlotte. Faulkner, true to a practice he followed throughout his writing life, is seeking a literary voice for his own bereavement—first, the loss of his romance with Meta Carpenter and its signification of passion, a passion that might have been capable of continuing;[8] second, the loss of what Judith Sensibar so convincingly calls "the power of the memory of interracial love, in the deeply conflicted and racially charged cultural terrain of his own Northern Mississippi,"[9] a power both originating and then figured in the death of Caroline Barr. Whether shaped as a screen image of a white mother, somewhat distantly beautiful, set against the persona of the warmly erotic black mother—or more simply as a desirable dark-skinned woman, Rider's great love is one Faulkner admits to understanding.

"Pantaloon in Black" is Faulkner's most eloquent evocation of human pain. Like Rider, the author's psyche walks a narrow line between sanity and madness, trapped into life by the very strength that has provided its former balance. In the case of Rider, the strength is physical, and Faulkner floods the narrative with images that describe that strength—strength used first creatively and then suicidally: "flinging the dirt with that effortless fury"; "handling himself at times out of the vanity of his own strength logs which ordinarily two men would have handled with canthooks"; "the man [Rider] moving almost as fast as a horse could have moved"; "rode the log down the incline, balanced erect upon it in short rapid backward-running steps"; "cast his cant-hook away as if it were a burnt match"; and then in the less literate vernacular, "throws the cot against the wall and comes and grabs holt of that steel barred door and rips it out of the wall, bricks hinges and all, and walks out of the cell toting the door over his head like it was a gauze window-screen."[10]

For Faulkner, the author as surrogate for the bereaved Rider, the strength is intellectual and emotional. It crumbles only during the bouts with drink, at the end of the worst of which Faulkner is allowed his return to a womblike regression.[11] But on a daily basis, month after month, year after year, tragedy after tragedy (and there were a great many tragedies in Faulkner's life),[12] William Faulkner, the oldest son, he who would have profited from the law of primogeniture, was condemned to be *responsible*. As he wrote in May of 1940, only a few months after sending the manuscript of "Pantaloon in Black" to his agent and less than four months after Caroline Barr's death, "Beginning at the age of thirty I, an artist, a sincere one and of the first class, who should be free even of his own economic responsibilities . . . began to become the sole, principal and partial support—food, shelter, heat, clothes, medicine, kotex, school fees, toilet paper and picture shows—of my mother, . . . brother and his wife and two sons, another brother's widow and child, a wife of my own, and two step children, my own child: I inherited my father's debts and his dependents, white and black."[13] Faulkner gives us the key here—"economic responsibilities." Oh, to be free of them. To be able to *be* a writer "of the first class," to be able to shut out the incorrigible details of the mundane dailiness of life, within not only one household—his own—but within those other households he felt rested on his tired shoulders as well.

"Pantaloon in Black" may well be a lament not only for a lost love, then, but for a lost life. There is a nostalgia in Faulkner's comment that suggests the days of the patron, the source of support allowing the artist, especially the artist "of the first class," to "be free even of his own economic responsibilities." Instead of freedom from those responsibilities, class, for Faulkner, brought a myriad of such obligations. As people of "a certain class," the Falkners/Faulkners lived a certain way, with a certain set of privileges: no matter what their real financial circumstances, they dressed and shopped so that the community thought they were well-off. (This is, of course, not only a Southern story; this is the life of the middle class, even before the days of credit card debt and personal bankruptcies, throughout the United States.) And it is a life the responsible son inherits—along with layers of debt—from his father, the tin coffee pot replacing the silver loving cup, coppers replacing the valuable gold coins,[14] the ill-equipped son left to cope with the aftermath of the vanished fortune.

As Faulkner was to write a few years later, in the Appendix to the reissue of *The Sound and the Fury*, and as he wrote in 1945 to Malcolm Cowley when he suggested that he use the "Jason" section of that novel in *The Portable Faulkner:* "That Jason is the new South too. I mean, he is the one Compson and Sartoris who met Snopes on his own ground and in a fashion held his own. Jason would have chopped up a Georgian Manse and sold it off in shotgun bungalows as quick as any man."[15] Faulkner's 1944 correspondence with Cowley reinforces this theme of economic struggle, telling him that he opens mail to "get the return postage stamps (if any)" and that he has accepted his working in Hollywood—"the salt mines"—six months each year. "I don't know when I will come East, I mean to New York. I would like to, but I never seem to have that much money anymore, as I try to save what I earn here to stay at home as long as possible on."[16]

By 1941, after the wearing years of the 1930s, when Faulkner was forced to plead with his publisher for enough money to have his electricity turned back on, not to mention a 1940 letter listing taxbills, living costs, insurance, etc.,[17] anger shapes the mood of at least some of his fiction. And this anger, like Rider's tragic behavior, has something to do with the failure of his work to achieve for him the American Dream. Who within his intimate culture has worked any harder? Who has taken the comparative abuse of that culture good-humoredly, or has at least stood that ridicule and abuse? When do the rewards start to come? Let me take a few minutes to read "Pantaloon in Black," the tale that (with parts of "The Fire and the Hearth") is the first-written segment of *Go Down, Moses*, as a tightly focused tragedy, the narrative of both Rider's great love and of his near-attainment of the evanescent American Dream.

What are the details Faulkner, as writer, foregrounds? In addition to Rider's immense physical strength, the reader learns about his simple yet enviably successful life. What Rider has: a successful marriage, complete with a fire on the hearth (134). A successful working life, as "head of the timber gang" (133). Successful economics: rent "paid promptly in advance" and enough left over so that "he [Rider] had refloored the porch and rebuilt and reroofed the kitchen . . . and bought the [kitchen] stove" (133). Faulkner emphasizes too the joy and surprise of the weekly Saturday love gift: "the first hour would not have passed noon when he would mount the steps and knock, not on post or doorframe but on the underside of the gallery roof itself, and enter and ring the bright cascade of silver dollars onto the scrubbed table in the kitchen where his dinner simmered on the stove and the galvanised tub of hot water and the baking powder can of soft soap and the towel made of scalded flour sacks sewn together and his clean overalls and shirt waited, and Mannie would gather up the money and walk the half-mile to the commissary and buy their next week's supplies and bank the rest of the money in Edmonds' safe and return and they would eat once again without haste or hurry after five days—the sidemeat, the greens, the cornbread, the buttermilk from the well-house, the cake which she baked every Saturday now that she had a stove to bake in." Rider's memory here is of the ritual of love, of the habits, the practices, of love—all stemming from the plenty of his earning ability, "the bright cascade of silver dollars" (134–35).

As the narrative proves, without that love and its rituals, he is literally without breath; Rider's hyperventilation punctures the shroud of grief that his society might have better understood. Just as we readers are swept through the classic three-day saga of his protagonist's bereavement, so does Faulkner make clear that in Rider the hero's tragic flaw is his capacity to be inordinately moved, rather than pacified or dulled, by his grief. Like a Shakespearian fool, or perhaps a Hamlet, Rider too loses his rational mind: he can't quit thinking, "just cant quit thinking" (154). Accordingly, like a true nobleman, at the grave scene he throws the spade "like a javelin" (132).

In this Aristotelian model, Rider buries Mannie (literally, himself buries her) on the morning of the first day, and then disappears into the woods, coming out only at dusk. Everyone else is at church, but that avenue does not attract him; his meditation has taken place alone. His experience is complete that evening when he sees the ghost of his beloved, walking in their home: he decides then that he must follow Mannie. Day two begins before sunrise, when he gets to work alone and early, ravenously eats the fireman's lunch as breakfast, handles the huge logs by himself, turns away from his uncle who brings a peach pie, leaves work, buys liquor, visits his aunt, and plays dice. There, at midnight between the second and the third day, Rider kills the crooked white overseer-dealer, and returns "home" where he is arrested as he sleeps in his back yard. With his aunt, he is jailed and after the melee of his destroying the cell, he is taken and eventually hanged by the overseer's relatives.

Parodic as this outline may seem, Faulkner intends no parody in this account of Spoot's [Rider's] reaction to his immense grief. The child of God-fearing people, who provide both spiritual and physical succor for him, Rider casts away the worldly success he has known during his brief twenty-four years: even his aunt and uncle cannot save him from himself. Lest we miss the tragedy, lest we miss the several ways Faulkner dignifies Rider's behavior, the author in a coda provides the sheriff deputy's misunderstanding analysis of the black man's behavior. Incomprehensible to the white man of law, Rider's willingness to give up his life (in order to both stifle his grief and rejoin Mannie), his willingness to opt out of the American Dream, is described by this observer as inhuman, as Rider's having no "normal human feelings" (150). Faulkner's irony makes clear his views about the shallowness of the judgments some whites make about some blacks, and returns the reader to the authorial comment at the burial scene, about the humble graves, "marked off without order about the barren plot by shards of pottery and broken bottles and old brick and other objects insignificant to sight but actually of a profound meaning and fatal to touch, which no white man could have read" (131–32).

"Go Down, Moses"

The structure of "Pantaloon in Black" is significant in part because it foreshadows that of the entire book, where the last section, the title story, gives the reader another view of white culture's misreading. Here the white leaders of this small-town Southern society are bemused if not embarrassed by the behavior of its black citizens. Set in motion by another sorrowful death, the plot of "Go Down, Moses" shows the grieving mixed-race Worsham "family" innocently getting the town to pay the costs of bringing home for burial Mollie Beauchamp's executed grandson, Samuel Worsham Beauchamp, alias "Butch" and, in Chicago, alias someone else, a name which remains unknown to us.

In this story Faulkner plays with the dichotomy between intellect and emotion, and uses levels of language to make clear the differences. Gavin Stevens here, like the character Gavin Stevens in Faulkner's detective stories, is a likable, well-intentioned bumbler—although he has a "thin, intelligent, unstable face," he has a Harvard doctorate and a Phi Beta Kappa key (353). Marked with the external trappings of success, Stevens explains the Worsham/Beauchamp situation to the rest of the town, taking on himself responsibility both moral and financial. Faulkner shows that, in effect, what Stevens does is complete an economic transaction—he provides funds for the return of Mollie's grandson, enacting the process of what Minrose Gwin calls his "paternalism."[18] Yet although Miss Worsham tells him the import of bringing "Butch" home, even though he hears from the start the impassioned refrain, "Roth Edmonds sold . . . him [Samuel Worsham Beauchamp] in Egypt," Stevens still misunderstands the act of returning the young man (353). Faulkner implies that Stevens would similarly misunderstand the concepts of "home," "kinship," and "family."

Stevens's logical and precise speech is always geared toward economics, but it is a mark of Faulkner's understanding of irony that Miss Worsham's comments are also economically based: "Mollie's and Hamp's parents belonged to my grandfather. Mollie and I were born in the same month. We grew up together as sisters would" (357). As slave owners, the Worshams profited from their holdings, no matter how sisterly Miss Worsham felt toward Mollie. Yet even as she tells Stevens that the deceased criminal was named after her father, even as she shows him how little race matters to her,[19] Stevens predictably fails to hear what her information means. He insists on coming to the house, to pay his respects and to share in their mourning. Shocked by the reappearance of the specter of slavery in their chanting refrain, "Roth Edmonds sold him . . . Sold my Benjamin," however, he bolts from the room, struggling to breathe.

As he does often in his fiction, Faulkner reminds the reader that the past is never past. Miss Worsham accepts Stevens's apology for coming and continues to serve as intermediary for the two races, saying simply, "It's our grief" (363).

Not only a racial matter—for Miss Worsham is as white as Stevens, and probably better placed by family position, the understanding that allows the comprehension of grief is born of unstudied, unlearned humanity. It is also born of human effort, for Miss Worsham, like Molly in "The Fire and the Hearth," has walked all the seventeen miles into town, carrying with her in small change and tattered bills the $25 she believes, hopes, will cover the "immediate expenses" (359). These formidable women, like Miss Worsham and Molly Beauchamp, that populate much of Faulkner's fiction stand at some variance with the view of Faulkner as misogynist. Perhaps the criticism that has attended Faulkner's creation of lovers and wives—romantic leads, so to speak—misses one set of issues. Here I quote Richard Gray, who warns us not to pay too much attention to "the complex issue of Faulkner's response to the women who inhabited his life and the images of womanhood they engendered. Women inhabited that life, certainly, but most of the time they inhabited its edges: nothing was more important to Faulkner than his work."[20] One might add to that proposal the suggestion that many of Faulkner's women characters might also stand as surrogates for the author and his own confused place in the world, which sometimes occasioned for him more than a little outright pain.

Observing Faulkner as he characterizes not only the older women in his fiction but also the way he works with women as daughters more generally shows a number of complex attitudes, most of them sympathetic to the roles women must play in a Western patriarchal system such as ours. I have written elsewhere of the stifling of Rosa Coldfield as daughter,[21] and the misuses of father power in not only *Absalom, Absalom!* but many of Faulkner's novels. Here, too, Lucas Beauchamp's daughter Nat, for all her intelligence and elan, ends her sleuthing, her tracking her father's adventures with various stills, by being stifled into a marriage—one that gives her neither a porch nor a stove. Faulkner's use of Nat in "The Fire and the Hearth" illustrates perfectly Levi-Strauss's paradigm of kinship systems, in nearly all of which "the exchangeable figure is the daughter" with the father—here, Lucas—in control of any exchange.[22]

Yet within *Go Down, Moses,* both novel and story, the plot dynamic turns on women characters' expressions of a kind of folk wisdom. At a basic level, Mollie is right that Roth Edmonds sold Butch—he at least turned him out—after he had broken into the commissary store; led by bigger dreams, far from family in Chicago, Butch lost his way. Even as Rider was protected by his kin (his aunt's presence within the jail cell might conceivably have saved his life), Butch had no one near to care about him. More centrally, in the novel *Go Down, Moses,* the never-expressed perspective of Lucius McCaslin's slave Eunice serves as the silenced—both repressed and absent—contextualizing story. Bereft of language, her behavior translated by others into subliterate expression in the elementary script of the commissary ledger, Eunice yet managed to serve notice on the white patriarchy that her days of servitude were over. Like Rider, Eunice willed her own death, and by it insisted that she would no longer accept her shattered life being defined—by others—as human. Her death announced to the world—if anyone could interpret her act—that her master had overstepped the bounds of even white male privilege.

In 1998, we think we are competent to read Eunice's silence. It is what Christine Froula terms "the hysterical cultural script: the cultural text that dictates to males and females alike the necessity of silencing women's speech when it threatens the father's power."[23] For Eunice, *her* daughter's betrayal by her father forced her renunciatory act, but ironically Eunice's suicide did not save Tomasina. It did not save anyone. In Faulkner's world, the daughter's power, like the mother's, is "suppressed and muted, while the father, his powers protected, makes culture and history in his own image."[24] This dilemma, then, of excavating the daughter's story and thereby breaking all known patriarchal rules is the reason nearly every essay about *Go Down, Moses* quotes Ike's halting reading of the commissary ledger. In it Faulkner creates the rationale for Ike McCaslin's renunciation of property—for, more valuable than the land he gives up, *Eunice* was property, and only that. Faulkner simultaneously presents the mind of the South beginning to come to terms with what possession meant. The revelation, cut away from the platitudes about economic and moral sanctions, is "withering," in Cleanth Brooks's terms.[25] But unlike Quentin Compson, who kills himself in disbelief that everything he has learned, everything his family has established as morality, is false, Ike makes active gestures to reclaim his vision of moral behavior. He searches for James and Fonsiba, Lucas's siblings; not understanding Fonsiba's paean to freedom, he pities her and arranges a small monthly payment. Then he publicly and, as Faulkner shows us, with great personal loss, gives up his land and with it his place in the world/community as he knows it. No version of the American Dream I know depends on being "uncle to half a county and still father to none" (286).

The power of Eunice's suicide reverberates through *Go Down, Moses*. The reader is prepared for it structurally, it seems to me, by the poignancy of Rider's story of his lost love. Despite an apparent but never purely comic opening (in both "Was" and "The Fire and the Hearth"), *Go Down, Moses* maintains a tragic tone throughout. Its tenor reflects Faulkner's own relentless worry about the direction the life of the South, like his own, was taking.

"The Fire and the Hearth"

My purpose in skirting the Eunice-Tomasina story, just as I have the Ike McCaslin narrative, is to draw from Faulkner's original schema for the novel. From the careful work of Joanne Creighton, James Early, Carol Clancey Harter, and Dirk Kuyk, Jr., among others,[26] we know that Faulkner began with "Pantaloon in Black," the segments of "The Fire and the Hearth," "Go Down, Moses," "The Old People," and "Delta Autumn," which he rewrote extensively once he had folded the five-part "The Bear" into the novel. So far as critics can tell, his early configuration for the book drew from "The Fire and the Hearth" and the Lucas Beauchamp charactrer; as he did later in *Intruder in the Dust,* he used the black Lucas as a focus of his interrogation of racist social opinion.

One of the most emphatic sections about the differences between black culture and white occurs in Faulkner's re-creation of Lucas's challenge to Zack Edmonds, his childhood "brother" in the way Mollie and Miss Worsham were "sisters," over his young wife, the same Molly. Even as the reader's attention is held by the meticulous description Faulkner provides, of Lucas realizing his rage over Zack's insult (which effectively destroyed Lucas's family unit in order that Molly would provide care for Edmonds's child), the author's language beats home the race theme. In the fifteen pertinent pages, Faulkner uses the locution "the white man" instead of Zack's name more than forty times.

> "Hah!" Lucas said. He flung the white man's left hand and arm away, striking the other backward from the bed as his own right hand wrenched free; he had the pistol in the same motion, springing up and back as the white man rose too, the bed between them. . . . He snapped the breech shut and faced the white man. Again the white man saw his eyes rush until there was neither cornea nor iris. *This is it,* the white man thought, with that rapid and even unamazed clarity, gathering himself as much as he dared. Lucas didn't seem to notice. *He can't even see me right now,* the white man thought. (55)

Word choice like this reminds the reader that Faulkner was first, and remained always, a poet, and his composing process shared much with romantic poetic frenzy. The origin of the language pattern above occurs during Lucas's plan for turning George Wilkins over to the law, some ten pages before the quoted scene. As Lucas laid his trap, he thought "The report would have to come from Edmonds, the white man, because to the sheriff Lucas was just another nigger" (43). What is most characteristic of Faulkner's irony here comes next: "and both the sheriff and Lucas knew it, although only one of them knew that to Lucas the sheriff was a redneck without any reason for pride in his forbears nor hope for it in his descendants" (43). Lucas as a proud McCaslin, regardless of the shade of pigmentation of his skin, provides a continuing narrative perspective throughout much of the novel.

As a proud man, Lucas stumbles on both that pride and on his vanity. Molly, in the scene above, calls him "fool" and despite Lucas's derogation of women (and of the clan Edmonds who are "woman-made" to their McCaslin lineage), the reader accepts Molly's view. But that Lucas is important is undeniable. What is most interesting in Faulkner's use of the Beauchamp figure is the fact that his sixty-seven-year-old black sharecropper has a number of traits in common with Ike McCaslin. Along with the unquenchable pride comes the surety of judgment. Neither character can believe he is liable either to being wrong or to being outsmarted. Whereas in several segments of the novel Isaac is old and therefore comes complete with veneration, Lucas—positioned in "The Fire and the Hearth" as young—is comparatively humorous. The disjunction between Lucas's own sense of self and society's view of him as an inferior black man ("an uppity nigger" as Zack suggests and the Clerk of Courts echoes, 124) provides the frame for the comedy. Being outsmarted by George Wilkins, being tricked by the planted gold piece, being ordered around by Roth Edmonds, Lucas evokes from us a grudging empathy, and a smile. He does so even in his statement to Roth, at the moment of decision about the divorce Molly wants from him, in his obsession with this purest form of the American Dream, the gold coin: "I'm a man. . . . I'm the man here. I'm the one to say in my house, like you and your paw and his paw were the ones to say in his" (116). Had we only heard these words, we might have thought their speaker was Ike McCaslin. Unilateral decisions, with no receptivity to anyone else's sense of justice or morality, mark the two McCaslin men's temerity. With the unnamed granddaughter of Tennie's Jim, we yearn to ask—of both of them—"Old man . . . have you lived so long and forgotten so much that you dont remember anything you ever knew or felt or even heard about love?" (346). In this woman's resistance to erasure, her scorn at Roth's attempt to not only silence but to disembody both her and their son, she defies both the patriarchy and the supposed limitations of her own race.

Lucas, too, understands relinquishment. Fired with his quest for gold, he rationally decides to change occupations: "he was a little sorry to give up farming. He had liked it; he approved of his fields and liked to work them, taking a solid pride in having good tools to use and using them well" (42). Lucas thinks of himself as a property owner as well as a businessman with a "regular clientele" for his liquor (35). He makes choices, and he also admits, at his age, that extraordinary effort leaves him weary. Perhaps most central of all to the characterizations of the two men is their priding themselves on being responsible. One of Lucas's endearing acts as he leaves to confront Zack Edmonds is exhuming the sack of gold and placing it in Molly's shoe. Should he die, or be hanged for Zack's death, he has provided for Molly. But then, Faulkner told us this too: "only Lucas was left, the baby, the last save himself of old Carothers' doomed and fatal blood which in the male derivation seemed to destroy all it touched" (280).

Faulkner's censure is much wider than its application to Ike and Lucas, however. Throughout *Go Down, Moses*, similarities among male characters abound. The scene above, when Ike echoes and passes on Roth's monosyllabic response and order to his beloved—"No"—shows the crass self-serving of the last generation of the Edmonds line (339, 341). Replicating the behavior of his great-grandfather, Roth Edmonds uses women, does, friends, and Uncle Ike with no regard for their feelings. In Ike's willingness to parrot Roth's cruel dismissal, the men are shown to be more like than unlike. In "The Fire and the Hearth," in the conflict scene we have already read, Zack Edmonds knows exactly why Lucas behaves as he does: Lucas and Zack are the same person. Like the understanding that exists between Lucas and George, to the detriment of the well-being of Nat, Lucas's daughter, the hunting camp friends in "Delta Autumn" are callous and impervious, finding only humor in the destruction of humane values—both female deer and human love. Recompense does not suffice. As the unnamed woman tells Uncle Ike, "That's just money" (341). So much for a conventional version of the American Dream.

The Readers of *Go Down, Moses*

One of our problems as readers of Faulkner, I think, has been that we are guilty of oversimplifying the biographical approach. Because Faulkner was the son of a family with a recognizable, and reasonably prestigious, ancestry—at least a storied one—a family of a certain class not to mention race, we read his sympathies and empathies from that limited perspective. In reality, William Faulkner repeatedly stood—or was forced to stand—very far from the center of any patriarchal design. If the Falkner family had not deteriorated to the extent of the Compsons in the 1929 *The Sound and the Fury*, it had at least lost enough ground to be a kind of model for that deterioration: recriminations, blame, crevices in the proud facade, almost desperate aspirations for the children. For *The Sound and the Fury* is, at its heart, about the kinds of pressures those foolish parental aspirations create for children, hungry-to-please children (and all children are hungry to please, especially first-borns like Billy Faulkner).

Never the apple of either of his parents' eyes, Faulkner by the time he was thirty and forced to take on a range of financial responsibilities for which he was—by both education and temperament—singularly *un*-suited, was then asked to move from the outside edge of the family structure to the center and, a bit like Jason Compson,[27] to do whatever he could to provide for the rotting family in the rotting house (or, worse, houses). The obvious theme of *Absalom, Absalom!*, and the less obvious one of both "Old Man" and "Wild Palms," given a particularly postmodern fillip in the latter, this being saddled with unwanted responsibility is another of the themes that threads together the *Go Down, Moses* "stories."

My suggestion here is that Faulkner has written about these themes before. Perhaps as Daniel Singal notes in his recent study, that *Go Down, Moses* has "a very different kind of tone" may be less a mark of the author's failing powers than it is a ramification of his attempt to reach readers so that they could not willingly misunderstand. Singal objects here to what he calls Faulkner's "moralistic pronouncements."[28] After more than twenty-five years of writing about essential issues in his own country, as well as his Yoknapatawpha, Faulkner may have thought that some sense of outrage—or at least clarity—was overdue. An analogy between the silencing of Eunice and the silencing of William Faulkner may not be amiss.

What do these comments mean for Faulkner readers? Just this. We tend to read his white characters in ways different from his black ones, even when he makes us question race and its ambivalences—as he does in *Light in August, Absalom, Absalom!*, and *Go Down, Moses.* We tend to read his male characters in ways different from his female ones, even when he shows us clearly the nobility and bravery of the latter. As readers, even today, we all too often reflect the American culture of Faulkner's times: we identify more easily with the white characters of a certain class and sensibility; we understand meeting conflict/adversity in gentlemanly (read *passive*) ways (we are Ike, not Rider, and most of all we are Quentin Compson); we identify with the paternalism that Gavin Stevens represents. Better located ourselves socially, economically, racially, we—like Stevens—will help our culture to "take care of things."

Go Down, Moses succeeds as a book because it does not allow us to be self-satisfied, knowing liberals. The Eunice-Tomasina story sticks in our consciousness, our life. I read this novel as Faulkner's most poignant, most revealing statement of what a man's life is forced to be like in

America. Faulkner's protagonist, however, does not fit the pattern. He cannot meet his lover's needs in Hollywood, or his wife's needs in Mississippi, or his daughter's needs anywhere. He watches the American Dream float by, and realizes what a sham it is. In his disillusion, he can only grieve for all the life that stands around him—and the people he sees that he admires most are black. No matter how whites want to explain and socialize their behavior, they do not have the power, or the understanding, to play that authoritative role. What is consistent is the black person's need to be a real person, with friends, rituals, beliefs, and love. Rider remains the hero of *Go Down, Moses,* because his personal authenticity is not diluted with the mongrelizing white blood that Lucas contends with every day of his life. In that key dialogue between Lucas and Zack Edmonds, when Lucas explains that he is driven by old Carothers McCaslin to avenge the insult to his male honor, he lays blame where most of us readers would try to find honor. As Faulkner knew so well, it is hard to escape our own boundaries of privilege, gender, and race. As he phrased it in *Go Down, Moses:* "I am what I am; I will be always what I was born and have always been" (286).

In this bitingly limiting admission, Faulkner's *Go Down, Moses* joins the great—and usually very strange, narratively—American literary works. As Lothar Hönnighausen claims, Faulkner's novels are like Melville's *Moby Dick* because of the author's "unorthodox blend of metaphoric ingenuity and richness reminiscent of metaphysical poetry."[29] Or, put so well by Terence Martin, "The swirling dialectic of *Go Down, Moses* reaches back to Adam, to Columbus, and to the American Civil War as Isaac McCaslin explores the implications of ownership and the exploitation of the wilderness in the Mississippi setting Faulkner knew so well. With immense range *Go Down, Moses* engages the turbulent issues of American history, alludes to the discovery of an already tainted promise in the New World, and appropriates the Biblical story of dispossession from Eden to its thematic purpose. Perhaps no other novel articulates the themes of American history so precisely."[30]

NOTES

1. Philip M. Weinstein, "Mister: The Drama of Black Manhood in Faulkner and Morrison" in *Faulkner and Gender*, ed. Donald M. Kartiganer and Ann J. Abadie (Jackson: University Press of Mississippi, 1996), 273–96; rpt. in his *What Else But Love? The Ordeal of Race in Faulkner and Morrison* (New York: Columbia University Press, 1996). Weinstein considers *Go Down, Moses* as well.

2. Among others, see Olga Vickery, *The Novels of William Faulkner* (Baton Rouge: Louisiana State University Press, 1964); Eric J. Sundquist, *Faulkner: The House Divided* (Baltimore: Johns Hopkins University Press, 1983); David L. Vanderwerken, *Faulkner's Literary Children: Patterns of Development* (New York: Peter Lang, 1997); Donald M. Karti-

ganer, *The Fragile Thread: The Meaning of Form in Faulkner's Novels* (Amherst: University of Massachusetts Press, 1979); James Early, *The Making of "Go Down, Moses"* (Dallas: Southern Methodist University Press, 1972); Thadious M. Davis, *Faulkner's "Negro": Art and the Southern Context* (Baton Rouge: Louisiana State University Press, 1983); Daniel J. Singal, *William Faulkner: The Making of a Modernist* (Chapel Hill: University of North Carolina Press, 1997); Paul S. Stein, "Ike McCaslin: Traumatized in a Hawthornian Wilderness," *Southern Literary Journal* 12 (Spring 1980): 65–82; Mick Gidley, "Sam Fathers's Fathers: Indians and the Idea of Inheritance," in *Critical Essays on William Faulkner: The McCaslin Family*, ed. Arthur F. Kinney (Boston: G. K. Hall, 1990), 121–31; Carol Clancey Harter, "The Winter of Ike McCaslin: Revisions and Irony in Faulkner's 'Delta Autumn,' "*Journal of Modern Literature* (1970–71): 209–25; David Walker, "Out of the Old Time: 'Was' and *Go Down, Moses*," *Journal of Narrative Technique* 9 (Winter 1979): 1–11; and especially Louis J. Rubin, Jr., "The Dixie Special: William Faulkner and the Southern Renaissance," in *Faulkner and the Southern Renaissance*, Faulkner and Yoknapatawpha, 1981, ed. Doreen Fowler and Ann J. Abadie (Jackson: University Press of Mississippi, 1982), 63–92, and Richard H. King, "Memory and Tradition," ibid., 138–57. As Terence Martin summarizes in "Telling the World Over Again: The Radical Dimension of American Fiction": Some critics see Ike McCaslin "as a lonely hero who seeks a private purity in the midst of a corrupt world"; to others, he is "one who flees to an impossible innocence to avoid the responsibilities of being human" (172) [*American Letters and Historical Consciousness*, ed. J. G. Kennedy and D. M. Fogel (Baton Rouge: Louisiana State University Press), 1988, 158–76].

3. William Faulkner, *Go Down, Moses* (New York: Vintage International, 1990), 298–301; hereafter cited in text.

4. William Faulkner, letter to Robert Haas, *Selected Letters of William Faulkner*, ed. Joseph Blotner (New York: Random House, 1977), 284.

5. See Joanne V. Creighton, *William Faulkner's Craft of Revision* (Detroit: Wayne State University Press, 1977); James Early, *The Making of "Go Down, Moses"*; Dirk Kuyk, Jr., *Threads Cable-Strong: William Faulkner's "Go Down, Moses"* (Lewisburg, Penn.: Bucknell University Press, 1983); Mark R. Hochberg, "The Unity of *Go Down, Moses*," *Tennessee Studies in Literature* 21 (1976): 58–65; Harbour Winn, "Lineage and the South: The Unity of Faulkner's *Go Down, Moses*," *Midwest Quarterly* 32 (Summer 1991): 453–73; and Michael Millgate, "William Faulkner: The Problem of Point of View," in *William Faulkner: Four Decades of Criticism*, ed. Linda Welshimer Wagner (East Lansing: Michigan State University Press, 1973), 179–91, and *Faulkner's Place* (Athens: University of Georgia Press, 1997).

6. See discussions above and also Cleanth Brooks, *William Faulkner: The Yoknapatawpha Country* (New Haven: Yale University Press, 1963), for whom the story is both "Wordsworthian" and reminiscent of Hemingway, 254–55; Karl F. Zender, *The Crossing of the Ways: William Faulkner, the South, and the Modern World* (New Brunswick, N.J.: Rutgers University Press, 1989); Richard Gray, *The Life of William Faulkner: A Critical Biography* (Oxford: Blackwell, 1994); Noel Polk, *Children of the Dark House, Text and Context in Faulkner* (Jackson: University Press of Mississippi, 1996), and Linda Wagner-Martin, ed., *New Essays on "Go Down, Moses"* (New York: Cambridge University Press, 1996).

7. See Judith L. Sensibar, "Who Wears the Mask? Memory, Desire, and Race in *Go Down, Moses*," in Wagner-Martin, *New Essays*, 101–27; for a less specific consideration, see Deborah Clarke, *Robbing the Mother: Women in Faulkner* (Jackson: University Press of Mississippi, 1994).

8. See Gray, *Life of William Faulkner*; Joseph Blotner, *Faulkner: A Biography* (New York: Random House, 1984); David Minter, *William Faulkner: His Life and Work* (Baltimore: Johns Hopkins University Press, 1980); and Meta Carpenter Wilde and Orin Borsten, *A Loving Gentleman: The Love Story of William Faulkner and Meta Carpenter* (New York: Simon & Schuster, 1976).

9. Judith Sensibar, "Who Wears the Mask? Memory, Desire, and Race in *Go Down, Moses*," *New Essays*, 101–27.

10. Page numbers for the excerpts from *Go Down, Moses* are given here rather than in the text: 131, 133–34, 138, 140, 141, and 153 (in the sheriff deputy's vernacular).

11. While a number of biographers have dealt with the issue of Faulkner's alcoholism, and see Noel Polk's *Children of the Dark House* and Judith Sensibar's "William Faulkner, Poet to Novelist: An Imposter Becomes an Artist" in *Psychoanalytic Studies of Biography,* ed. George Moraitis and George H. Pollock (Madison, Conn.: International Universities Press, 1987), 305–35, none has so relied on assessments of the effects of that alcoholism to interpret Faulkner's writing as Daniel J. Singal in *William Faulkner: The Making of a Modernist.*

12. See above, particularly the two-volume Joseph Blotner biography as well as biographies by David Minter, Frederick A. Karl, and Richard Gray; see also Minrose C. Gwin, *The Feminine and Faulkner: Reading (Beyond) Sexual Difference* (Knoxville: University of Tennessee Press, 1990).

13. Quoted in Joseph Blotner, *Faulkner: A Biography* (1984), 417.

14. *Go Down, Moses*, 287; of interest here is Minrose Gwin's essay, "(Re)Reading Faulkner as Father and Daughter of His Own Text," *Refiguring the Father, New Feminist Readings of Patriarchy*, ed. Patricia Yaeger and Beth Kowaleski-Wallace (Carbondale: Southern Illinois University Press, 1989), 238–58.

15. William Faulkner to Malcolm Cowley, August 16, 1945, in Cowley's *The Faulkner-Cowley File, Letters and Memories, 1944–1962* (New York: Viking, 1966), 15.

16. Ibid., William Faulkner to Malcolm Cowley, May 7, 1944, 7.

17. *Selected Letters of William Faulkner*, ed. Joseph Blotner (New York: Random House, 1977); William Faulkner to Harold Ober, January 18, 1941, 138–39; see also Faulkner to Robert K. Haas, June 1, 1940 (*Letters,* 126–29). The situation was hardly new: as he had written Morton Goldman sometime in April of 1935, "$1000.00 is least that would help me. What I really need is $10,000.00. With that I could pay my debts and insurance for two years and really write. I mean, write. The man who said that the pinch of necessity, butchers and grocers bills and insurance hanging over his head, is good for an artist is a damned fool" (91); in a late July letter to Goldman, he fears bankruptcy (92). And in 1941, to Harold Ober, a letter received November 10, "Please sell it ["The Bear"] for something as soon as you can. I am in a situation where I will take almost anything for it or almost anything else I have or can write" (144). In this personal context, Richard Godden's 1997 book, *Fictions of Labor: William Faulkner and the South's Long Revolution* (Cambridge: Cambridge University Press) seems strangely ironic.

18. Minrose C. Gwin, "Her Shape, His Hand: The Spaces of African American Women in *Go Down, Moses*," *New Essays on "Go Down, Moses"* (1996), 73–100; 81. Gwin's comments are in alignment with Susan V. Donaldson's reading of the work as master narrative, "Contending Narratives: *Go Down, Moses* and the Short Story Cycle," *Faulkner and the Short Story*, ed. Evans Harrington and Ann J. Abadie (Jackson: University Press of Mississippi, 1992), 128–48.

19. Among the excellent criticism that focuses upon race in *Go Down, Moses* is Eric J. Sundquist, *Faulkner: The House Divided* (Baltimore: Johns Hopkins University Press, 1983); Philip M. Weinstein, *Faulkner's Subject: A Cosmos No One Knows* (New York: Cambridge University Press, 1992); Richard C. Moreland, *Faulkner and Modernism: Rereading and Rewriting* (Madison: University of Wisconsin Press, 1990); John T. Matthews, "Touching Race in *Go Down, Moses*," *New Essays on "Go Down, Moses"* (1996), 21–47; John Carlos Rowe, "The African-American Voice in Faulkner's *Go Down, Moses*," *Modern American Short Story Sequences*, ed. J. Gerald Kennedy (New York: Cambridge University Press, 1995), 76–97; Thadious M. Davis, "The Game of Courts: *Go Down, Moses*, Arbitrary Legalities, and Compensatory Boundaries," *New Essays on "Go Down, Moses"* (1996), 129–54 as well as her *Faulkner's "Negro": Art and the Southern Context* (1983). Note also Frederick Karl's comment that *Go Down, Moses* evinces "a new turn in Faulkner's thinking about race . . . the linkage of race by way of Molly" (*William Faulkner: American Writer*, 654); see following note for criticism that chronicles issues of Faulkner's characterization of women.

20. Richard Gray, *The Life of William Faulkner: A Critical Biography* (1994), 76. See in

particular the work of Minrose Gwin and Elisabeth Muhlenfeld, "The Distaff Side: Women of *Go Down, Moses*," in *Critical Essays on William Faulkner: The McCaslin Family*, 198–211, Diane Roberts, *Faulkner and Southern Womanhood* (Athens: University of Georgia Press, 1994), Deborah Clarke, *Robbing the Mother: Women in Faulkner*, and essays by Davis, Gwin, and Sensibar in *New Essays on "Go Down, Moses."*

21. Linda Wagner-Martin, "Rosa Coldfield as Daughter: Another of Faulkner's Lost Children," *Studies in American Fiction* 19:1 (Spring 1991): 1–13; see also Noel Polk, *Children of the Dark House*.

22. Lynda E. Boose, introduction to *Daughters and Fathers*, ed. Boose and Betty S. Flowers (Baltimore: Johns Hopkins University Press, 1989), 19.

23. Christine Froula, "The Daughter's Seduction: Sexual Violence and Literary History," *Daughters and Fathers*, 111–35; here, 112.

24. Ibid. And see Wesley and Barbara Alverson Morris's discussion of the racism in *Go Down, Moses* as "supplementations of the primal sin against the father. . . . Racism is a version of paternalism" (*Reading Faulkner*, Madison: University of Wisconsin Press, 1989), 231.

25. Cleanth Brooks, *William Faulkner: The Yoknapatawpha Country* (New Haven: Yale University Press, 1963), 248.

26. Joanne V. Creighton, *William Faulkner's Craft of Revision* (1977); James Early, *The Making of Go Down, Moses* (1972); Carol Clancey Harter, "The Winter of Ike McCaslin: Revisions and Irony in Faulkner's 'Delta Autumn,'" *Journal of Modern Literature* (1970–71), and Dirk Kuyk, Jr., *Threads Cable–Strong* (1983).

27. Linda W. Wagner, "Jason Compson: The Demands of Honor," *Sewanee Review* 79:4 (Winter 1971): 554–75; see also my *Hemingway and Faulkner: inventors/masters* (Metuchen, N.J.: Scarecrow Press, 1975).

28. Daniel J. Singal, *William Faulkner: The Making of a Modernist*, 256.

29. Lothar Hönninghausen, *William Faulkner: The Art of Stylization in His Early Graphic and Literary Work*, 184.

30. Terence Martin, "Telling the World Over Again: The Radical Dimension of American Fiction," *American Letters and Historical Consciousness*, 171.

Our Land, Our Country: Faulkner, the South, and the American Way of Life

CHARLES REAGAN WILSON

Our text is Faulkner 1955. In his essay "On Privacy: The American Dream: What Happened to It?," Faulkner complained of the invasion of his privacy by a writer who penned a story on him against his wishes. He blamed corporate America: the magazine company, not the writer, was at fault. This experience led Faulkner to speculate on the decline of individual liberty in a world increasingly dominated by "powerful federations and organizations and amalgamations like publishing corporations and religious sects and political parties and legislative committees," which use "such catch-phrases as 'Freedom' and 'Salvation' and 'Security' and 'Democracy' " to delude the public. The ultimate danger was mass conformity and the intimidation that went with it. He feared that someday anyone who was individualist enough to want privacy "even to change his shirt or bathe in, will be cursed by one universal American voice as subversive to the American way of life and the American flag." He had a wonderful description of the voice of public conformity: "that furious blast, that force, that power rearing like a thunder-clap into the American zenith, multiple-faced yet mutually conjunctived, bellowing the words and phrases which we have long since emasculated of any significance or meaning other than as tools, implements, for the further harrassment of the private individual human spirit, by their furious and immunised high priests: 'Security'. 'Subversion'. 'Anti-Communism'. 'Christianity'. 'Prosperity'. 'The American Way of Life'. 'The Flag'."[1]

Faulkner's 1955 essay is a telling commentary on American culture of the 1950s, a time of the organizational society, the man in the gray flannel suit, McCarthyism, and pietistic patriotism. His overt use of the term "American Way of Life" is also most appropriate, as Americans used the term often in the decade to reify an ideology of the United States that would define what this country represented on the cultural front of the Cold War with the Soviet Union. If the Soviets had Communism, we had the American Way.

The term "American Way of Life" is a useful one in providing a structured way to investigate an aspect of Faulkner's understanding of America. Public interest in an "American Way" rose simultaneously with the beginning of Faulkner's most creative years in the 1930s and lasted into the 1950s, when he was reflecting most explicitly in public statements about contemporary issues of American culture. I want to place Faulkner's attitude toward America in the context of the history of the terms American Way of Life and a variant of it, the Southern Way of Life. Faulkner, of course, inherited this latter term as well and understanding its meanings can also help us appreciate Faulkner's efforts to relate his little postage stamp of native soil to broader regional and national issues. I want to position him, then, in terms of these concepts, and also in relation to the term the "American Dream," which he used in two key essays in the 1950s. This essay is a study of Faulkner the intellectual and his views at a particular moment in time.

Mitford M. Mathews, in the *Dictionary of Americanisms* (1951), identified the earliest use of the term "American Way" in 1885, when a magazine writer observed: "To use an expression made popular, we believe, by General Hawley some years ago in regard to a very different question, dynamiting is 'not the American way!' " It is good to know that blowing up things was not seen as peculiarly American in 1885, but Mathews's other references suggest that the term did not come into popular use until the 1930s and 1940s. The term appeared in at least four titles in those years. It served as the title, for example, of a Kaufman and Hart theatrical play about an immigrant family, and the play ended with a patriotic flourish. The phrase "American Dream," which Faulkner used as the subtitle in his 1955 essay, also came into widespread use during the Depression. The American Way and the American Dream suggested something about the collective nature of the people of the United States, something abiding in their culture.[2]

These terms surely grew out of a related term, Americanism, which was in vogue in the early twentieth century. The new order that emerged from Progressive era modernization and the pressures toward conformity and idealism during World War I were institutionalized by the ideology of Americanism, which, according to historian Warren Susman, "replaced the older Protestant ethic as an ideological foundation of corporate capitalism." In one sense, Americanism of the early twentieth century stood for industrialism. It might even be called *Fordimus*, to honor Henry Ford, the saint of mass production. Rationality, order, science, respect for productivity, efficiency, discipline, work, planning, organization, and bureaucracy—these were the values of Americanism associated with the modern way and represented by the United States in the 1920s. But

Americanism was more than that. It also represented an embrace of mass culture, another form of modernity in this period. The manipulation of public opinion through advertising and the measurement of public opinion through polling brought attention to the outlook of the masses more than ever before, at the time when consumer culture was emerging as a new stage of capitalism. Technological developments such as the photograph, the radio, and the motion picture created the potential to influence and shape a conformist society as never before. Americanism was an idealistic statement of the American version of modernity, expressed with a moralistic tone that traced back to the Puritans.[3]

The Depression era, then, inherited the idea of Americanism and its values of industrial order, mass culture, consumer capitalism, and moralistic idealism. As Susman has noted, the 1930s saw an "effort to find, characterize, and adapt to an American way of life as distinguished from the material achievements (and the failures) of an American industrial civilization." The economic catastrophe of the decade promoted a stress on cultural homogeneity among middle-class Americans. "Amid the psychic ravages of the Great Depression," writes historian Jackson Lears, "widespread longings for a secure sense of identity led to a quest for a sense of belonging in some comforting collective whole," and the term American Way captured this aspiration. In the 1930s, Americans were less inclined than in the Progressive era to identify their way simply with industrialism. Instead, democracy emerged as the central concept. At a 1939 forum entitled "Can We Depend Upon Youth to Follow the American Way," for example, moderator George V. Denny Jr. commented on the term: "I take it that by that phrase we mean the democratic way—the idea of 'giving everybody a chance to share in making the rules.' " The Depression era rediscovered an America rooted in democracy and in the nation's history, symbolized by filiopietistic biographies such as Carl Sandburg's Lincoln and Douglas Southall Freeman's Lee, the New Deal's cultural programs that documented the lives of the poor and brought American culture to communities of all sorts, and the enormous popularity of historical sagas of the past such as Margaret Mitchell's novel *Gone with the Wind* (1936) and the 1939 film made from her book. The key term in describing the American Way in the 1930s, democracy, often implied a call to social action, as the nation rallied to fight the chaos of economic disaster but also reasserted the need to reform its democracy in a world where Americans faced competition with fascists, socialists, and communists.[4]

World War II reinforced the idea of a peculiarly American national culture that all could affirm. In this time of challenge and trial for American society, the American Way validated a belief in the homogeneity of the American people and in the social ideals of conformity and consensus. Commentators on the American Way emphasized cultural issues such as lifestyles, patterns of belief and behavior, and the distinctive values and attitudes that represented the traits of a special people. The Cold War further reinforced the belief in a unitary American culture that could serve as a counterweight to Communism. The era's ideologists adapted the traditional belief system associated with middle-class Americans—including a commitment to individualism, democratic rights, and private enterprise. Faith emerged as an even more central concept than before. Since materialism was the distinctive philosophical component of the Soviet enemy, Americans elevated respect for religion to a new position of authoritativeness, even in a seemingly secularized society. But in 1950s America religion itself became a part of the capitalist economy, through the selling of religion. In 1954, the Ideal Toy Company marketed a doll with flexible knees that could be made to "kneel in a praying position," the company's response, it said, to "the resurgence of religious feeling and practice in America today."[5]

Frances FitzGerald's study of American school textbooks of this era found that "democracy," the central term of the American Way construction that had developed in the 1930s, had become simply a synonym by the 1950s for the status quo, in opposition to fascism and communism, rather than a call for social justice, as commentators in the 1930s used the term. The American Way appeared now as fixed and static, so entrenched, as historian Stephen Whitfield notes, that "it could not have been changed with a lug wrench."[6]

A leading student, and advocate, of the American Way of Life in the 1950s was religious sociologist Will Herberg. He wrote of it in 1955:

> The American Way of Life is, at bottom a spiritual structure, a structure of ideas and ideals, of aspirations and values, of beliefs and standards; it synthesizes all that commends itself to the American as the right, the good, and the true in actual life. It embraces such seemingly incongruous elements as sanitary plumbing and freedom of opportunity, Coca-Cola and an intense faith in education—all felt as moral questions relating to the proper way of life. The very expression 'way of life' points to its religious essence, for one's ultimate, over-all way of life is one's religion.[7]

Herberg argued for a civil religion that grew out of a shared folk culture and projected an idealism that provided unity amidst the conflicts of American life. His American Way was especially significant in reconciling religion and democracy. As he noted, the American Way, with its stress on a generalized acceptance of religious faith, rather than validating any one particular religious tradition, had enabled Catholics and Jews, as well as Protestants, to be accepted in American culture.

One more meaning of the term "way of life" was relevant in Faulkner's cultural background. Southerners of his generation appreciated the ideological meanings of the American Way. In the decades from 1930 to 1960, the South was surely moving closer to embracing its tenets. The challenges and turbulence of the Depression, World War II, and the Cold War did work to nurture a sense of American unity that affected the South as well as other places in the nation, and economic development and changes in transportation and communication surely contributed to the Americanization of Dixie. But the South had its own sense of regional identity as well, created by the cultural elite in the early nineteenth century during the sectional crisis and perpetuated for generations thereafter. Southerners and Americans in general used the term "Southern civilization" in that era to represent the South with images of a hierarchical, paternalistic, racially conscious society, a familiar mythic place of Cavaliers and their ladies.[8]

Although the idea of a regionally distinctive Southern life goes back into the nineteenth century, writers did not generally use the term "Southern Way of Life" until *I'll Take My Stand* (1930), or at least that is the earliest I have found after sustained searching. In the introductory "Statement of Principles," the Twelve Agrarians noted that all the essays in their symposium tended "to support a Southern way of life against what may be called the American or prevailing way," and they insisted "that the best terms in which to represent the distinction are contained in the phrase, Agrarian *versus* Industrial." I have found over a dozen uses of the term "way of life" in the book, reflecting the pervasiveness of the idea in their discourse, which drew a distinction between industrial civilization and agrarian culture. Genuine humanism, they insisted, "was deeply founded in the way of life itself—in its tables, chairs, portraits, festivals, laws, marriage customs." The unreconstructed Southerner, according to John Crowe Ransom, was the only American with a real sense of the past, persisting, he wrote, "in his regard for a certain terrain, a certain history, and a certain inherited way of living."[9] The Agrarians were passionate in dismissing the mass culture of the American Industrial Way, especially for its effect on art. Donald Davidson had much fun in sketching the evil scene. "The industrialists in art . . . will naturally make their appeal to the lowest common denominator. They know the technique of mass-production, which, if applied to the arts, must invariably sacrifice quality to quantity." Thus, "the shop-girl does not recite Shakespeare before breakfast." Rather, "the shop-girl reads the comic strip with her bowl of patent cereal and puts on a jazz record while she rouges her lips. She reads the confession magazines and goes to the movies." Issues of humanism and the arts were driving forces in the Agrarian manifesto, which posited a Southern Way as nurturing those qualities of civilization far better than the American Way.[10]

If the Vanderbilt Twelve created an enduring argument for Agrarianism as the Southern Way, the 1950s saw a furious defense of racial segregation as the Southern Way. W. J. Cash's classic *Mind of the South* (1941) assessed the centrality of segregation to the Southern life. The South, he wrote, lived "under the sway of a single plexus of ideas of which the center was an ever growing concern with white superiority and an ever growing will to mastery of the Negro. And of which the circumference was a scarcely less intense and a scarcely less conscious concern with the maintenance of all that was felt to be southern, a scarcely less militant will to yield nothing of its essential identity." By the 1950s and 1960s, the term "Southern Way of Life" was virtually synonymous for most Americans with racial segregation, an identification reinforced in white public opinion by black challenges to Jim Crow. An August 1964 editorial in the Meridian, Mississippi *Star*, for example, vowed to fight integration, to "keep up the sacred obligation to . . . fight for our precious Southern way of life." The term "sacred obligation" reflected that this was a regional civil religion equivalent to Herberg's American civil religion of the postwar years.[11]

After winning the Nobel Prize, William Faulkner began to speak out more openly than before on public issues, and many of his comments reveal his awareness of the issues involved in the constructed cultural configurations called the American Way of Life and the Southern Way of Life. As we have seen, the American Way evoked industrialism, nationalism, civil religion, mass culture, consumerism, materialism, yet also paradoxically idealism, and above all, democracy. The Southern Way had taken on meanings of Agrarianism and racial segregation. How did Faulkner construct a public ideology related to these issues in the 1950s? What was the Faulkner Way?

Faulkner would have thunderously dismissed, of course, the very idea of a Faulkner Way, or any other Way in capital letters, a unitary cultural idea that supposedly represented a group identity. Faulkner lampooned, ridiculed, and otherwise demolished terms that he believed had become shibboleths, associated with troubling features of the human psyche en masse. "In fact," he wrote, "we must break ourselves of thinking in the terms foisted on us by the split-offs of that old dark spirit's ambition and ruthlessness: the empty clanging terms of 'nation,' and 'fatherland' or 'race' or 'color' or 'creed.' " As I noted at the beginning of this paper, Faulkner indicted the "furious and immunised high priests" of America, the theocratic celebrants of the civil religion, for "bellowing the words and phrases" which had been emptied of meaning: " 'Security'. 'Subversion'. 'Anti-Communism'. 'Christianity'. 'Prosperity'. 'The American Way'. 'The Flag'." One could hardly imagine a more incisive, rigorous, thorough critique of the American Way of Life in the 1950s than in that brief litany. The terms show Faulkner's dismissal of the nation's mindless anti-communism, soulless materialism, superficial religion, and bogus patriotism, and they suggest Faulkner would not have been a likely sunny spokesman for the well-scrubbed and cheerful Father Knows Best America of that decade.[12]

If Faulkner derided the idea of an American Way, he did claim the related concept of the American Dream, as seen in his using that term as the subtitle for two essays in the mid-1950s, which were part of an uncompleted series. He defines the term for us: "This was the American Dream: a sanctuary on the earth for individual man." The term "American Dream" did have a specfiic meaning to Faulkner that he could embrace, that of individual liberty. Faulkner put the American Dream in the perspective of history, seeing it emerging as "a condition in which the individual human being could be free not only of the old established closed-corporation hierarchies of arbitrary power which had oppressed him as a mass, but free of that mass into which the hierarchies of church and state had compressed and held him individually thralled and individually impotent." He thus contrasts American liberty with Old World hierarchies of power from above, but he also emphasizes that American liberty enables individuals to escape entrapment as part of an anonymous mass, a condition to which hierarchies of power reduced human beings. He imagines "the individual men and women who said as with one simultaneous voice: 'We will establish a new land where man can assume that every individual man—not the mass of men but individual men—has inalienable right to individual dignity and freedom within a fabric of individual courage and honorable work and mutual responsibility.' " In Faulkner's ideological imagination, the American Dream of individual liberty is inalienable and offers dignity and freedom as part of a system that in turn demands from the individual courage, work, and responsibility.[13]

But Faulkner strikes a pessimistic tone in these essays from the mid-1950s, arguing that the Dream has been lost. "It is gone now. We dozed, slept, and it abandoned us." He sets up, in effect, a dichotomy between the American Dream of individual liberty and a collective American Way of Life, even a democratic way, which he sees based in fear. "Because now what we hear is a cacophony of terror and conciliation and compromise babbling only the mouthsounds; the loud and empty words which we have emasculated of all meaning whatever—freedom, democracy, patriotism—with which, awakened at last, we try in desperation to hide from ourselves that loss."[14]

In discussions of the American Way by other observers from the 1930s to the 1950s, individual liberty was surely seen as a part of the American Way, albeit one aspect of a broader assemblage. Faulkner argued that tendencies in American life associated with an American Way had eroded individual liberty. Faulkner identified two interactive forces in American life of the 1950s that had claimed and distorted the idea of America—"the giants of industry and commerce," on the one hand, and, on the other, "the manipulators for profit or power of the mass emotions called government, who carry the tremendous load of geopolitical solvency, the two of which conjoined are America." Like Eisenhower's warning about the military-industrial complex a few years later, Faulkner's critique of the American Way zeroed in on its underlying danger to the basis of political authority. Despite its central value of democracy, the American Way represented to Faulkner a dramatic undermining of it. Instead of meaningful individual self-determination, Americans had to live with "what might be called almost a universal will to regimentation, a universal will to obliterate the humanity from man even to the extent of relieving him not only of moral responsibility but even of physical pain and mortality by effacing him individually into any, it does not matter which as long as he has vanished into one of them, nationally-recognised economic group by profession or trade or occupation or income-tax bracket or, if nothing else offers, finance-company list." These identities offered only "the anonymity of a group where he will have surrendered his individual soul for a number."[15]

While these giant institutions exercised their power, the mass of Americans were bought off with the commodities of consumerism. Gavin Stevens insists in *Intruder in the Dust* that "we in America have debased" the idea of the divinity of the individual soul "into a national religion of the entrails in which man owes no duty to his soul because he has been absolved of soul to owe duty to and instead is static heir at birth to an inevictible quit-claim on a wife a car a radio and an old-age pension." As Faulkner noted in his "On Privacy" essay, a "sickness" in American culture went "back to that moment in our history when we decided that the old simple moral verities . . . were obsolete and to be discarded," replaced by meaningless group identities and actions that represented the impulses of an eroding mass culture, consumer capitalism, and centralized government.[16]

Faulkner's critique of American corporate industrialism, materialism, and mass culture could have come from the pages of *I'll Take My Stand*, expressing a Southern conservative view of modernity. He is not asserting, though, an Agrarian solution. Little of Agrarianism is found in Faulkner's public rhetoric of the 1950s. In *Intruder in the Dust* he does have Gavin Stevens admiringly lift up the simplicity of the black man's aspirations: "not an automobile nor flashy clothes nor his picture in the paper but a little of music (his own), a hearth, not his child but any child, a God in heaven which a man may avail himself a little of at any time without having to wait to die, a little earth for his own sweat to fall on among his own green shoots and plants." This passage does not really reflect Faulkner's public voice of the 1950s, though, and we do not want to enter into the well-worn debate of whether Stevens speaks for Faulkner. Traditional agrarian culture in the South, in any event, even by the early 1950s was a vanishing form and Faulkner did not seem inclined to use it as a metaphor to critique the dominant American Way.[17]

Nonetheless, Faulkner does present a meditation on the Southern Way of Life in his 1950s public rhetoric. Writing after the Brown decision of 1954, Faulkner saw the coming conflict between the Southern Way that whites were embracing in defending Jim Crow and the American Way as symbolized by the national government's new resolve to end it; or as he put it, "the impasse of the two apparently irreconcilable facts which we are faced with in the South: the one being the decree of our national government that there be absolute equality in education among all citizens, the other being the white people in the South who say that white and Negro pupils shall never sit in the same classroom." This formula left out the group who would in fact bring about the change, namely African Americans who worked through community organizations and direct action in the South. However, few whites, even moderates and liberals, recognized this fact in the mid-1950s.[18]

Faulkner tried to carve out a position as a moderate. In a letter to the Memphis *Commercial Appeal*, he criticized the dual school system of the South, necessitated by the regional commitment to Jim Crow, earning in the process irate letters and late-night phone calls from other white Southerners who were, as he said, grasping "at such straws for weapons as contumely and threat and insult to change the views or anyway the voice which dares to suggest that betterment of the Negro's condition does not necessarily presage the doom of the white race." Yet Faulkner also, of course, criticized black leaders and Northern liberals for going too fast on integration. He predicted in 1956 that blacks would indeed gain their civil rights, but he urged civil rights leaders to allow Southern whites to adjust to changes to prevent bloodshed against their people. He was convinced, like many other white moderates and liberals, that a racial war would result if blacks continued pressing for their rights, although their gradualism never fixed a date when civil rights would indeed be accomplished with black agitation in abeyance. Faulkner believed that Southern white identity in the 1950s was "an emotional condition of such fierce unanimity as to scorn the fact that it is a minority within the country and which will go to any length and against any odds at this moment to justify and, if necessary, to defend that condition and its right to it."[19]

Economics were the basics of the racial obsessions underlying the Southern Way, in Faulkner's view. The Southern white fear was "not of the Negro as an individual Negro nor even as a race, but as an economic class or stratum or factor, since what the Negro threatens is not the Southern white man's social system but the Southern white man's economic system," which Faulkner pointed out was "established on an obsolescence—the artificial inequality of man." He confessed "our southern white man's shame" of denying blacks economic opportunity and the "double shame" of fearing that social equality would lead to economic advance. The "bugaboo of miscegenation" was a "triple shame" because whites raised the issue only to obfuscate the underlying economic basis of the Southern Way of Life.[20]

In response, Faulkner also sketched a vision of the Southern Way that transcended economics and racism, a bicultural dream that later became common among liberal Southern whites. He was no segregationist, yet he could affirm Southern culture as a lived experience inherited from the past, a shared experience of the region's blacks and whites. "In fact, there are people in the South, Southerners born," he wrote, and would have included himself in this group, "who . . . Love our land—not love white people specifically nor love Negroes specifically, but our land, our country: our climate and geography, the qualities in our people, white and Negro too, for honesty and fairness, the splendors in our traditions, the glories in our past." Those people, including himself, he wrote, loved the South enough to work, in effect, to save the South by changing it, even if they earn along the way "the contempt of Northern radicals who believe we dont do enough" and the "contumely and threats of our own Southern reactionaries who are convinced that anything we do is already too much."[21] His phrases "our land, our country" reveal his ownership of the South as a part of America.

Faulkner was among a group of white Southerners who claimed a biracial Southern identity, explored its burdens, and saw significance in it related to its tragic history of race relations. South Carolina farmer, Presbyterian layman, and social activist James McBride Dabbs was a liberal Southerner who worked more actively than Faulkner for social change, but he and Faulkner represented a similar effort to reconcile, in effect, an American Way and a Southern Way in the 1950s and 1960s. "They say we are defending our way of life," Dabbs wrote in 1958. "What is our way of life? They say segregation," but he would have none of it. He insisted there was "the Southern way of life which men have longed for when absent and fought for when challenged." It was not the separation of segregation, and, he added, "it's more than hot biscuits"—although I have a feeling Dabbs loved hot biscuits, too. Like the Vanderbilt Agrarians and Faulkner, Dabbs rejected industrialism as a source of values and urged Southerners not to accept "the straight American religion" and forget their past. "It seems to me sheer waste to throw away so much only to gain—more shares in General Motors!" The South should look at its own people and their experience to understand the meaning of any Southern Way. The "Entity called the South was hammered out by black man and white man working together." The land was the setting for building a biracial community, which was at the heart of any talk of a Southern Way. "Through the processes of history and the grace of God we have been made one people," he wrote, adding that now "there is no telling what great age might develop in the South." The South would show the way to the rest of the world.[22]

Faulkner and Dabbs thus saw the Southern story of race relations as abiding in its broad human significance, having something to offer the nation and, indeed, the world. One of the most revealing aspects of Faulkner's thought concerning the American Way of Life, the Southern Way, and the American Dream was his consideration of the international context, as well as a regional one, in exploring the meaning of America in the 1950s. This is the final aspect of decoding Faulkner's attitude toward an American Way. Faulkner traveled overseas after winning the Nobel Prize, and his observations reflected his understanding of America. He went to Japan, the Middle East, North Africa, and Europe. Communism was on his mind. Given the economic blight he often saw, he was surprised that the people of many of the nations he visited were not more inclined toward communism. "Then suddenly I said to myself with a kind of amazement: It's because of America. These people still believe in the American dream." They followed the American lead, "not because of our material power: Russia has that: but because of the idea of individual human freedom and liberty and equality on which our nation was founded, which our founding fathers postulated the word 'America' to mean." Faulkner's explicit definition of the American Dream identified "individual liberty" as the Dream, but in considering the international ramifications in his own age, he broadens the American Dream to include equality as well as liberty. He noted, writing in 1956, that the countries he had visited were still free of communism because of "that belief in individual liberty and equality and freedom which is the one idea powerful enough to stalemate the idea of communism."[23]

Faulkner used his peculiar position as an internationally celebrated American writer from the South to draw connections in the 1950s between his region, nation, and world. At the center of these connections was race relations. The fundamental issue was liberty. "And if we who are still free want to continue so," Faulkner wrote, "all of us who are still free had better confederate and confederate fast with all others who still have a choice to be free—confederate not as black people nor white people nor blue or pink or green people, but as people who still are free, with all other people who are still free: confederate together and stick together too, if we want a world or even a part of a world in which individual man can be free, to continue to endure." Faulkner understood the force of history, which in the era after World War II meant the rise of nonwhite peoples expelling imperialists from their colonial empires. Into this vacuum of departing imperialists communism rushed, "that other and inimical power which people who believe in freedom are at war with," as Faulkner put it. Communism was an ideology that offered to nonwhites not freedom "because there is no such thing as freedom; your white overlords whom you have just thrown out have already proved that to you. But we offer you equality, at least equality in slavedom; if you are to be slaves, at least you can be slaves to your own color and race and religion."[24]

If the American Dream was to be believed abroad, it must be practiced at home, in his country, in his South. Faulkner fell back on racist imagery in marking the progress of African Americans under the idea of America, writing of "the people who only three hundred years ago were eating the carrion in the tropical jungles," but he did laud "the Phi Beta Kappas and the Doctor Bunches and the Carvers and the Booker Washingtons and the poets and musicians." He praised their embodiment of what was an important part of Faulkner's own ideology, "that to gain equality, one must deserve it, and to deserve equality, one must understand what it is: that there is no such thing as equality *per se*, but only equality *to*: equal right and opportunity to make the best one can of one's life within one's capacity and capability, without fear of injustice or oppression or violence." In the international competition between communism and freedom, Faulkner was confident that if America lived up to its ideals with its own nonwhite people, then it could educate the world's nonwhite peoples about the American Dream. "We don't need to sell the Negro on America and freedom," Faulkner wrote," because he is already sold." Faulkner understood the centrality to American liberty of what was happening to African Americans. Consideration of African Americans led him to broaden his understanding of the American Dream from liberty to include equality as well. This was part of his broader reflection on the relationship between western culture and the third world, on the necessity of free people practicing freedom in their own countries if they wanted to extend its sway.[25]

Thus Faulkner became an inadvertent spokesman for the American Way of Life. His travels overseas for the United States government, his work with the People-to-People program, his reflections on incorporating nonwhite peoples into free society, his anticommunist stance—all made him a figure of the American Way as the *Saturday Evening Post* so often wrote about it. This was ironic given his impassioned strictures against so many of its manifestations. Remember his litany of shibboleths: Security. Subversion. Anti-Communism. Christianity. Prosperity. The Flag. To the degree that Faulkner perceived the American Way of Life as a term for McCarthesque fear, mindless anticommunist hysteria, consumer materialism, pious Christian patriotism, he could dismiss it. He saw the American Dream as a category of the American Way, and he could endorse its ideals of liberty and equality, even if he was pessimistic about their survival in American culture.

Faulkner consistently wrote against the regimentation he identified as a characteristic feature of 1950s America, which the term American Way evoked for him, with its overtones of a strangling orthodoxy. His recurrent reference to being not of "the mass of men but individual men" suggests the crucial point. The term American Way of Life implied to Faulkner the collective orthodoxy of a fearful 1950s American culture. It reflected democracy but a democracy that combined the worst instincts of the right wing conspiratorial populist rage of a Senator Joseph McCarthy and the soulless materialism of a Flem Snopes. That was a democracy he did not care for. But Faulkner discovered in his world travels that American democracy still represented the ideals of individual freedom and equality. Reform of the Southern Way to extend these principles to African Americans would be essential for the promise of America to continue to resonate. Faulkner thus linked region, nation, and world in defining an ideology of 1950s America.

NOTES

1. "On Privacy (The American Dream: What Happened to It?)," in *Essays, Speeches, and Public Letters, by William Faulkner*, ed. James B. Meriwether (London: Chatto and Windus, 1967), 73.

2. Mitford M. Mathews, *A Dictionary of Americanisms on Historical Principles* (Chicago: University of Chicago Press, 1951), 1:26; Warren I. Susman, *Culture as History: The Transformation of American Society in the Twentieth Century* (New York: Pantheon, 1984),

302. See also Merle Curti, "The American Exploration of Dreams and Dreamers," *Journal of the History of Ideas* 27 (July-September 1966), 391–416.

3. Susman, *Culture as History*, 76–85.

4. Ibid., 156 (quote), 164–66; Warren Susman, "The Thirties," in *The Development of an American Culture*, ed. Stanley Coben and Loren Ratner (Englewood Cliffs, N.J.: Prentice-Hall, 1970), 227–31; Jackson Lears, "A Matter of Taste: Corporate Cultural Hegemony in a Mass-Consumption Society," in *Recasting America: Culture and Politics in the Age of Cold War*, ed. Lary May (Chicago: University of Chicago Press, 1989), 41; George V. Denny, Jr., et al., "Can We Depend upon Youth to Follow the American Way?" in *Conversations with Richard Wright*, ed. Keneth Kinnaman and Michael Fabre (Jackson: University Press of Mississippi, 1993), 22.

5. Susman, *Culture as History*, 155; J. Ronald Oakley, *God's Country: America in the Fifties* (New York: Dembner Books, 1986), 320.

6. Frances Fitzgerald, *America Revised: History Textbooks in the Twentieth Century* (Boston: Little-Brown, 1979). See Stephen Whitfield, *The Culture of the Cold War* (Baltimore: Johns Hopkins University Press, 1990), 57.

7. Will Herberg, *Protestant-Catholic-Jew: An Essay in American Religious Sociology* (1955; Garden City, N.J.: Anchor Books, 1960), 75.

8. For the South in the 1950s, see Numan V. Bartley, *The New South, 1945–1980* (Baton Rouge: Louisiana State University Press and the Littlefield Fund for Southern History of the University of Texas, 1995).

9. Twelve Agrarians, *I'll Take My Stand: The South and the Agrarian Tradition* (1930; Baton Rouge: Louisiana State University Press, 1977), xxxvii, xliv, 1.

10. Ibid., 35.

11. Meridian (Mississippi) *Star*.

12. "Address to the Graduating Class of Pine Manor Junior College," *Essays*, 141–42; "On Privacy," 73.

13. Ibid., 62.

14. Ibid., 65–66.

15. "Address upon Receiving the National Book Award for Fiction," and "Address to the English Club of the University of Virginia, *Essays*, 144, 162.

16. William Faulkner, *Intruder in the Dust* (New York: Modern Library, 1948), 202; "On Privacy," 71.

17. *Intruder in the Dust*, 156.

18. "On Fear: Deep South in Labor: Mississippi," *Essays*, 94–95.

19. Ibid., 91, 93, 95. See also "Letter to a Northern Editor," *Essays*, 86–91.

20. Ibid., 95–96, 105.

21. Ibid., 95.

22. James McBride Dabbs, *The Southern Heritage* (New York: Knopf, 1958), 24–36 (quotes 24).

23. "On Fear," 101–2.

24. Ibid., 102–3.

25. Ibid., 104, 105. For background on this point, see Paul Carter, *Another Part of the Fifties* (New York: Columbia University Press, 1983), and William Manchester, *The Glory and the Dream: A Narrative History of America, 1932–1972* (Boston: Little-Brown, 1974).

The Portable Eclipse: Hawthorne, Faulkner, and Scribbling Women

KATHRYN B. MCKEE

In 1877, Mark Twain was invited to speak at John Greenleaf Whittier's seventieth birthday party, along with most of the period's other literary lights. He proceeded to tell the august gathering a story featuring "certain of [America's] biggest literary billows" in which he poked fun at everything from their anatomies to their poetry, using modified versions of their own lines to create what he intended as humorous effect.[1] Among his targets were Ralph Waldo Emerson, Oliver Wendell Holmes, and Henry Wadsworth Longfellow, all members of his rapidly reproving audience. Later Mark Twain himself would describe the reception of his speech as "a sort of black frost."[2] Of the three men he good-naturedly abused, only Emerson has sailed into the twentieth century with his "literary billow" status intact, and in the canon of American literature Mark Twain himself has come to outrank the man he had been asked to honor. Although the political nature of canon formation is a well-established topic, the fact remains that we read and teach the work of certain authors instead of others, and we turn to a relatively narrow range of voices in describing the "American experience," a term which in itself, critics have repeatedly demonstrated, has no fixed meaning. Consistently consulted among those voices is that of Nathaniel Hawthorne, whose nineteenth–century stories and novels of New England are consulted by readers for what they reveal about America's Puritan past and about human reactions to guilt, ambition, and hypocrisy. Hawthorne and the power of his reputation find striking parallels in the twentieth–century prominence of William Faulkner, whose tales of North Mississippi are generally understood to embody a universality that extends beyond region to address an American audience concerning its national heritage and its membership in a larger human community.

Pairing Hawthorne and Faulkner is in itself no original enterprise: critics frequently place them on a stylistic and thematic continuum that constitutes a rubric for establishing classic American literature of the last one hundred years. Most readers of their work can quickly compile a list of their similarities: both men essentially wrote of what they knew and found themselves heavily invested in recording the collective pasts of their regions. They both probed darker aspects of humanity, ushering their readers into the subterranean impulses of individual psychology. Both evoked a world and a set of characters now firmly entrenched in our classrooms, and each lived long enough to see himself become a canonical figure, a writer against whom other writers were—and still are—measured. Both men are also noted for the strong and almost haunting female characters they created, about whom each seemed to feel a certain amount of ambivalence—Hester Prynne and Zenobia, Caddy Compson and Judith Burden. The relationship of Hawthorne and Faulkner to the women *authors* of their era forms another parallel between them and suggests that each was ambivalent toward his prolific female contemporaries, who were subsequently relegated to the status of literary blips rather than literary billows.

My aim is not to deflate the literary billowhood of either Hawthorne or Faulkner, a strategy guaranteed to cast a black frost in the midst of a mid-summer Mississippi heat wave, but rather to examine the consequences of their reputations for our understanding of American literature. Most particularly, Faulkner's renown has overshadowed the contributions of female modernists who shared his region but not his lasting fame, notably Evelyn Scott and Frances Newman. Yet Scott and Newman engage in narrative experimentation equally daring to that of Faulkner's. That their fiction has been limited by its association with region demonstrates an ongoing critical tendency to link female writing with less than universal concerns. It also reveals the function of the idea of "Faulkner" in determining if and how a work makes the transition from being one limited by its ties to the South to one encompassing the American experience.

In 1946, Malcolm Cowley compiled *The Portable Faulkner* for Viking Press, and by most accounts, including that of Lawrence Schwartz in *Creating Faulkner's Reputation*, launched Faulkner's career as a writer of national proportions. By 1950, Schwartz maintains, Faulkner "had moved from the category of unappreciated Southern novelist to become the major American literary voice of the mid-twentieth century."[3] The accessibility provided by the *Portable* edition accounts for only a small part of its impact; Cowley's strategies for presenting Faulkner to the academy are undoubtedly more significant factors in the rapid escalation of Faulkner's reputation. Richard Brodhead, in *The School of Hawthorne*, essentially argues that Cowley admitted Faulkner to American literature by linking to him to Hawthorne, thus establishing Faulkner as a twentieth-century manifestation of ongoing American literary traits. Their connection, Cowley asserts, rests in their attitude toward region and in their ability to recreate the particularity of place. Hawthorne's New England and Faulkner's Mississippi were for each "a lump of history and a permanent state of consciousness."[4] To Cowley subsequent critics have attributed the all-important theory that Faulkner, like Hawthorne, wrote of his subject matter in pieces that when properly aligned reveal a "living pattern," a design that unveils more in it entirety than its individual components can attest to alone.[5] Two years later, in 1948, Cowley edited *The Portable Hawthorne*; it did not, of course, substantially alter Hawthorne's canonical standing. As Brodhead observes, Hawthorne "is the only American fiction writer never to have lived in the limbo of the non-elect."[6]

For all his fame, Hawthorne's fuming about the success of some of his female contemporaries has become legendary. Centered mainly in a single comment he made in a letter to his publisher and friend, William Ticknor, in 1855, Hawthorne's reputation as an enemy of female writing, suggests Nina Baym, may be exaggerated.[7] Naming Maria Cummins's sentimental novel *The Lamplighter*, a best-seller of its time, as a prime example, Hawthorne exploded: "America is now wholly given over to a d—d mob of scribbling women, and I should have no chance of success while the public taste is occupied with their trash—and should be ashamed of myself if I did succeed."[8] His frustrations did not prevent Hawthorne's reading with a discerning eye, however; a few weeks later he wrote again to Ticknor, this time praising Fanny Fern's novel, *Ruth Hall*. Fern, Hawthorne, observed, wrote "as if the devil was in her"; he observed that when female authors "throw off the restraints of decency, and come before the public stark naked, as it were—then their books are sure to possess character and value."[9] His provocative language suggests that women writers succeed most often when they abandon the external trappings of gender, in this case by tempering the conventions of that era's wildly popular sentimental fiction.

Yet Hawthorne admirably made his way in a market saturated by such literature. As Jane Tompkins convincingly argues in *Sensational Designs*, the explanation for Hawthorne's success lies not in a discerning readership but rather in the fact that, given the mid-nineteenth century world view, "there *was* no difference" between the work of the sentimentalists and that of Hawthorne.[10] Their audiences understood both as exemplifying human sympathy; both probed the intricacies of the human heart; both stressed the role of spirituality in living a fulfilled life. Modern readers, because of the cultural context that informs their reading, are simply attracted to different facets of *The Scarlet Letter*, for example, than were its initial readers. Beyond the cultural context of reading, Tompkins maintains, Hawthorne succeeded in large part because he reaped the benefits of well-established connections in the literary world. He was part of a publishing network that continued to promote his reputation—and its investment in it—long after his death. Susan Warner, author of the celebrated novel *The Wide, Wide World*, on the other hand, just knew the wrong people and faded steadily from prominence even within her own lifetime. By the early to mid-twentieth century, "sentimental fiction" was itself a pejorative label, used to dismiss the entire careers of female writers enormously popular within their own time.

Identifying Hawthorne with the sentimentalists usefully complicates the continuum of American letters and challenges common approaches to studying women's literature. Central to the latter pursuit is a strategy Baym terms "literary essentialism"—the assumption "that at every time and place where women write there will be ways of writing allotted specifically to them and that in these ways of writing an idea of gender will be constructed."[11] We have often and profitably undergone the process of identifying a particularly female way of writing, recognizing that the predominance of male writing risks eclipsing concurrent female patterns. The function of sentimental fiction, for instance, was to act in part as a training manual, to illustrate the duty of young women to submit to father, husband, and God, while, at other times, to demonstrate the need to retain a sense of individuality in the midst of a divinely-ordered society. At the same time, however, Baym cautions against reading women's literature as a phenomenon isolated from male writing, maintaining that "considerable influence flowed across the gap in both directions."[12] Adopting Baym's viewpoint means that *The Scarlet Letter* can be understood as "deeply marked by domestic sentimentality [; it] can be read either as a story of the development of feminine autonomy in a patriarchal world or as a story of the retention of one's womanhood despite tremendous obstacles—in other words, it can be read as a woman's fiction."[13] We learn, after all, that despite its ostracizing power, "the scarlet letter had not done its office."[14] Hester has essentially redefined its role, remaking her badge of shame into an emblem of mercy and compassion that admits her to the bedsides of the very community that condemned her. By the novel's close, Hester, the sexual creature and fallen woman, has become a light to other women "in the continually recurring trials of wounded, wasted, wronged, misplaced, or erring and sinful passion,—or, with the dreary burden of a heart unyielded, because unvalued and unsought."[15] Knowing herself to be too sullied to act as its priestess, Hester still predicts the coming of a new order—"when the world should have grown ripe for it"—in which men and women establish relations "on a surer ground of mutual happiness."[16] As members of Hawthorne's twentieth-century audience, we admire Hester's quiet defiance, even as earlier readers may have first noticed her defiant submission. Hester's ties to the nineteenth-century's "cult of domesticity" mean that to understand Hawthorne aright, we need to understand sentimentalism as practiced by the "damned mob of scribbling women."

Yet just as Hawthorne—and not the sentimentalists—continues to dominate our understanding of mid-nineteenth-century New England, so Faulkner controls America's perceptions of the early and mid-twentieth-century South. Readers approach his work as a nearly nonfictional accounting of the nation's most storied and darkly intriguing region. We read it as representative of the Southern Renascence; we read it as the South's greatest contribution to literary modernism. Faulkner emerges as one of America's most skilled practitioners of the latter movement, steadily transforming himself, according to Daniel Singal, from the largely Victorian poet of *The Marble Faun* to the high modernist of *The Sound and the Fury*.[17] That Faulkner tapped willingly and expertly into the cultural drift of the international literary scene is surely in large part responsible for his intimidating stature. In fact, Michael Kreyling argues that by mid-century Faulkner had come to live "with an additional burden not often considered: himself as an institutionalized cultural force."[18] In the realm of Southern literature, Faulkner obviously marks not just an era in time—pre- and post-Faulkner—but also provides a highwater mark by which we measure achievement—someone reminds us of Faulkner, someone deviates from Faulkner, someone parodies Faulkner, no one is Faulkner. Flannery O'Connor's often-quoted observation still rings true: "The presence alone of Faulkner in our midst makes a great difference in what the writer can and cannot permit himself to do. Nobody wants his mule and wagon stalled on the same track the Dixie Limited is roaring down."[19] Kreyling makes much of O'Connor's word choice. She does dub Faulkner "the Dixie *Limited*," suggesting that O'Connor and others, particularly those outside the dominant white, male understanding of the South, saw other Souths to write about, and other literary styles and strategies to explore. Thus by extension O'Connor's remark provides a foundation for Kreyling's fruitful contention that the literature of women and African Americans in the South has been engaged in "the complicated enterprise of getting out from under one burden of cultural assumption . . . and trying out the viability of another. . . ."[20] In arguing for the identification of a female tradition within the context of Southern literature, Kreyling maintains that women writers "imagine their traditions and identities aslant to (or quite separate from) the officially imagined South."[21] Indeed the work of many nineteenth– and twentieth–century female authors suggests that for women the realities and abstractions of region have functioned differently than they have for men.

Kreyling's assertions are provocative when paired with Anne Goodwyn Jones's and Susan V. Donaldson's *Haunted Bodies: Gender and Southern Texts*. In their introduction, Jones and Donaldson suggest "that gender in the end may be as important an analytic category for making sense of the South as race itself has traditionally been acknowledged to be."[22] Jones and Donaldson challenge two assumptions fundamental to the study of Southern literature: the South is a place resistant to change; and the South maintains a collective identity, distinct from the American one. Fixed assumptions about the way gender is constructed and maintained in the South, despite their promotion in the region's texts, are a poor match for the ambivalence actually characterizing such operations, with the result being that "seemingly stable categories of manhood and womanhood . . . are everywhere inevitably susceptible to destabilization and alterity."[23] In actuality, claim Jones and Donaldson, the South's regional identity is inextricably bound to national efforts to understand the role of gender, so that "manhood and womanhood in the South cannot be examined apart from general American notions of masculinity and feminity."[24] Thus conventional images of belles and cavaliers, of male and female lascivious slaves, oversimplify gender relations, both in life and in the region's literary texts. The contributors to *Haunted Bodies* find that male and female Southern writers influence and react to one another in much the same way that scholars now understand mid-nineteenth–century writers to have cross-pollinated one another's work. Consequently, if we better understand Hawthorne by identifying the function of sentimentalism, we likewise may better understand Faulkner by identifying how contemporary female writers came "aslant" to "the officially imagined South" that critics and readers have now long identified as Faulkner's South—a South obsessed by race, by its collective past, and by the stains on the hands of the young men who inherited the ledger books and the memories of their ancestors. We may also come to understand better the women writers in and of themselves and to notice how male and female notions of gender undermine and undergrid one another in the South and in America.

The shadow Faulkner now casts over those launching careers simultaneously with or even before his own, would not, of course, have been so apparent to his female contemporaries. Among others, Elizabeth Madox Roberts, Caroline Gordon, Katharine Anne Porter, Evelyn Scott, and Frances Newman frequently took their native South as their subject matter, and all reflect in their treatments of it an increasing distance on the region's nineteenth–century image. Yet of the five, the two least–known figures—Scott and Newman—most nearly approximate the modernist literary experimentation that distinguishes Faulkner's work and aligns it with national and international literary trends. Readers and critics of the time recognized the inventiveness of these women and were befuddled by their styles, much as they were by Faulkner's. Scott's unconventional Civil War novel, *The Wave*, published in 1929, the same year as *The Sound and the Fury*, led Robert Morss Lovett to conclude in *The New Republic*: "The reader will need patience to integrate a world presented in fragments, and to correlate a mass of constantly shifting shapes and colors. But he will have his reward."[25] Newman's biting, satirical style often inspired less patience; T. S. Matthews found her second novel, *Dead Lovers Are Faithful Lovers*, exhibiting "genuine, implicit, and restrained" tragedy, but wryly observed that "if Miss Newman pursues this method further . . . her next book will have to be translated."[26] Such criticism precedes similar responses to Faulkner's work, particularly to *The Sound and the Fury*, the first of his high modernist novels. Of it, Clifton Fadiman rails in *The Nation*: "one hundred pages of an inbecile's simplified sense perceptions and monosyllabic gibberings, no matter how accurately recorded, are too much of a good thing."[27] Indeed Scott, Newman, and Faulkner were largely considered writers' writers. The two women were established literary critics of the 1920s and for this reason, as much as for their creative work, they were well known in the world of American letters. Scott's *The Wave* was also a popular success; Faulkner would have been pleased to have earned half so much attention for *The Sound and the Fury*.

In his work, Faulkner exemplifies many of the characteristics of male modernists outlined by Bonnie Kime Scott in *The Gender of Modernism*: his fiction is experimental in its use of form and language, with an overt intention to challenge the processes by which its audience typically creates meaning.[28] Scott and Newman unquestionably and successfully share those goals, producing, not an isolated strand of women's fiction, but a body of work fully participatory in the sweep of literary modernism. Although Anne Goodwyn Jones notes that Newman's "models were modernists like Virginia Woolf," she is careful to establish that Newman "identified herself as part of a male literary tradition, hoping to be accepted within it, while at the same time paradoxically asserting that her own literary value rested in her distinctly female voice."[29] That paradox is fundamental to understanding both Scott and Newman; each saw herself as bringing a decidedly female way of seeing to the lens her male counterparts were using to record and to re-imagine the world they saw. Experimental literary form, then, provides Scott and Newman the means to reflect the destabilized state of gender in their native South.

Scott's technique as a modernist is most accessible to contemporary audiences through the form and content of two of her twenty book-length works: *Escapade*, published in 1923, and *The Wave*, published in 1929. *Escapade* is thinly veiled autobiography that chronicles the emergence of Evelyn Scott, born Elsie Dunn in 1893, in Clarksville, Tennessee. Despite the use of fictional names, the narrative recounts the years she spent in Brazil as a young woman after escaping America on the arm of Frederick Creighton Wellman, the much older, married, dean of Tulane University's School of Tropical Medicine. The couple change their names to Evelyn Scott and Cyril Kay Scott, although they are never legally married. In Brazil, Scott gives birth to her only child, a son. Much of *Escapade* is devoted to his harrowing birth and the complications Scott suffered in a medically primitive country. The volume is composed mainly of impressionistic, kaleidoscopic images that rely heavily on color and sensation for their effectiveness in transporting the reader on Scott's journey into what she calls "the enigma of myself,"[30] marked by the farthest reachings of pain, despair, and self-doubt.

Scott's *The Wave*, by contrast, focuses on a public event, the Civil War. With the exception of historical figures, including Robert E. Lee and Ulysses S. Grant, no character appears in more than one of the novel's more than one hundred vignettes. The reader is thereby plunged into detailed scenarios and becomes heavily invested in them because of Scott's minute rendering of place and character. Other authors adopt a similar strategy in recreating the chaos of this conflict—Stephen Crane in *The Red Badge of Courage*, Michael Shaara in *Killer Angels*, Shelby Foote in *Shiloh*—but Scott's purpose extends beyond depicting the chaos of war and the necessarily individualized perspectives of its participants. Many of her characters never see a battlefield; the voices she records are those of women, children, African Americans, businessmen, chaplains, prostitutes, flag-bearers, mental patients, and teenagers, many of whom remain outside the battle's core but are unable to withstand the rippling effect of its consequences. Although the historical events to which Scott refers are presented chronologically, moving from the shots fired on Fort Sumter to the shots fired at Lincoln, the lasting impression offered by *The Wave* is that of a montage, marked by ambivalence, suffering, and crossed purposes. Scott shows no favoritism in her depiction; both North and South are represented, and neither is morally superior. The novel's epigraph, taken from a scientific study called *Physical Geography*, demonstrates the novel's stylistic and thematic link to modernism. Observes the scientist: "waves travel in some definite direction, but a cork thrown into the water does not travel with the waves. It moves up and down, to and fro, but unless it is blown by the wind or carried by a current it returns to the same position with each wave and does not permanently leave its place."[31] Buoyed pointlessly by the wave of war, the characters of Scott's novel and their real-life nineteenth-century counterparts live the modern predicament: a search for meaning that lends little consolation, an absence of perspective that results in no understanding of the world beyond self, a nightmarish immobility that compromises any sense of individual autonomy. The reader is buffeted by the same wave, able to retain from the fragments of Scott's narrative only pieces of individual lives and causes that offer no final coherence. Instead, they merge into an impressionistic portrait of an un-won war that called forth both the most human and the most animalistic traits of its participants. *The Wave* was Scott's greatest achievement as a modernist.

Frances Newman died unexpectedly in 1928 and left behind fewer works than did Scott, but critics clearly align her with the experimental literature of the 1920s. The subject matter and style of Newman's two novels, *The Hard-Boiled Virgin*, published in 1926, and *Dead Lovers Are Faithful Lovers*, published in 1928, vary widely from Scott's approaches but are equally provocative. Most distinctive about them is the caustic wit Newman employs to satirize her characters, her own experiences, and her South. *The Hard-Boiled Virgin* uses no dialogue; *Dead Lovers Are Faithful Lovers* incorporates it minimally; both novels rely on the detached perspective of an ironic third-person narrator to record the absurd inability of love—as learned in a society founded on romanticism—to meet the needs of women. Like Scott's work, Newman's novels use short, untitled chapters that provide a disjointed reading experience, requiring an alertness that surely discouraged some readers. Her unabashed use of black humor—reflected clearly in the titles of her books—indicates that Newman felt comfortable stepping into a realm typically reserved for men. Certainly she could hold her own as a humorist; her work is witty, irreverent, and merciless, and she offers no more hope for women who challenge the forms that confine them than she does for women who submit willingly to convention. Her life, however, like Scott's, tells a different story, one of a woman who boldly used the techniques of modernism to allow for her presence and perspective as a female writer.

Beyond their ties as female modernists and incisive critics, Scott and Newman share one additional bond: they were likely known and read by their fellow Southerner, William Faulkner. Scott's ties to Faulkner are well-documented and retold by every Scott scholar as part of the argument that she deserves a revival of interest. In 1929, the publishing house of Cape and Smith asked Scott to review *The Sound and the Fury* prior to its publication. Cape and Smith so liked what she had to say about it that they printed her remarks in pamphlet form for distribution with the novel. Praising both Faulkner's themes and his stylistic innovation, Scott essentially acts as a precursor to Cowley, recognizing in Faulkner's seemingly disjointed narrative the story of the South and Dilsey's inextricable role in its future. In their introduction to Scott's critical piece, Cape and Smith express the hope that her kind remarks will elevate Faulkner to Scott's company. The irony of their wish is inescapable for modern audiences. Compounding it is Faulkner's later response to Scott's own achievements. Asked in a 1940 interview to name female novelists whose work he admired, Faulkner replied: "Evelyn Scott is pretty good . . . for a woman."[32] Like Hawthorne, then, Faulkner was aware of the women scribbling around him, not just by way of reputation, but surely because he had read them, at least this one. To a feminist ear, Faulkner's comment constructs a pejorative category of women's writing. Yet as Peggy Bach maintains, "because of her high artistic standards and her treatment of themes, similar to his own, perhaps [Faulkner] admired her."[33] Nonetheless, Scott witnessed her literary star steadily decline as Faulkner saw his ascend. Her work was uneven in quality and her personal life perpetually teetered on the brink of disaster. By the time of her death in 1963, Evelyn Scott was well on her way to being forgotten; more than twenty years had passed since her last published novel. When Bach began her research, only Scott's essay about *The Sound and the Fury* remained in print. What Faulkner knew of Newman's work is less clear. Blotner's catalogue of his library, however, records the presence of an inscribed copy of *The Hard-Boiled Virgin* in the library at Rowan Oak.[34] But certainly other prominent Southerners knew of her. In 1930, James Branch Cabell wrote: "I today believe, simply and quite surely, that had some five more years of living been accorded to Frances Newman she would have stayed remembered, not merely as unique, but as supreme among the women writers of America."[35] Despite his invocation of a "women writers of America" subculture to which Newman might belong, Cabell clearly respected her work. Her subsequent decline was steady, however, and as Anne Firor Scott points out: "her name is hardly recognized even by serious students of southern literature."[36] Recent publication of full-length biographies about each woman—*Fighting the Current: The Life and Work of Evelyn Scott* by Mary Wheeling White and *Frances Newman: Southern Satirist and Literary Rebel* by Barbara Ann Wade—surely heralds a renewed interest in them.[37]

Despite all of their stylistic similarities to Faulkner, Scott and Newman obviously boast reputations completely inferior to his. One of the laments of Newman's heroine Katharine Faraday is that any work she produces as an aspiring writer will necessarily fall into the vastly inferior category of American—rather than British—literature. Her creator has not even that to worry about; those who read her work now tend to be interested primarily in Southern literature, and hence Newman and Scott have regressed to regional stature while Faulkner claims attention as a national writer. Yet it is precisely because they complicate our understanding of region that Scott and Newman command our attention. They are engaged, finally, in a completely different endeavor than the one that Faulkner pursued. Failing to recognize their departures from Faulkner is a failure to recognize the significantly different impact of region on men and women. Failing to recognize their similarities to him is a failure to recognize fully their participation in a national literary scene. The South Faulkner stayed home to write about was not, after all, the one that Scott and Newman physically left behind, although they, like Quentin, could never really escape it. Both women use their fiction to castigate and challenge the idea of the South as it limited the evolution of their womanhood. In *The Wave*, Scott acknowledges the burden of the white South's past. But her interests lie ultimately in individual portraits, the most strikingly rendered of which are particular women's lives—the poor white character Mrs. Stoner, who, ill from childbirth and unable to cope with the incessant demands of her other children, hangs herself; Aunt Nancy Green, the African American woman who joins the procession of other freed slaves following the Union troops toward Savannah, only to die shortly after she is underway; the upper-class Amy whose suitor seems to have deserted both her and the military, leaving her pregnant and mentally unable to withstand the strain of her life. This is not the South of the Cavalier myth, of Colonel Falkner, of Ike McCaslin's ledgers or Quentin Compson's haunted memories. In the work of Scott and Newman we hear Caddy Compson's literal voice, wooed by the power of her own sexuality but comprehensively forbidden by her culture from exploring it. Through the kaleidoscopic lens of Quentin's vision, and that of other male characters, Faulkner offers at a remove what is central to the fiction of Scott and Newman.

The concerns of their fiction often seemed dissatisfying to critics who found that it lacked the sort of universal appeal heralded in Faulkner's writing. Using standards by which male autobiography was evaluated, a number of critics found *Escapade* too self-absorbed, too limited and limiting. They failed to recognize Scott's efforts to transmit her sense of claustrophobia stemming from what Mary Wheeling White understands as a feeling of confinement, brought on by pregnancy, illness, and motherhood. Of *Escapade*, Ludwig Lewisohn observed in *The Nation*: "here is art which seems to [the reader] cramped, fettered, enfeebled by causes not rooted in the author's creative vision or faculty, but arising from a passing mood and fashion."[38] Yet in truth it is Scott who has been "cramped, fettered, enfeebled" by preconceptions concerning her behavior. *Escapade* is the process by which she frees herself of those limitations, confronting directly the meaning of her gender by appropriating the audacity of the male gaze and the linguistic innovation of the male writer. Scott's fascination with her pregnant body is riveting in its frankness, and her open acknowledgement of sexuality striking for the ease of its expression. Whereas Noel Polk points out that "the connection between sexuality and corruption . . . is as common as words in Faulkner's work,"[39] Scott is pleased by reports from home of her lost reputation and encourages herself to "consider sex more factually and with less mystical solemnity" (7). What she resents in the gossip that drifts her way from America is the implication that she has been taken advantage of, efforts, she indignantly exclaims "to deprive me of responsibility for my own acts. To have John [her fictional name for Cyril] sent to prison as though I had not equally selected the condition to which we have been brought!" (17). In many ways, Scott would seem a direct contradiction to Peggy Whitman Prenshaw's findings about Southern female autobiographies—texts marked, in her view, by "indirection and obliquity in her revelations of self," thus avoiding the stigma of unladylike self-absorption.[40] Like Hester, Scott commands and reshapes her self-perception and the perception of those who regard her. Like Caddy, she understands that much male interest in her originates in the protectiveness pinned to an abstraction: her Uncle Alec's "sense of responsibility in regard to me related only to my virginity. . . . The love among whom one has been reared is usually not love at all. One can die inwardly without any of them being aware of it" (77). Thus she articulates, as Caddy does in actions but not in words, the South's suffocating presence in the evolution of her identity and her efforts to see herself physically as a woman. Unlike Judith Sutpen, Scott would seem to circumvent the male presence that saves her from her own sexuality.

But despite the escape of her *Escapade*, Scott fails to transform her persona into the model of independence her early declarations herald. Physically and psychologically she can at last only see herself refracted through the vision of others, most particularly men. For the Southern female, maintains Prenshaw, identity is relational, derived from how she sees herself in juxtaposition to other people, and the ensconcement of the self within a web of relationships tends to be the subject of her autobiographies. Scott resents the intruding male gaze unavoidably accompanying the doctor who attends her labor and delivery. After Dr. Januario's initial examination, Scott notes: "I wanted to get away from my body that he had touched—to leave it to him. To have one's individuality completely ignored is like being pushed quite out of life. Like being blown out as one blows out a light. I began to believe myself invisible" (51). Yet as one male gaze withers her, another male gaze restores her sense of physical existence. She continues: "However, as long as John can see me I continue to exist" (51), and "because [John] believed in me, I was actual to myself" (50). As the first flash of independence from her daring escapade evaporates and her pregnancy becomes increasingly visible, Scott struggles to know herself outside of the structured Southern society she left behind. She is uncertain, as was Caddy, whether to embrace defiantly its judgment of her or rage against it, yet she is at a loss for words to name herself beyond its reaches. "I wonder who I am," Scott muses some pages earlier as preface to a consideration of her pregnant body and the unknown child within it. "I want John here to give me a name to see myself with," she concludes (41), observing her tendency to shrink from the probing glances of men on the street because "I can feel satisfied in my own body only when I am with people who do not question it" (38). What Scott seeks is connected to the world Hawthorne's Hester describes, one free of entrapping gazes, one in which men and women look one another in the eye nonjudgmentally.

From the Southern culture in which she was reared, which she discusses more directly in her second autobiographical volume, *Background in Tennessee*, Scott learns to turn first to men to see herself.[41] Yet her dilemma and her emotions, finally, are not limited by regional space. Her birthing process contrasts strikingly with the birthing rituals of the native women. After a villager washes Scott's baby for her, Scott feels compelled to wash it again, fearful of the woman's lack of hygiene, but also attentive to the need to purify the baby from its attachment to the impurity of birth. Scott is horrified by the primitive nature of the servant Petronilla's birth-giving: "the midwife tore the naval cord from the child with her bare hands" (93). When the child later dies, Petronilla feigns grief. In the servant's quick return to the life of a prostitute, Scott glimpses total female submersion in a sexual lifestyle in which children are but unfortunate incidents. America's sanitization of sex and of motherhood gives her no way to grasp the world of tropical indulgence.

Escapade, then, is no "cramped, fettered, enfeebled" narrative, but a powerful rendering of a distinctively female experience, universal in the subject matter it adopts, if particularly American in the attitudes it reflects. It dares us to see the world as women do and as few women had in earlier literature. Of Doctor Januario, Scott concludes: "If he and I gazed with the same eyes we should perceive different things" (56). This, perhaps, is her most important finding, for herself personally, and for us as readers of Southern and American literature and culture. Faulkner and

Scott gazed with Southern eyes on many of the same issues. They both recognized that womanhood, particularly as nurtured in the South, combined an element that separated a woman's body from its femininity. While both expose that chasm, they "perceive different things." From Faulkner we learn most clearly the nature of Quentin's obsession with the abstractions of honor and virginity; from Scott's perspective we lock eyes with the male gaze, witnessing the pleasure of female self-discovery, but discovering the inability of language to preserve the distinctiveness of that experience. To understand the nature of sexuality in the South—and in America—we need to look both ways.

Frances Newman's accounting of male-female relations strikes remarkably similar chords, particularly in female susceptibility to be created by forces outside of herself. Both of Newman's novels are in some ways about hard-boiled virgins; the first, actually called *The Hard-Boiled Virgin*, is the story of Katharine Faraday's studied resistance to male advances in keeping with her romantic notions about what deflowerment should be, while the second, *Dead Lovers Are Faithful Lovers*, is an accounting of Evelyn Cunninghan's twelve-year, childless marriage which ends triumphantly in her husband's death, thus sparing Evelyn from having to tend relentlessly to his fidelity. Both novels rely on a clear demarcation of the public and private selves of the protagonist. Katharine, for example, frequently views her actions from a detached perspective, as though she is performing in a play, indicated by the narrator's use of stage terminology and by Katharine's eventual decision to become a playwright. She is aware that as a dark-haired woman keenly interested in reading and writing she is markedly different from the other belles of Atlanta and from her siblings. In fact, Katharine Faraday explores sexuality and the constraints her society places on it in a way few earlier Southern characters could have, at the same time illustrating Anne Goodwyn Jones's contention that Newman's fiction is concerned "obsessively . . . with the role of the southern lady."[42] Although, as Reginald Abbott maintains, Katharine gleans her romantic notions in part from the British literature she reads,[43] she lives in a culture that encourages her to believe that life can be lived successfully by a code. It is the same society, after all, that Mark Twain claimed was wrecked by its subscription to the fancies of Sir Walter Scott. Consequently, Katharine "did not often doubt that a fortunately timed spraining of an ankle would shortly introduce her to her destined husband, or that her destined husband was a tall young Englishman who sprang from [an ancient] family."[44] Her romanticism is tinged with particularly Southern notions: "She had known for eight years that no southern lady ever allows any man to touch so much as her pocket handkerchief until he has begged her to become his wife"

(115–16), and "she knew that in Georgia no lady was supposed to know she was a virgin until she had ceased to be one" (174–75).

Yet for all of her interest in proper frocks and the armor of her virginity, Katharine Faraday knows a few other things as well. She knows, the narrator tells us, "that southern ladies and gentlemen respect the polite fictions of society" (51), suggesting that Katharine may know how to lead a private life as well as a public one. Her first substantial attraction of note is to a young married man, Robert Carter, whom she meets at her family's vacation spot. Katharine fashions a voodoo doll of his ailing wife and sticks it full of pins, then hopefully scans the obituaries until "she decided that the story of Katharine Faraday and Robert Carter was complete" (83). From her experience with Carter, Katharine learns that when she goes to bed at night it is possible to call forth "a fountain [that] rose and fell and dropped its electric spray through her thin brown body" (75). Katharine Faraday may well be the first Southern heroine, maybe the first American heroine, to masturbate, at least in print.

Katharine is intensely conscious of both her sexuality and of the role it plays in aligning her society. From a young age, "she knew that any boy is born to a more honorable social situation than any girl." She attributes his special status to a negated capability: his ranking "seemed to be the result of his inability to produce a baby rather than his ability to produce an idea" (30). After ascertaining that "a southern lady's charms are estimated entirely by their agreement with tradition and her intelligence is judged entirely by her ability to disagree with tradition" (244), Katharine learns to play her social role to its fullest, having cracked the code of gender she sees as its basis. Although she eventually begins "to fear that she was really a southern lady and that she would never be swept off her feet" (253), Katharine does finally have sex with a male playwright named Alden Ames—remarkably similar in name to Caddy's lover, Dalton Ames. Unlike Caddy, whose veins pulse against Quentin's hand at the mere mention of Dalton's name, the sexual act with Alden seems to Katharine "more remote than a kiss after he had given it to her" (273). She finds that, like Evelyn Scott, she should have been more concerned with the practical aspects of love-making that with its "mystical solemnity." The unbearable suspense of wondering if she is pregnant dogs her every effort "and [leaves her] suffering because she did not know what was happening in her own body, and because she could not control her own body" (275). For Katharine, the withholding of sexual contact passes from frigid coquetry to power—power to control and possess her gender, outside of relations with men and outside of the social forms that suggest she must relinquish her body permanently to another.

But Katharine's defiance of social expectation by choosing to remain unmarried also illustrates, in Jones's words, how "the twenties for women in the South gave more the appearance of liberation than the fact."[45] Like Evelyn Scott, Katharine Faraday depends upon the reflection of self she can see in the eyes of others, namely theater audiences. In the novel's closing chapter, Katharine basks in the attention of a younger man who reflects in his awe of her the admiration of the crowd at large. She essentially writes the script of their future conversations and blocks the actions of their lovemaking, which she expects to shatter the illusion she currently subscribes to of being "hopelessly virginal" (285). Recognizing her illusion as such, Katharine Faraday lives in a hall of mirrors that offers up different versions of herself. She has understood that the Southern lady is simply one of the roles that she might adopt, but she has crafted for herself no more stable alter-ego in the guise of playwright. "Hard-boiled virgin" is simply another mask; her sexuality will have to be returned to her again by each illusion-shattering lover rather than asserted by her. Outside of playacting the roles society offers her, Katharine Faraday cannot define herself.

Evelyn Cunningham, the central character of *Dead Lovers Are Faithful Lovers*, likewise understands herself as playing a role, but only one—that of doting wife to railroad executive Charlton Cunningham. To create the image she wants Charlton to see requires a great deal of work on Evelyn's part; she slips out of bed each morning, for example, to rearrange and perfume herself so that she appears to her husband's waking eyes just as she did before he closed them the night before. Evelyn refers to the transformation of her self from a "figure" on which to hang clothes into a "body" immediately after the honeymoon begins,[46] but it is partly to preserve this body and her husband's perception of it that Evelyn shuns motherhood. She feels sure that after she gave birth "her husband could not possibly go on looking at her as if he were looking at Cleopatra . . ." (86). Charlton's admiring gaze sustains her sense of self.

In this second novel, Newman aims her satire at the figure of the Southern gentlemen as well. Approximately half-way through the text, she introduces the perspective of the mistress Charlton does indeed have, Isabel Ramsey, a young, unmarried librarian, who displays an independence remarkably different from Evelyn's limited scope of action. She and Charlton meet in the library, and she recalls his eyes examining her "as if they were looking through a glass case at a Gutenberg Bible" (182). She is an object he has heard about but seldom seen—a woman making her way independently from a male definitions and expectations of her. Eventually he comes to see her as "a woman instead of a Holy Bible" (202–3), suggesting that he considers leaving behind the sanctity of the near untouchable womanhood that his wife embodies. Yet Charlton and Isabel's love remains unconsummated because Charlton actually knows how to love a woman only one way—as an image he holds at a remove. He repeats to Isabel exact lines he has used in conversation with his wife, and the narrator employs similar wording to describe the intensity of Charlton's physical contact with both women, leaving the reader to wonder about the actual state of his private marital relations. Isabel Ramsey's Southern training explains to her his reluctance: "she was thinking that if Charlton Cunningham went on saving her from himself for himself, she would be like the letter which she had once dropped down on that hearth, and which had become ashes without ever becoming fire" (266). Charlton Cunningham, finally, is as tightly wound into the abstractions of virginity and honor as is Evelyn Scott's uncle and Caddy Compson's brother. He believes himself to be the force that preserves Isabel from knowledge of her own sexuality, but she penetrates the veneer of his rationale to recognize his egocentric motivation: he is saving her not *from* him but *for* him so that she remains, to his mind, "in the legal and immaculate state in which a southern gentleman thinks he should receive his bride" (271). His insistence on image rather than physicality "saves" Isabel from the sexual desire both feel. Charlton falls ill and dies, leaving behind a never-revealed tryst with Isabel and a triumphant widow in Evelyn, who dons black crepe as the perpetual symbol of having served well a husband who never left her. Isabel's excruciating wait for word from Charlton mirrors Evelyn's anxious waiting from the novel's beginning, signalling that both women, despite their vastly different lifestyles, have come to depend upon Charlton to give shape and meaning to their lives. The source of their self-worth dead, Evelyn may actually fare better than Isabel, reflected back to herself as triumphant widow in the eyes of the community. Newman's indictment of gender relations in her native South is complete; no one escapes.

No one escapes in Faulkner's fiction either—the reader finds him dismantling Southern ladies and gentlemen, Southern attitudes toward race and tradition, Southern class structures and time-honored patterns of human interaction. But fundamental to the South that Faulkner projects is a profound ambivalence about what it means to be Southern, about what the South means to the imagination of his characters. Missing from the South that Scott and Newman offer is ambivalence about how the region has shaped the women who come from it; they resoundingly condemn constraints imposed on female sexuality and selfhood, more pronounced in their Southern experience, but endemic to America at large. Missing is any hint of Gavin Stevens's admonition to go slow in expiating the sins of the South. Missing is even the hint of a desire to call forth "that July afternoon in 1863" with the latent and frustrated hope that this time the battle might be won. The battles Newman, Scott, and their female protagonists fight are different ones, and from their perspective the reader looks out, as she had earlier in the fiction of Kate Chopin, for example, from the small space allotted to women. What we have seen more often is the South that Faulkner gave America. But in the "cramped, fettered" spaces of Scott's narratives, and in the merciless wit of Newman's, we find the South Faulkner did not know from the inside and thus could not have offered to the nation. Scott and Newman match Hawthorne's criteria: here are women who "throw off"—gladly—"the restraints of decency," who "come before the public stark naked, as it were," whose books "possess character and value." They literally give—not just to Southern women, but to women more generally—bodies, their fiction dovetailing with national and international efforts to express through literary modernism the sensations of femininity, the power of sexuality, and the value of self-creation. If their efforts finally show the marks of regional upbringing, then our knowledge of the South is both enriched and connected to the struggles of American females to embrace without penalty their womanhood. A full understanding of gender as it operates in constructing and propelling the South's self-image and the image America holds of it requires the insights of both the men and the women who have lived within and beyond the region.

NOTES

1. Paul Fatout, ed., *Mark Twain Speaking* (Iowa City: University of Iowa Press, 1976), 110.

2. Mark Twain's remark is cited in "Mark Twain" in George McMichael, ed., *Anthology of American Literature*, vol. 2, 3rd ed. (New York: Macmillan Publishing Company, 1985), 345.

3. Lawrence, Schwartz, *Creating Faulkner's Reputation: The Politics of Modern Literary Criticism* (Knoxville: University of Tennessee Press, 1988), 10.

4. Malcolm Cowley, introduction to *The Portable Faulkner* (New York: Viking Press, 1946), 4.

5. Ibid., 8.

6. Richard H. Brodhead, *The School of Hawthorne* (New York: Oxford University Press, 1986), 11.

7. Nina Baym, "Rewriting the Scribbling Women," *Legacy*, 2.2 (Fall 1985): 3–12.

8. Hawthorne to William Ticknor, Liverpool, 19 January 1855, *The Letters 1853–1856*, ed. Thomas Woodson, et al., vol. 17 of *The Centenary Edition of the Works of Nathaniel Hawthorne*, ed. William Charvat (Columbus: Ohio State University Press, 1962), 304.

9. Hawthorne to William Ticknor, Liverpool, 2 February 1855, *The Letters 1853–1856*, 308.

10. Jane Tompkins, *Sensational Designs: The Cultural Work of American Fiction 1790–1860* (New York: Oxford University Press, 1985), 18.

11. Baym, "Rewriting the Scribbling Women," 6.

12. Ibid., 11.

13. Ibid.

14. Nathaniel Hawthorne, *The Scarlet Letter*, ed. Fredson Thayer Bowers, vol. 1 of *The Centenary Edition of the Works of Nathaniel Hawthorne*, ed. William Charvat (Columbus: Ohio State University Press, 1962), 166.

15. Ibid., 263.

16. Ibid.

17. Daniel J. Singal, *William Faulkner: The Making of a Modernist* (Chapel Hill: University of North Carolina Press, 1997).

18. Michael Kreyling. *Inventing Southern Literature* (Jackson: University Press of Mississippi, 1998), 130.

19. Flannery O'Connor, "Some Aspects of the Grotesque in Southern Fiction," in *Mystery and Manners*, ed. Sally and Robert Fitzgerald (New York: Farrar, Straus & Giroux, 1962), 45.

20. Kreyling, *Inventing Southern Literature*, 112.

21. Ibid., 78.

22. Anne Goodwyn Jones and Susan V. Donaldson, "Haunted Bodies: Rethinking the South through Gender," in *Haunted Bodies: Gender and Southern Texts*, ed. Anne Goodwyn Jones and Susan V. Donaldson (Charlottesville: University Press of Virginia, 1997), 16.

23. Ibid., 6.

24. Ibid., 17.

25. Robert Morss Lovett, "The Wave," *New Republic*, 7 August 1929, 319.

26. T. S. Matthews, "Fancy Goods," *New Republic*, 27 June 1928, 153.

27. Clifton Fadiman, "Hardly Worth While," *Nation*, 15 January 1930, in *William Faulkner: The Contemporary Reviews*, ed. M. Thomas Inge, vol. V of *American Critical Archives*, ed. M. Thomas Inge (Cambridge: Cambridge University Press, 1995), 39.

28. Bonnie Kime Scott, ed., *The Gender of Modernism: A Critical Anthology* (Bloomington: Indiana University Press, 1990), 4.

29. Anne Goodwyn Jones, *Tomorrow Is Another Day: The Woman Writer in the South, 1859–1936* (Baton Rouge: Louisiana State University Press, 1981), 274–75.

30. Evelyn Scott, *Escapade* (New York: Thomas Selzer, 1923), 123. Subsequent references appear parenthetically in the text.

31. Evelyn Scott. *The Wave* (1929; Baton Rouge: Louisiana State University Press, 1996). Subsequent references appear parenthetically in the text.

32. Mary Wheeling White, *Fighting the Current: The Life and Work of Evelyn Scott* (Baton Rouge: Louisiana State University Press, 1998), 1.

33. Peggy Bach, "A Serious Damn: William Faulkner and Evelyn Scott," *Southern Literary Journal* 28.1 (Fall 1995): 133.

34. Joseph Blotner, *William Faulkner's Library: A Catalogue* (Charlottesville: University Press of Virginia, 1964).

35. James Branch Cabell, *Some of Us: An Essay in Epitaphs* (New York: Robert M. McBride & Company, 1930), 30.

36. Anne Firor Scott, foreword to *The Hard-Boiled Virgin* (1926; Athens: University of Georgia Press, 1993), xv.

37. The biographies are White, *Fighting the Current,* and Barbara Ann Wade, *Frances Newman: Southern Satarist and Literary Rebel* (Tuscaloosa: University of Alabama Press, 1998).

38. Ludwig Lewisohn, "Defiance," *The Nation*, 8 August 1923, 141.

39. Noel Polk, "Around, behind, above, below Men: Ratliff's Buggies and the Homosocial in Yoknapatawpha," in *Haunted Bodies: Gender and Southern Texts*, 359.

40. Peggy Whitman Prenshaw, "The True Happenings of My Life: Reading Southern Women Autobiographers," in *Haunted Bodies: Gender and Southern Texts*, 445.

41. Evelyn Scott, *Background in Tennessee* (1937; Knoxville: University of Tennessee Press, 1980).

42. Jones, *Tomorrow Is Another Day*, 272.

43. Reginald Abbott, "A Southern Lady Still: A Reinterpretation of Frances Percy Newman's *The Hard-Boiled Virgin*," *Southern Quarterly* 27.4 (Summer 1989): 49–70.

44. Frances Newman, *The Hard-Boiled Virgin* (1926; Athens: University of Georgia Press, 1993), 70. Subsequent references appear parenthetically in the text.

45. Jones, *Tomorrow Is Another Day*, 271.

46. Frances Newman, *Dead Lovers Are Faithful Lovers* (New York: Boni & Liveright, 1928): 12. Subsequent references appear parenthetically in the text.

Contributors

Richard Godden, professor of American literature at the University of Keele, is the author of *Fictions of Capital: The American Novel from James to Mailer* and *Fictions of Labor: William Faulkner and the South's Long Revolution,* as well as numerous essays and reviews on American fiction and poetry.

Catherine Gunther Kodat is assistant professor of English and American studies at Hamilton College. Her doctoral dissertation, at Boston University, was "Southern Modernists in Black and White: Jean Toomer, Allen Tate, William Faulkner, and Zora Neale Hurston"; she has also published essays and lectured on Hurston, Faulkner, Morrison, Lorraine Hansberry, and American ballet and modern dance.

Kathryn B. McKee is McMullan Assistant Professor of Southern Studies and assistant professor of English at the University of Mississippi. Her doctoral dissertation at the University of North Carolina at Chapel Hill was "Writing in a Different Direction: Postbellum Women Authors and the Tradition of Southwestern Humor, 1875–1920." She has published essays and lectured on Channing and Emerson, Hawthorne, Glasgow, Kaye Gibbons, Bobbie Ann Mason, and Sherwood Banner.

Peter Nicolaisen, professor of English at the Padagogische Hochschule Flensburg, has written books on Edward Taylor, Hemingway, Faulkner, Conrad, and Thomas Jefferson. He has been a visiting professor at the University of Virginia, University of California, Berkeley, Pennsylvania State University, and Winthrop University in South Carolina.

Charles A. Peek is associate professor of English at the University of Nebraska at Kearney. He is coeditor, with Robert W. Hamblin, of *A William Faulkner Encyclopedia* and author of "Order and Flight" in *Approaches to Teaching Faulkner's "The Sound and the Fury."*

Noel Polk, professor of English at the University of Southern Mississippi, is the author of *Faulkner's "Requiem for a Nun": A Critical Study, An Editorial Handbook for William Faulkner's "The Sound and the Fury," Eudora Welty: A Bibliography,* and *Children of the Dark House: Text and Context in Faulkner.*

Hortense J. Spillers, professor of English, Cornell University, is coeditor of *Conjuring: Black Women, Fiction, and Literary Tradition* and coeditor of *Comparative American Identities: Race, Sex, and Nationality in* *the Modern Text*, as well as numerous essays on black writers and black feminist criticism.

Joseph R. Urgo is professor and chair of the Department of English at the University of Mississippi. He is the author of *Faulkner's Apocrypha: "A Fable," Snopes, and the Spirit of Human Rebellion*; *Willa Cather and the Myth of American Migration*; *Novel Frames: Literature as Guide to Race, Sex, and History in American Culture*; and, most recently, *In the Age of Distraction.*

Linda Wagner-Martin is Frank Borden and Barbara Lasater Hanes Professor of English and Comparative Literature at the University of North Carolina, Chapel Hill. She has written or edited over forty books, including studies of Hemingway and Faulkner, W. C. Williams, John Dos Passos, Ellen Glasgow, Sylvia Plath, and Gertrude Stein.

Charles Reagan Wilson is professor of history and Southern studies and director of the Center for the Study of Southern Culture at the University of Mississippi. He is the author of *Judgment and Grace in Dixie: Southern Faiths from Faulkner to Elvis* and *Baptized in Blood: The Religion of the Lost Cause, 1864–1900*. He is also coeditor of the *Encyclopedia of Southern Culture*.

Index